Ernest G. Bormann *University of Minnesota*

Communication Theory

Holt, Rinehart and Winston
*New York   Chicago   San Francisco   Atlanta   Dallas
Montreal   Toronto   London   Sydney*

Library of Congress Cataloging in Publication Data

Bormann, Ernest G.
  Communication theory.

  Includes index.

  1. Communication—Philosophy. I. Title.
P91.B68   001.5'1   79-24333

ISBN 0-03-019086-X

Acknowledgments

Portions of chapters 5 and 6 have been revised and adapted from Ernest G. Bormann, *Theory and Research in the Communicative Arts,* New York: Holt, Rinehart and Winston, 1965.

Portions of chapters 7, 8, and 9 have been modified and adapted from Ernest G. Bormann, "Generalizing About Significant Form: Science and Humanism Compared and Contrasted" and "Rhetorical Criticism and Significant Form: A Humanistic Approach," in Karlyn Kohrs Campbell and Kathleen Hall Jamieson, eds., *Form and Genre: Shaping Rhetorical Action,* (Falls Church, Va.: Speech Communication Assn., 1978), and are reprinted by permission of the Speech Communication Association.

Figure 1 (top): From Claude E. Shannon and Warren Weaver, *The Mathematical Theory of Communication.* Copyright 1949. Reprinted by permission of the University of Illinois Press, Urbana, Ill.

Figure 1 (middle): From Wilbur Schramm, "How Communication Works," in Wilbur Schramm, ed., *The Process and Effects of Mass Communication.* Copyright 1955. Reprinted by permission of the University of Illinois Press, Urbana, Ill.

Figure 1 (bottom): From *The Process of Communication: An Introduction to Theory and Practice* by David K. Berlo. Copyright © 1960 by Holt, Rinehart and Winston, Inc. Reprinted by permission of Holt, Rinehart and Winston.

Figure 2 (top): From Dean C. Barnlund, "A Transactional Model of Communication," in Johnnye Akin, Alvin Goldberg, Gail Myers, and John Stewart, eds., *Language Behavior: A Book of Readings,* The Hague: Mouton & Co., Publishers, 1971. Figure adapted from Figure 3.7, p. 49 in *Fundamental Concepts in Human Communication* by Ronald Applbaum et al. Copyright © 1973 by Ronald Applbaum, Karl W. E. Anatol, Ellis R. Hayes, Owen O. Jenson, Richard E. Porter, and Jerry E. Mandel. Reprinted by permission of Harper & Row, Publishers, Inc.

Figure 2 (bottom): From *Communication in Everyday Use,* Third Edition, by Elizabeth G. Andersch, Lorin C. Staats, and Robert N. Bostrom. Copyright 1950, © 1960, 1969 by Holt, Rinehart and Winston, Inc. Reprinted by permission of Holt, Rinehart and Winston.

Preface

This book examines the current state of representative theorizing about communication. In addition to providing a summary of the content of essays and courses in communication theory, I examine critically the conceptualizations, root assumptions, and explanatory power of major accounts of the nature and practice of communication. My purpose is not only to give the reader an understanding of the content of communication theory but also to express a position on controversial issues and to stimulate the student to work through personal positions on key issues. Given the state of contemporary knowledge about communication, I believe that critical analyses and assessments are as important to a good course as are summaries of current theory and surveys of current research results.

Scholars studying communication tend increasingly to supplement their thinking with rhetorical theory and criticism. I, therefore, give attention to humanistic studies wherever I feel they relate usefully to communication theory. My emphasis, however, is upon what is generally thought of as communication theory.

Evidence has been piling up in the last decade that the research tradition of searching for laws that govern relevant variables is not adequate as a disciplinary perspective for the study of communication. In the 1970s the scholars making humanistic and social scientific studies of communication began to examine alternative approaches to the development of communication theory. Transition points such as this are ideal for the sort of thorough critique which seeks to retain the significant and discard the trivial.

These are clearly exciting times for the student of communciation, for the discipline is once again going to its root assumptions and asking such basic questions as: How do we know? What is the nature of our current knowledge? What should be the nature of knowledge in our discipline? How can we best study the things we are concerned about? How can we organize our discoveries into coherent explanations to provide the best understanding of communication?

My framework of analysis divides the general field of communication theory into two major sorts of theories: (1) special, predominantly artistic, theories of limited scope, restricted to communities of people who have learned the standard usages, rules and exemplars of the style; and (2) general social scientific theories designed to provide explanations based upon lawfulness or strong probabilities.

Part One of the book traces the beginnings and rise of communication theory in the twentieth century and summarizes some of the representative materials that typically have been and are included in courses in communication theory. Part Two provides the framework of analysis and compares and contrasts the nature of special and general theories of communication with rhetorical theories and scientific theories. Part Two also presents a thorough description and analysis of three contemporary special theories: (1) public speaking theory, (2) relationship communication theory, and (3) the message communication theory. Part Three deals with general communication theories. It begins with a basic discussion of the nature of science and of social science, and of social scientific approaches to studying communication in particular. Part Three also contains a summary of leading critiques of current communication theory and practice, including my own critique focused on variable analytic studies. The part also contains an examination of rhetorical theory, history, and criticism and their relationship to communication theory. The book concludes with an afterword which summarizes my analysis with a discussion of current tendencies and evaluates their promise for the future.

January 1980

Ernest G. Bormann
University of Minnesota

Contents

PART TWO

Special Communication Theories

3 Communication Styles and Special Theories   59

4 Contemporary Special Communication Theories   81

PART THREE

General Communication Theories

5 The Analysis of General Theories of Communication   105

6 Science and the Nature of Knowledge About Communication   128

PART ONE

Background and Survey of Contemporary Communication Theories

1

The Development of Contemporary Communication Theory

Introduction

The study of communication has had a long, varied, and sometimes honorable tradition in western culture. The scholars of classical Greece and Rome studied rhetoric intensively, and from that time until the present the process of how one person communicates with others has been a topic of fascination—in some historical periods more than others, to be sure, but never has the study of communication ebbed to insignificance. History thus gives us a complex and detailed account of human efforts to discover the nature, essence, and dynamics of communication.

Human beings have communicated for the aesthetic experience, for moral purposes, and for practical ends. They have studied communication in order to appreciate the art and become better artists, to learn what communication is and how it works, to develop means of communicating more effectively for practical ends, and to satisfy their curiosity.

The years from 1920 to the present have seen an increasing interest in the study and practice of communication. Indeed, in the middle decades of the twentieth century, *communication* became for North Americans a "god term" which served much as had the term *education* in previous years. Where the popular solution had been "more education," by the 1960s it was often "more and better communication" for problems as diverse as juvenile delinquency, marital breakups, and loss of faith in political institutions. The general public as well as the scholarly community often referred to "communication problems" as the most basic and important in all areas of society.

My purpose in this book is to examine the current state of knowledge about human communication. The following chapters provide a summary and critique of the major perspectives, conceptualizations, hypotheses, models, and philosophical analyses which constitute current thinking about communication.

My argument is that as a result of historical developments in the United States in the twentieth century, the old rhetorical traditions which influenced speaking and writing in the nineteenth century became inadequate; they could no longer serve as a theoretical basis for the practice, criticism, and explanation of "communication episodes," both informal and formal. Consequently there were a number of new formulations about communication. Some of those interested in the study of communication were predominantly teachers and critics of applied communication, while others were more interested in general social scientific accounts of human symbol-using. Their diverse interests were expressed in midcentury writings about communication which frequently included an indiscriminate mixture of elements. Some of this material related to general explanations of communication processes, some to definitional problems, some to philosophical concerns, and some to practice. As a result, the representative formulations of knowledge about communication varied widely in terms of their purpose, nature, level of abstraction, and scope.

My analysis sorts out these various elements and divides communication theories into two major groups: (1) style-specific artistic formulations which relate to the communication practices of communities clearly bounded by patterns of general usage; and (2) general, more universal formulations which account for the communication features common to several or many or all such communities. I call the style-specific formulations *special* theories of communication and the more universal formulations *general* theories of communication.

Both special and general theories are important and necessary to the scholarly study of communication, but they serve different functions and should be evaluated according to different criteria. For example, a typical textbook on public speaking provides an artistic special theory of communication that is concerned with a group of communication episodes characteristic of set occasions in contemporary North American culture. On the other hand, a discussion of "persuasion" in terms of a "universal tendency to strive for cognitive consistency" is an attempt to provide a general theory which relates not only to public speaking but sales conferences, mass-media advertising, and many other types of communication. We should not expect a special theory—of public speaking or of any other specific type of communication—to provide the same kind of explanation of communication processes that we have a right to expect of a general theory. Nor should we expect a general theory to anticipate and explain all the idiosyncratic, arbitrary, and conventional stylistic features which can accompany the actual specific communication practices of the members of a community.

4

The Development of
Contemporary
Communication Theory

The remainder of this chapter is a survey of the study of communication in this century, with special attention to research approaches. It also touches on the relationship between communication and rhetoric; the topic will be discussed at length elsewhere in the book, but is appropriately introduced here because of the strong current interest in it.[1]

Twentieth-Century Study of Communication

Rhetoric was from colonial times until the late nineteenth century an important subject for study in American colleges and universities. Originally the emphasis had been upon the study of rhetorical principles for oral communication, but during the nineteenth century the orientation changed to writing. With the adoption of the department as the basic administrative unit for institutions of higher learning in the nineteenth century, the study and teaching of rhetoric became the province of departments of English.

As English departments began to stress written argument and the study of literature, the elocution movement grew and flourished. The teachers of elocution emphasized the study of voice, articulation, and gesture. This concern with manner rather than content led some elocutionists into excessive attention to the details of delivery, and consequently elocution was drawing criticism by the turn of the century. In 1892 when the National Association of Elocutionists was formed, strong opposition developed among the membership to the use of the word "elocutionists" in the name for the organization.[2]

College and university teachers of elocution and English who were dissatisfied with the emphasis on delivery in the elocution movement, with the position of oral communication in English departments, and with the philological research that was influential in these departments banded together in various national organizations, and eventually founded the Speech Communication Association and many of the early departments of speech. The move for a separate association and separate departments was motivated partly by the research interests of the dissidents. One of the leaders in the movement, James M. O'Neill, speaking at a banquet of the English Council in 1913, said, "The issue splits on the rock of standards of scholarship. The German Ph.D. ideal is not for Public Speaking, which must have its own standards of scholarship and teaching. . . ."[3] James A. Winans, writing in the first issue of *The Quarterly Journal of Public Speaking*, reflected the same dissatisfaction. "We shall not," he wrote, "for some time be driven to the painful emendation of the text of Demosthenes or to studying the influence of Quintilian on Patrick Henry. We ought not to be led into dry-as-dust studies. . . ."[4]

Despite the fact that the research traditions in the departments of English had irritated some of the dissidents, the study of rhetoric was well established, and a number of them began to revitalize the traditional studies of rhetorical history and theory. They turned particularly to such classical sources as Aristotle's *Rhetoric*.[5] In 1925, Wichelns wrote a seminal essay entitled "The Literary Criticism of Oratory." After examining in detail the literary criticism of a number of speakers, he contrasted such studies with rhetorical criticism and suggested that the latter "is not concerned with permanence, nor yet with beauty. It is concerned with effect. It regards a speech as a communication to a specific audience, and holds its business to be the analysis and appreciation of the orator's method of imparting his ideas to his hearers."[6] From these beginnings came a tradition of humanistic rhetorical theory and rhetorical criticism that formed the backdrop for the emergence of communication theory.

The Influence of Nineteenth-Century Natural Science

Those scholars who were seeking to define a new discipline that would make communication, particularly oral communication, its central focus were searching for appropriate ways to study and account for human communication at a time when science was much respected. Research, particularly scientific research, was an avenue to personal and professional status. With the sciences at this height of power and prestige, the intellectual communities tended to consider communication a second-class intellectual chore. Certainly this was the case when communication was seen as typified by the elocutionist's concern with making well-rounded tones or the instructor's concern with teaching freshman composition or public speaking.

Whether they were teachers of composition, journalism, elocution, public speaking, or radio broadcasting, scholars concerned with communication did not enjoy their comparative lack of status. Winans proclaimed, "I have no great humility before teachers in other lines. Toward them we bristle with defiance." However, he also wrote, "It [the scholarship which is the product of research] will make us orthodox. Research is the standard way into the sheepfold."[7]

Seeking to study the subject of their interest, many took the advice of the Research Committee of the newly formed National Association of Academic Teachers of Public Speaking, which suggested that they take courses "in the departments of physiology, psychology, sociology" in order to gain "a working knowledge of a technique of inquiry which they could adapt to their own field without great difficulty."[8]

The chemists and physicists of the turn of the century practiced their sciences by discovering invariable relationships among carefully quantified factors. Their method was to discover the *relevant* variables (those discernible features of the phenomenon under study which were causally related), to control some of them, to vary some, and to leave some alone. The experimenter observed the effect of the manipulation of some variables upon those that remained. The investigator then attributed the changes in the variables that were not manipulated to the changes in those that were.

The rigorous control and manipulation of relevant variables required laboratory conditions that allowed the investigators to seal off the processes they were investigating. Chemists and physicists at the turn of the century were approximating closed systems for the phenomena they were studying and doing so with such care that laboratory conditions were often a necessity.

Generally the experimenters measured the variables carefully to quantify the changes in them during the course of the experiments. Because investigators measured changes numerically, they could use the mathematics of functions for the deductive interpretation of such data.

When experimentation developed several mathematically valid functional relationships, theoreticians could manipulate the mathematical functions deductively and compute new applications as well as check for the logical consistency of all the laws relating to a given field of investigation.

The challenge to early communications theorists was therefore to discover relevant variables, to develop techniques of controlling and manipulating them, and to devise systems of numerical measurement.

Behaviorism

Behaviorism, perhaps the most experimentally oriented of the schools of psychology which flourished in the early years of the twentieth century, applied the model of the natural sciences sketched above to the study of human beings. Pavlov's experiments with animals in which he conditioned a dog's response to a bell so that the animal responded to the stimulus of the signal as it had to the stimulus of food struck some as the equivalent of Newton's law of gravity. Could the conditioned response provide the basic principle of animal (and human) learning, and could the scientific study of human beings then proceed in terms of finding the appropriate ways to apply the principle to more and more complicated behavioral repertoires?

The study of learning and behavioral modification principles pushed ahead vigorously from the 1920s to the 1950s. So-called "learning theory" became a central concern of behaviorism, and the development of Skinnerian psychology, which accounted for human learning and behavior in terms of reinforcement schedules, came to be a dominant school of psychology at the time investigators began to study communication scientifically. The exemplar of the behavioristic experiment was a study in which the investigator manipulated a stimulus under controlled conditions in order to discover its effect on a response. As more and more puzzles surfaced using the example of stimulus-response experiments, the investigations grew more complicated. The researcher would manipulate the stimulus, and note the response, then manipulate a reinforcement of the response and observe the result of the manipulation of both original stimulus and subsequent reinforcement upon the animal's behavior.

In the decades before World War II a number of psychologists put forth general theories to account for all learning. In the 1940s a substantial number of psychologists still believed that comprehensive theories of learning would soon be developed, and leading psychologists such as Guthrie, Tolman, and Hull offered such theories. Perhaps as influential as any was the formulation of Clark L. Hull, who presented a complex and detailed account of learning based upon the concept of *habit strength*, which developed as a function of practice. Another basic concept in Hull's theory was that of *habit*, which was defined as a stimulus-response connection based upon reward. Hull and his followers attempted to quantify the basic variables involved in the theory; for example, they defined habit strength in terms of the number of times a response was rewarded. But by the 1970s it was clear that the hope of a grand theory of learning on the lines of Newton's theory of physics had come to naught. Learning theory turned out to be a set of hunches or hypotheses of limited applicability. G. A. Kimble summed up the search of twentieth-century psychologists for a theory of learning as follows:

> A final fault in much learning theory stems from earlier tendencies to use the laws of physics as a model. Theorists once sought general laws of wide applicability that tended to obscure differences among individuals. For example, so complete was Hull's faith in universal 'laws' of animal behavior, that he based his hypothesis about the optimal interval for classical conditioning in humans, other mammals, and birds on the pattern of nerve conduction in the optic nerve of the horseshoe crab. . . . it was believed that, by studying many subjects and by computing averages, basic laws of learning could be found. However, so-called laws were developed in this way that failed to represent even one individual whose behavior contributed to the average.[9]

When investigators began to study communication scientifically, they often applied the model of the behavioristic school of psychology to their efforts. Thus, at one step removed they were heirs to the general approach of the sciences of physics and chemistry. They tried to develop experiments that would yield functional laws, laws that would predict outcomes in the same precise way that the laws of physics and chemistry do. They moved into line behind the learning "theorists" in their effort to use the laws of physics as a model and find a "grand" theory of the Newtonian type to cover human communication behavior.

Attitude Change Studies

Early researchers of communication tried to isolate relevant variables, control some, manipulate others, and observe in some measurable way the effect on the dependent variables. In the 1920s such researchers as Charles Woolbert, Giles Gray, Sara Stinchfield, Robert West, Andrew Weaver, Alan Monroe, William Utterback, and Franklin Knower published findings on empirical research relating to oral communication. As early as 1935, Hollingworth's book *The Psychology of the Audience* drew on as many as seventy-five research studies.[10] By 1943, Howard Gilkinson could comment in his *Outlines of Research in General Speech*, "Over a period of years, and particularly during the last decade, an increasing number of statistical and experimental investigations of interest to teachers and students of speech have appeared in publication."[11] Gilkinson's bibliography contained 354 items.

Early investigators explored a number of different topics. Some studied the relationships between personality traits and communicative skills, while others examined the effect of courses in public speaking.[12] Some made content analyses of various messages both oral and written, while others examined the effects of oral propaganda on different types of audiences.[13]

One of the early important lines of inquiry was directed to the study of opinion and attitudes. Psychologists such as Thurstone developed scales to discover the gross effects of movies on the attitudes of viewers or to chart attitudes toward blacks or toward public issues such as capital punishment.[14] A number of researchers began to study the shift of opinion or change in attitude that resulted when an audience heard a speech or listened to a debate. Woodward formulated a shift-of-opinion ballot to be used in studying the effects of a message on an audience.[15] Willey and Rice, using a five-point scale, studied the reaction of Dartmouth students to a speech by William Jennings Bryan on evolution.[16] Gilkinson compared the responses of Democrats and Republicans to a radio speech against the New Deal by General Hugh Johnson.[17]

After the early studies that treated the entire message as a unit and attitudes or opinions as unitary responses, the next step was the development of investigations that examined the effect of various kinds of communication content on attitudes, opinions, and retention of information. As early as 1924, Collins was studying the effectiveness of condensed and extended emotional appeal.[18] One of the most extensive of the early studies was that of Knower in the 1930s. He studied the effect of emotional and logical-factual arguments on attitudes of college students toward prohibition. Knower compared both oral and written messages.[19] In 1940 Lull reported the results of his research on the effects of humorous and nonhumorous speeches on the attitudes of students toward state medicine.[20]

World War II stimulated and encouraged the impulse to study propaganda and persuasion empirically. Feldman in a brief historical survey of attitude change research noted:

> Rapid advances were made in this area during the decade between 1945 and 1955. As with many other advances in the social psychology of that era, they issued largely from the collaboration and research that had taken place during World War II, in the research branch of the Information and Education Division of the War Department. . . .[21]

Feldman attributes the rapid advances to "well-planned attacks isolating the effects of carefully controlled variations in the communicator, the message, and the audience."[22]

By the late 1940s the investigators were still studying attitudes as unitary responses, but they were dividing the stimuli which resulted in the change responses into parts. They began to ask what parts of the communication were causing the changed responses and what combinations of parts were most effective in causing attitude changes. Moreover, they began to conceptualize the phenomenon they were studying as a *process* and to think of the parts of that process as *variables*. If attitude change is a process in which important elements change through time as the interaction unfolds, then by analogy with nineteenth-century chemistry, research designs should begin with the discovery or stipulation of relevant variables. Once the investigators have determined the relevant variables, they can go on to specify some which are to be manipulated, some which are to be controlled, and some which are to be left free to be changed by the experimental manipulation.

9

Attitude Change Studies

Haiman's 1949 study of ethos is an important exemplar of the emerging research norms. The field of communication is not a scientific discipline and is in what Kuhn calls a preparadigmatic state.[23] However, Haiman's study is a benchmark in an emerging school of investigation which has many of the characteristics of a paradigm. I shall refer to the school of communication study as the quasi-paradigm of variable analytic studies.[24] Haiman's study assumed at least three relevant variables: (1) the ethos of the speaker, (2) the message, and (3) the audience's attitude toward the topic. He held the message constant (controlled the variable) but changed the introduction of the speaker (manipulated the independent variable). He attributed the speech for some listeners to a communist, for some to a sophomore at Northwestern University, and for some to the surgeon general of the United States. By attributing the speech to different speakers he tried to change the variable of speaker ethos, and he administered pre- and post-tests of audience attitude toward the topic in order to quantify the effect of manipulating the variable of listener attitudes.[25]

Another benchmark study in variable analytic studies of attitude change was that of Hovland and Weiss in 1951. They presented four communications to each subject and attributed each communication to either a high- or low-credibility source. They indexed changes in attitudes toward the topic of each communication immediately after its receipt and after three weeks.[26] In general the influential work of Hovland and his associates at Yale University proved to be sufficient to convert a considerable group of investigators to follow the exemplar.[27]

Thus in the twenty years from 1950 to 1970, many social psychologists and communication scholars adopted the exemplar of manipulating variables of credibility of the message's source, variables of the message's content, or variables of the message's structure; controlling other variables; and assessing the effect of the manipulation on some remaining variables—generally the audience's attitude. They examined the interactions among message variables such as order of arguments; use of evidence; emotional materials such as fear appeals, language intensity, and obscene language; source credibility variables; and audience variables such as sex, dogmatism, ego involvement in the subject of the message, and so forth.[28]

The studies based upon the exemplar of Haiman and Hovland came to be grouped under the label "attitude change." Members of the "attitude change" school sought to discover functional relationships (lawfulness) that could be expressed quantitatively. When such relationships were discovered, investigators hoped to integrate them mathematically and manipulate them deductively to yield prediction and control. The general goal of the research program was a science of communication complete with theoretical formulations along the model of Newtonian mechanics.

Group Dynamics Studies

Psychological Abstracts first indexed research articles under the term *group dynamics* in 1945. The references were to work by the social psychologist Kurt Lewin and his associates. Under Lewin's direction, the Research Center for Group Dynamics was set up at the Massachusetts Institute of Technology in 1945; another Research Center for Group Dynamics was established at the University of Michigan. Dorwin Cartwright and Alvin Zander at the Michigan Center edited a collection of research articles entitled *Group Dynamics: Research and Theory* in 1953.[29]

An influential early study was one by Lewin, Lippitt, and White that varied styles of leadership and examined the effect on group outputs.[30] In the 1950s many investigators used variable analytic research designs to study the influence of leadership styles, such as autocratic, authoritarian, democratic, group-centered, and production-oriented on group productivity and morale.

Much research in group dynamics and small-group communication in the years since 1950 exhibited the earmarks of the quasi-paradigm of variable analytic studies. The exemplar research designs involved the identification of important group variables, the manipulation of some variables prior to brief experimental group sessions in a laboratory setting, the control of other variables, and the indexing of changes in specified dependent variables after the meetings. Usually the investigators used some pre- and post-testing procedures, some control groups, or a design feature to estimate the influence of variables other than the independent and dependent ones, and sought to discover functional relationships that could be integrated into a consistent theoretical structure.

Other Research Approaches

Although the variable analytic school came to dominate communication research in the years after World War II, it was by no means the only research perspective used by social scientific investigators. Among the more influential of the early techniques was the quantitative and statistical study of message content.

Content Analysis Studies Investigators using a content analysis procedure define units of the discourse that they feel are comparable on some important dimension they wish to study. They also develop a category system into which they can sort the units. Hayworth in 1930 did an extended study of 145 speeches made in presidential campaigns from 1884 to 1920.[31] His study was concerned with amounts of space devoted by speakers to various persuasive stratagems. Runion did an early study of the speech style of Woodrow Wilson by making a content analysis of fifty speeches.[32]

Much research in the content of print media has been in the form of quantified analyses. A number of investigators have analyzed the content of the electronic media in the same fashion.[33]

An important line of research in small group analysis has utilized content analysis of the communication in group meetings. Bales pioneered in this line of investigation with his interaction process analysis method for the study of group process.[34] Subsequently a number of other investigators have developed content analysis studies of small group communication, particularly as it relates to decision-making.[35]

More recently some investigators have been making content analysis studies of two-person conversations and interviews.[36]

Survey Studies   Scholars interested in studying communication and its influence on opinion were also active in surveying audiences to discover the readership of various print media or the size and nature of the listening audience for the electronic media.[37] The practice of public-opinion polling developed into an industry which assessed and publicized the opinions of various segments of the public. Scholars interested in studying pedagogical practices related to communication also used survey studies to determine the nature and extent of various teaching methods.[38]

Field Studies   By the time of World War II a number of investigators used such observational techniques as questionnaires and interviews to study complex communication events which had occurred naturally, as opposed to creating communication events in the laboratory for the purposes of a specific study.

Merton and his associates studied the psychological response to a radio appeal by Kate Smith to buy war bonds.[39] They used a structured-interviewing technique called the "focused interview." Another group of scholars studied the panic caused by a 1939 radio broadcast which dramatized H. G. Wells' *War of the Worlds*.[40]

Among the forerunners of studies in small-group communication were those of Newcomb, who studied the operations of social norms and influence processes by means of attitude scaling, sociometric indexes, and interviews of students at Bennington College; and Whyte, who went into the field in the slums of Boston and spent over three years studying social clubs, political organizations, and racketeering using the method of participant observation.[41]

My sketch of other approaches than the variable analytic to the study of communication is by no means complete. My point is essentially that as growing numbers of scholars became interested in the empirical study of communication, they opened up a variety of research programs and used in often eclectic fashion a number of different investigative methods.

The Rise of Communication Theories

As might be expected as a new intellectual impulse matured into a consistent tradition, communication scholars who were establishing new courses and developing handbooks and textbooks for such courses wanted to find appropriate formulations for a scientific account of communication.

One of the first conceptual schemes which caught the scholars' attention was known as the mathematical theory of communication (sometimes called information theory). Engineers designing communication systems and working in the newly emerging field of cybernetics formulated the mathematical theory of communication. They used the theory to explain and to aid in designing sending-and-receiving equipment of maximum efficiency. Shannon and Weaver published the seminal essays relating to the theory under the title *The Mathematical Theory of Communication* in 1949.[42]

Shannon and Weaver divided the communication event into components such as *information source, transmitter, signal,* and *receiver.* The concepts and language of the theory reflect the electronic terminology of engineers working with wired and wireless transmission of "signals." Schramm used such terms are *source* and *signal* but modified the concepts somewhat to provide a more general description of communication. In a series of models Schramm described communication events by using such terms as *source, encoder, message, signal, channels, decoder, destination,* and *interpreter.*[43]

Shannon and Weaver presented a diagram of their description of communication, and subsequent scholars tended to portray their modification of the original formulation in similar fashion. These graphic depictions came to be known as *communication models.*

Berlo's influential book carried the process of elaborating models further by building on the Schramm formulation and adding models of subprocesses such as the interpreter model.[44] The elaboration and modification of communication models became an important form of "theorizing" in the years when communication theory was emerging as an identifiable entity.

In the 1950s a number of scholars put forward the hypothesis that human beings strive to keep their thinking and behavior logically consistent and when their sense of logical consistency is disturbed they strive to change their ideas, attitudes, or behavior to bring them back into balance. Heider presented an early balance or consistency account.[45] Osgood and Tannenbaum put forward a congruity hypothesis.[46] But perhaps the most popular of the balance notions was Festinger's, which came to be known as cognitive dissonance theory.[47] McGuire developed an elaboration of the consistency theme with a medical analogy which suggested that people could be inoculated against attitude change if they were exposed to counterarguments.[48] Another related line of research investigated the effect of advocating a position counter to a person's attitude.

As the level of research increased after World War II, a number of scholars attempted to develop theory by summarizing and integrating research results. Following their assumptions about nineteenth-century physics, they believed that after sufficient study of communication events they would be able to develop lawful generalizations which would then serve as a theory from which they could derive further hypotheses for investigation.[49]

In the 1960s, therefore, those interested in the scientific study of communication had developed a considerable body of material which sought to explain communication. Much of the material consisted of an accounting of communication in terms of definitions of its essence and amplification of the definitions in terms of descriptive models which focused attention upon components of the process and how they interrelated in the total system. In addition, communication theory included some basic assumptions about the nature of human beings and how they responded to and initiated communication including such matters as whether or not they were innately logical and consistent. Generally the theory also dealt with research results by providing summaries and syntheses that sought to draw out functional relationships.

Critical Evaluations of Communication Theory

As more and more scholars attempted to make sense out of the accumulating research into various aspects of communications, a feeling of dissatisfaction with communication theory and research surfaced in the mid-1960s. The issue was drawn around the relative usefulness of laboratory experiments versus field studies. One group of dissidents charged that too many communication studies were being conducted in laboratories and that the artificial laboratory setting meant that the results of such studies could not be generalized to "real-life" communication events. They attributed the apparent barrenness of the research results to the emphasis on laboratory research and urged more studies in the field. Defenders of communication experiments in the laboratory answered by pointing to the unscientific nature of descriptive field studies. How could investigators test hypothesis if they could not manipulate and control variables? To be sure, investigators could on occasion intervene in real-life events and manipulate variables, in which case the result was a field experiment, but such opportunities were rare, and field experiments posed many difficulties which the laboratory setting could easily surmount.[50] Nevertheless, although experimental studies remained popular, a number of investigators did turn to field studies, and the controversy tended to die out.

The dissatisfaction with the state of communication research and theorizing, however, continued on into the 1970s, and by 1975 a much more sophisticated analysis than the discussion of field versus experimental laboratory studies was underway. Lack of progress in developing adequate theories relating to communication despite four decades of intensive empirical investigation resulted in a comprehensive analysis of the research enterprise that examined not so much methodological issues as basic philosophical questions.

The first strong expression of the dissatisfaction came in the mid-1970s with a number of convention programs and journal articles that made a three-part analysis of alternative assumptive systems for developing communication theory. Various partisans compared and contrasted the "covering law" perspective, the systems approach, and the rules viewpoint as possible and useful conceptual frames for the study of communication. The "covering law" perspective came to symbolize the typical research practices, and attacks on it can be viewed as attacks on the status quo.[51]

The early discussion was confused somewhat because the participants tended to use the term *theory* in an indiscriminate way by referring to *covering law theories, systems theories,* and *rules theories.* As the controversy continued, however, it became clearer that what was at issue was not a competition among well-formulated theories which provided alternative accounts of communication, but philosophical questions about being and knowing.

At roughly the same time, dissatisfaction with current communication theory and research began to express itself in a self-consciously philosophical attack on what some scholars saw as the tacit and sometimes contradictory philosophical assumptions of investigators conducting communication research.

They leveled their heaviest attacks on the philosophy of logical positivism. They argued that most of the tacit assumptions underlying communication theory and research were drawn from logical positivism. They then proceeded to discredit logical positivism and suggest some other philosophical position as a better perspective from which to do research and develop theoretical explanations for communication.[52]

Rhetorical Theory and Communication Theory

In the decades that saw the burgeoning interest in the social scientific study of communication, humanistic studies of rhetoric also experienced a growing popularity. Scholars studying rhetorical theory tended to find their models of research excellence in the practice of historians, literary critics, philosophers, and classicists. As a result of their differing approaches to scholarship, the two communities interested in the study of oral communication in the 1950s and 1960s often found themselves in conflict when they shared an academic department or a regional or national professional association. The two groups were interested in different things and saw themselves as practicing different kinds of scholarship. Members of one community tended to argue against the usefulness of the interests and methods of the other. As the conflicts over proper curriculums, proper standards for publication, proper research methods, proper assignment of organizational resources, and the comparative value of communication theory versus rhetorical theory grew in the decades from 1950 to 1970, the more extreme partisans of both communities tended to view the two approaches as inimical.

In the decade of the 1970s, however, an impulse developed of seeking a rapprochement if not an integration of the two communities.[53] The conflict between the partisans of social science and of humanism within the scholarly organizations and associations concerned with the study and practice of communication in contemporary society has generally been unproductive. Far from furthering the study of communication, it has too often degenerated into recriminations, backbiting, and intradepartmental and intra-associational conflict and political maneuvering, which dissipated energy, generated bitterness, and disrupted the time and climate for productive work for too many scholars. The impulse to seek an end to the conflict or at least to the destructive aspects of the feud is a healthy one. However, the possibility of achieving an integrated approach by using the insights of humanism as the basis for hypotheses that can then be subjected to scientific study is probably a vain one. That social science and humanism might be brought into some symbiotic relationship to provide a useful explanation of communication is, however, a possibility that deserves serious examination. In their preface to *Drama in Life: The Uses of Communication in Society*, the editors, Combs and Mansfield, write:

> The most promising tack, combining the humanistic concerns of the dramatists and symbolic interactionists with the rigor of behavioral models, may be communications theory. Probably, the disparate concerns of the many social sciences

may discover some threads of unity, and some acceptance of the humanities, in the development of new and fertile communication theories (or hypotheses) that may recognize the complexity of human behavior as manifest in symbols.[54]

After my survey and analysis of special and general communication theories, I will turn to the nature of humanism and discuss what it can contribute to our understanding of human communication and some ways in which humanistic and social scientific research can profitably supplement one another in general communication theories.

Summary

Although the study of human communication has had a long tradition in western culture, the study of rhetoric, particularly as oral communication, waned somewhat in the latter years of the nineteenth century and in the early decades of the twentieth. The years following World War I, however, starting at approximately 1920, saw the beginning of a rising tide of interest in the study of communication.

As early as 1915, dissidents within the established departments who were primarily interested in oral communication gathered together to form a national association, and shortly thereafter a number of new departments of public speaking or speech were formed. Searching for ways to do research and develop theory, some turned to traditional studies of rhetorical history and theory and some developed the scholarly practice of rhetorical criticism, but a substantial number turned to social scientific models for research methods.

By the 1930s, when the new interest was maturing, the influence of behaviorism in social science was strong, and many investigators who wished to study communication scientifically began to apply the model of behaviorism to their efforts. They often tried to isolate such variables as audience changes of opinion, or attitude, or the source of a message, or its organization or content.

After World War II the rapid advances by social psychologists and communication scholars in the study of attitude changes resulted in the emergence of an influential school of investigation and theorizing about communication called the attitude change studies. Following the models of research by Haiman and Hovland, a number of investigators sought to discover functional relationships which could be expressed quantitatively by isolating relevant variables, manipulating some, controlling some, and observing the effect of the independent variables upon the dependent ones.

Although influential and popular, the attitude change studies were only an important part of the larger research scene. Another group of investigators of small group process and communication also utilized the basic variable analytic approach to study their concerns. In addition, a number of other research strategies and theoretical formulations grew out of content analysis, survey studies, and field studies.

By the 1950s, a number of theorists had put forward explanatory accounts for phenomena more or less directly associated with human communication. Among the first important conceptual schemes for students of human communication were the mathematical theory of communication and consistency or balance explanations of attitude change.

The 1960s saw some unrest among scholars concerned with communication because of shortcomings in both research and theory. In the 1970s a widespread effort was underway to critically evaluate philosophical assumptions undergirding research and theory as well as to reorient research practices into what the dissidents felt would be more productive directions.

Notes

1. See, for example, Walter B. Weimer, "Communication, Speech, and Psychological Models of Man: Review and Commentary," in Brent D. Ruben, ed., *Communication Yearbook 2* (New Brunswick, N. J.: Intercultural Communication Assn., 1978), pp. 57–77; Herbert W. Simons, "Generalizing About Rhetoric: A Scientific Approach," in Karlyn Kohrs Campbell and Kathleen Jamieson, eds., *Form and Genre: Shaping Rhetorical Action* (Falls Church, Va.: Speech Communication Assn., 1978), pp. 33–50.
2. Frank Rarig and Halbert S. Greaves, "National Speech Organizations and Speech Education," in Karl Wallace, ed., *A History of Speech Education in America* (New York: Appleton-Century-Crofts, 1954), p. 491.
3. Quoted in Rarig and Greaves, p. 498.
4. James A. Winans, "The Need for Research," *Quarterly Journal of Speech* 1 (1915): 22. (The name of the *Quarterly Journal of Public Speaking* was changed in 1918 to the *Quarterly Journal of Speech Education* and in 1928 to the *Quarterly Journal of Speech*. I refer to all volumes of the publication as the *Quarterly Journal of Speech*.)
5. See, for example, the reports of early research work at Cornell University in *Quarterly Journal of Speech* 9 (1923): 237–238 and 365–368.
6. In Donald C. Bryant, ed., *The Rhetorical Idiom* (Ithaca, N. Y.: Cornell University Press, 1958), p. 35.
7. Winans, pp. 17–18.
8. *Quarterly Journal of Speech* 1 (1915): 195.
9. *Encyclopedia Britannica*, 15th ed., Macropaedia 10: 759.
10. H. L. Hollingsworth, *The Psychology of the Audience* (New York: American Book Co., 1935).
11. Howard Gilkinson, *Outlines of Research in General Speech* (Minneapolis: Burgess, 1943), p. 1.
12. For a summary of early studies in personality and communication ability, see Gilkinson, pp. 5–12.
13. For a summary of some early studies see Jack M. McLeod, "The Contribution of Psychology to Human Communication Theory," in Frank E. X. Dance, ed., *Human Communication Theory: Original Essays* (New York: Holt, Rinehart and Winston, 1967), pp. 202–235; see also Gilkinson, pp. 14–17.
14. See, for example, L. L. Thurstone, "The Measurement of Social Attitudes," *Journal of Abnormal and Social Psychology* 26 (1931): 249–269.
15 Howard S. Woodward, "Measurement and Analysis of Audience Opinion," *Quarterly Journal of Speech* 14 (1928): 94–111.
16. Malcom M. Willey and Stuart A. Rice, "William Jennings Bryan as a Social Force," *Journal of Social Forces* 2 (1924): 338–344.

17. Howard Gilkinson, "The Influence of Party Preference Upon the Responses of an Audience to a Political Speech," *Sociometry* 5 (1942): 72–79.

18. Rowland Collins, "The Relative Effectiveness of the Condensed And Extended Motive Appeal," *Quarterly Journal of Speech* 10 (1924): 221–230.

19. Franklin H. Knower, "Experimental Studies of Changes in Attitude: I. A Study of the Effect of Oral Argument on Changes of Attitude," *Journal of Social Psychology* 6 (1935): 315–347; Franklin H. Knower, "Experimental Studies of Changes in Attitude: II.A Study of the Effect of Printed Argument on Changes in Attitude," *Journal of Abnormal Social Psychology* 30 (1936): 522–532; Franklin H. Knower, "Experimental Studies of Changes in Attitude: III. Some Incidence of Attitude Changes," *Journal of Applied Psychology* 20 (1936): 114–127.

20. P. E. Lull, "The Effectiveness of Humor in Persuasive Speeches," *Speech Monographs* 7 (1940): 26–40.

21. Shel Feldman, "Motivational Aspects of Attitudinal Elements and Their Place in Cognitive Interaction," in Shel Feldman, ed., *Cognitive Consistency: Motivational Antecedents and Behavioral Consequents* (New York: Academic Press, 1966), p. 78.

22. Ibid.

23. Thomas S. Kuhn, *The Structure of Scientific Revolutions*, 2nd ed. (Chicago: University of Chicago Press, 1970), pp. 10–22.

24. I borrow the term *variable analytic* from Delia, who uses it in a somewhat similar way in Jesse G. Delia, "Alternative Perspectives for the Study of Human Communication: Critique and Response," *Communication Quarterly* 25 (1977): 48.

25. Franklyn S. Haiman, "An Experimental Study of the Effects of Ethos in Public Speaking," *Speech Monographs* 16 (1949): 190–202. For earlier studies of the prestige of message sources, see Claude E. Arnett, Helen H. Davison, and Harriett N. Lewis, "Prestige as a Factor in Attitude Changes," *Sociology and Social Research* 16 (1931): 49–55; I. Lorge, "Prestige, Suggestion, and Attitudes," *Journal of Social Psychology* 7 (1936): 386–402.

26. See Carl Hovland and Walter Weiss, "The Influence of Source Credibility on Communication Effectiveness," *Public Opinion Quarterly* 15 (1951): 635–650.

27. Carl Hovland, Irving Janis, and Harold Kelly, *Communication and Persuasion* (New Haven, Conn.: Yale University Press, 1953).

28. A bibliography of such studies would include hundreds of items. For some recent studies in the continuing tradition, see Ronald F. Applbaum and Karl W. E. Anatol, "The Factor Structure of Source Credibility as a Function of the Speaking Situation," *Speech Monographs* 39 (1972): 216–222; E. Scott Baudhuin and Margaret Kis Davis, "Scales for the Measurement of *Ethos*: Another Attempt," *Speech Monographs* 39 (1972): 296–301; Raymond G. Smith, "Special Reports: Source Credibility Context Effects," *Speech Monographs* 40 (1973): 303–309; Christopher J. S. Tuppen, "Dimension of Communicator Credibility: An Oblique Solution," *Speech Monographs* 41 (1974): 253–260.

29. Dorwin Cartwright and Alvin Zander, *Group Dynamics: Research and Theory* (New York: Holt, Rinehart and Winston, 1953).

30. See Kurt Lewin, Ronald Lippitt, and Ralph White, "Patterns of Aggressive Behavior in Experimentally Created Social Climates," *Journal of Social*

Psychology 10 (1939): 271–299; see also Ralph White and Ronald Lippitt, "Leader Behavior and Member Reaction in Three Social Climates," in Dorwin Cartwright and Alvin Zander, eds., *Group Dynamics: Research and Theory*, 3rd ed. (New York: Harper & Row, 1968), 318–335.

31. Donald Hayworth, "An Analysis of Speeches in Presidential Campaigns from 1884–1920," *Quarterly Journal of Speech* 16 (1930): 35–42.

32. Howard L. Runion, "An Objective Study of the Speech Style of Woodrow Wilson," *Speech Monographs* 3 (1936): 75–94.

33. For a discussion of content analysis, see Bernard Berelson, *Content Analysis in Communication Research* (Glencoe, Ill.: Free Press of Glencoe, 1952).

34. Robert F. Bales, *Interaction Process Analysis* (Cambridge, Mass.: Addison-Wesley, 1950).

35. See, for example, David M. Berg, "A Thematic Approach to the Analysis of the Task-Oriented Small Group," *Central States Speech Journal* 18 (1967): 285–291; B. Aubrey Fisher, "Decision Emergence: Phases in Group Decision-Making," *Speech Monographs* 37 (1970): 53–66; Thomas M. Scheidel and Laura Crowell, "Idea Development in Small Discussion Groups," *Quarterly Journal of Speech* 50 (1964): 140–145.

36. See, for example, Leonard C. Hawes, "The Effects of Interviewer Style on Patterns of Dyadic Communication," *Speech Monographs* 39 (1972): 114–123; Donna M. Jurick, "The Enactment of Returning: A Naturalistic Study of Talk," *Communication Quarterly* 25 (1977): 21–29; L. Edna Rogers and Richard V. Farace, "Analysis of Relational Communication in Dyads: New Measurement Procedures," *Human Communication Research* 1 (1975): 222–239; Robert E. Nofsinger, Jr., "A Peek at Conversational Analysis," *Communication Quarterly* 25 (1977): 12–20.

37. See, for example, Clifford F. Weigle, "Two Techniques for Surveying Newspaper Readership Compared," *Journalism Quarterly* 18 (1941): 153–157; Donald G. Hileman, "The Young Radio Audience: A Study of Listening Habits," *Journalism Quarterly* 30 (1953): 37–43; Forest L. Whan, "Special Report: Daytime Use of TV by Iowa Housewives," *Journal of Broadcasting* 2 (1958): 142–148.

38. Harrison B. Summers, "Instruction in Radio and Television in Twenty-Five Selected Universities," *Journal of Broadcasting* 2 (1958): 351–368; Gordon Hostettler, "Rising College Enrollments and Teaching Methods: A Survey," *Speech Teacher* 7 (1958): 99–103; Arthur J. Bronstein, "The Study of Phonetics in American Colleges and Universities," *Speech Teacher* 6 (1957): 237–239.

39. Robert K. Merton, Marjorie Fiske, and Alberta Curtis, *Mass Persuasion: The Social Psychology of a War Bond Drive* (New York: Harper & Row, 1946).

40. Hadley Cantril, Hazel Gaudet, and Herta Herzog, *The Invasion from Mars* (Princeton: Princeton University Press, 1940).

41. Theodore M. Newcomb, *Personality and Social Change* (New York: Dryden, 1943); William F. Whyte, *Street Corner Society* (Chicago: University of Chicago Press, 1943).

42. Claude E. Shannon and Warren Weaver; *The Mathematical Theory of Communication* (Urbana: University of Illinois Press, 1949).

43. Wilbur Schramm, ed., *The Process and Effects of Mass Communication* (Urbana: University of Illinois Press, 1954), pp. 4–8.

44. David K. Berlo, *The Process of Communication* (New York: Holt, Rinehart and Winston, 1960).

45. Fritz Heider, *The Psychology of Interpersonal Relations* (New York: Wiley, 1958).

46. Charles G. Osgood and Percy Tannenbaum, "The Principle of Congruity in the Prediction of Attitude Change," *Psychological Review* 62 (1955): 42–55.

47. Leon Festinger, *A Theory of Cognitive Dissonance* (Stanford: Stanford University Press, 1957).

48. William J. McGuire, "Cognitive Consistency and Attitude Change," *Journal of Abnormal and Social Psychology* 60 (1960): 345–353; William J. McGuire, "The Effectiveness of Supportive and Refutational Defenses in Immunizing and Restoring Beliefs Against Persuasion," *Sociometry* 24 (1961): 184–197.

49. For some typical attempts to summarize and synthesize research findings, see Kenneth Andersen and Theodore Clevenger, Jr., "A Summary of Experimental Research in Ethos," *Speech Monographs* 30 (1963): 59–78; Erwin P. Bettinghaus, "Structure and Argument," in Gerald R. Miller and Thomas R. Nilsen, eds., *Perspectives on Argumentation* (Glenview, Ill.: Scott, Foresman, 1966), pp. 130–155; James C. McCroskey, "A Summary of Experimental Research on the Effects of Evidence in Persuasive Communication," *Quarterly Journal of Speech* 55 (1969): 169–179; Gary Cronkhite, *Persuasion and Behavioral Change* (Indianapolis: Bobbs-Merrill, 1969); Barry E. Collins and Harold Guetzkow, *A Social Psychology of Group Processes for Decision Making* (New York: Wiley, 1964); C. David Mortensen, *Communication: The Study of Human Interaction* (New York: McGraw Hill, 1972).

50. For some typical commentaries on laboratory studies, see Roger E. Nebergall, "A Critique of Experimental Design in Communication Research," *Central States Speech Journal* 16 (1965): 13–16; and essays by Theodore Clevenger, Jr., Gerald R. Miller, and Franklyn Haiman in Robert J. Kibler and Larry L. Barker, eds., *Conceptual Frontiers in Speech-Communication* (New York: Speech Association of America, 1969), pp. 144–165, 51–68, 136–139. For a survey of the controversy, see W. Charles Redding, "Research Setting: Field Studies," in Philip Emmert and William D. Brooks, eds., *Methods of Research in Communication* (Boston: Houghton Mifflin, 1970), pp. 105–159.

51. Important essays in setting up the three-part analysis include Charles R. Berger, "The Covering Law Perspective as a Theoretical Basis for the Study of Human Communication," *Communication Quarterly* 25 (1977): 7–18; Peter R. Monge, "The Systems Perspective as a Theoretical Basis for the Study of Human Communication," *Communication Quarterly* 25 (1977): 19–29; Donald P. Cushman, "The Rules Perspective as a Theoretical Basis for the Study of Human Communication," *Communication Quarterly* 25 (1977): 30–45.

52. For a leading exposition of the position, see Jesse G. Delia, "A Constructivist Analysis of the Concept of Credibility," *Quarterly Journal of Speech* 62 (1976): 361–375; Jesse G. Delia, "Constructivism and the Study of Human Communication," *Quarterly Journal of Speech* 63 (1977): 66–83.

53. See, for example, Gerald R. Miller, "Humanistic and Scientific Approaches to Speech Communication Inquiry: Rivalry, Redundancy, or Rapproche-

ment," *Western Speech* 39 (1975): 230–239; Donald C. Shields and John F. Cragan, "Miller's Humanistic/Scientific Dichotomy of Speech Communication Inquiry: A Help or a Hindrance?" *Western Speech* 40 (1976): 278–283.

54. James E. Combs and Michael W. Mansfield, eds., *Drama in Life: The Uses of Communication in Society* (New York: Hastings House, 1976), p. xxix.

21

Notes

2

The Nature
of Communication
Theory

By the 1950s, scholars in many disciplines had joined the rhetoricians with their traditional interest in the study of communication. Sociologists, psychologists, anthropologists, linguists, psychiatrists, philosophers, engineers, information systems specialists, and a number of other people in and out of academic circles began to study communication as a central concern.[1] However, the departmental structure of higher education that these scholars had inherited from late-nineteenth-century educational reforms could not provide an integrated organizational framework for the study of communication. The intellectual style, training, and scholarly traditions of the various disciplines and departments influenced the research and theorizing of communication scholars. Some sociologists were influenced by the school of symbolic interaction, some psycholinguists by developments in linguistics, some psychologists by the attitude change studies. A psychiatrist tended to conceptualize communication in one way, a psycholinguist in another. Even within departmental boundaries or within disciplines, scholars differed. Psycholinguists influenced by Chomsky conceptualized communication differently from those influenced by Skinner. As the bibliographies of works from various perspectives studying communication ballooned, the communication scholar had increasing difficulty keeping up with developments in the field.

Scholars who saw themselves as specialists in communication found the question of what should be included in courses and books on theory more and more pressing by the middle of the twentieth century. How eclectic should the communication theorist be? When theorists developed a course should the latest developments in all fields and disciplines be integrated into it? How much diverse conceptualization could be handled without causing confusion or at the very least oversimplification? Should theorists pick and choose in eclectic fashion and try to relabel and integrate a consistent and coherent conceptualization out of the best of the various schools of study? What was to be done with research results? Should they find their way into courses and books on communication theory?

The problems were difficult, and few writers came forward to present books of integrated and coherent human communication theories.[2] Several scholars compiled anthologies of essays, and many more wrote essays sketching in theories, approaches to theories, or frameworks which might lead to the development of theories.[3] Judging from the books and essays on communication theory, most of the scholars tried to borrow what seemed to them to be the best of the thinking about communication no matter what discipline or research tradition provided the assumptive system for the analysis.

The diversity of interest in and the sense of excitement about communication resulted in a plethora of research, conjectures about possible theories, and projections into the future. Communication theorists often seemed to be scrambling to keep up with the latest and most popular formulations. There is an excitement about being in the vanguard of a significant theoretical breakthrough. As a result, many approaches came to the attention of communication theorists, grew in popularity, and then waned. How then does one sort out what should be included in a discussion of communication theory and what should be omitted as too specialized, esoteric, passé, or unpromising?

The historical problems remain today and beset the writing of a chapter such as this one. What I propose to do is to allude to some of the important lines of theorizing in the study of human communication. I will give brief summaries of the form and content of those I judge to be the more historically significant. I will not have room to develop each approach in all its subtlety.[4] However, the chapter should provide a sense of the nature of what has typically been considered communication theory.

If the future resembles the past, communication theorists will continue to search for new approaches, and some of those currently on the horizon may soon become popular. Quite possibly I will have misjudged their potential and omitted them from my survey. Inevitably what some specialists consider to be the latest or the best theoretical approaches will be omitted as well. The future reader may, therefore, find some then currently attractive approaches slighted or omitted. My purpose is not to provide a comprehensive guide to everything that has, is, or will become popular for scholars and students of communication theory; I confine myself to giving the reader a general historical sense of the nature of communication theory. Such a general historical sense should help to set up the remainder of the book, in which I provide ways to study, analyze, think about, and evaluate communication theories. The ability to evaluate theories will stand one in good stead no matter how rapidly conceptualizations change and what forms the communication theories of the late twentieth century take.

The Many Senses of Communication Theory

Communication theory is a particularly confusing subject for study because the scholars formulating the knowledge base for the new field have used the term *theory* to refer to so many different kinds of thought structures. In addition, they have often shifted meanings for the term within the same book or article. They have used the term in all of the typical dictionary senses such as (1) *theory* as a proposed explanation whose status is still conjectural when compared to established propositions ("I have a theory that if a person advocates a position that is counter to his or her attitude the individual will change to a position closer to the advocated one"); (2) *theory* as the part of a science or an art that deals with principles and methods as opposed to applications or practices ("That may be all right in theory but it won't work in practice"); (3) *theory* as a conception of how things ought to be done or a method for doing them, including the rules and principles relating to the practice ("According to communication theory, good communicators provide lots of feedback"); (4) *theory* as a coherent and deductively consistent set of general laws which account for a broad class of phenomenon ("According to Newton's theory, the law of gravity is applicable everywhere in the universe").

The most general use of the term *theory* refers to the abstract analysis of matters of interest to scholars without much attention to applications. Theory as organized ideas unrelated to observations or practices serves little purpose for the student trying to understand the interrelationship between theory and research. When scholars use the term to denote all abstract discussions of ideas relating to a field of study, they blur some important distinctions. For example, the distinction between a hunch and a well-established explanation is important. Another important distinction is that between a coherent and deductively consistent set of general laws, assumptions, and axioms that accounts for a broad class of phenomenon on the one hand, and a coherent account of principles and methods associated with artistic practices on the other.

Communication experts often use the term *theory* in an indiscriminate way, sometimes in its scientific sense and sometimes in its artistic sense. In one important form of scientific theory we can explain things by accounting for them as specific instances of a general covering law. Why did the apple fall to earth? Because of the pull of gravity. Such scientific explanations also permit planning our affairs so that we can achieve our goals. We can anticipate the effect of gravity on a bridge while we are designing it and make plans so the structure will not fall of its own weight when we build it. An example of the sort of confusion that can result from such an indiscriminate way of using the term *theory* is furnished by the fact that communication theorists sometimes use the term in the sense of a body of organized principles and methods in contrast to a body of covering laws and mathematical applications. They then sometimes expect social scientific or artistic theories to result in the same kinds of explanations and the same predictions as are provided by the covering laws of the natural sciences.

What is the best way to deal with such confusions? One could single out the covering law theory as developed in the natural sciences for special treatment and reserve the honorific term *theory* for that particular sense of its typical dictionary meaning. Such a move leaves one with the problem of deciding how to label all the other conceptualizations that are important in thinking about, practicing, and explaining communication. I will take another course here. When using the term in the remainder of the book I will follow the more general usage of scholars in the field and make it the umbrella term for all careful, systematic, and self-conscious discussion and analysis of communication phenomena. Using the term *theory* as an umbrella does, of course, leave the original problem of making clear distinctions among its many possible meanings. My approach will be to draw the distinctions with qualifers, modifying phrases, and, when necessary, extended explications.

Rhetorical Theory and Communication Theory Compared

One of the major issues facing those who are involved in research and theory building in communication is the relationship between theories about rhetoric and theories about communication.

Rhetorical theory is the accumulated body of writings by experts in various rhetorical communities down through recorded western history. Scholars have, on occasion, treated the writings on rhetoric of such classical figures as Aristotle and Cicero as similar to scientific theories such as Newton's. Scholars have studied the classical rhetorics as though they expressed, if not invariable relationships, at least important principles which were applicable across time, geography, and cultures.[5]

Scholars sometimes studied rhetorical theory by collating various texts, searching for similarities in subsequent writings, and tracing influences back to older times whenever possible.[6] The history of rhetorical theory thus often contains interpretative structures that explain the unfolding of ideas in terms of continuity from past to present, in terms of the influence of previous writers upon subsequent thinkers, and in terms of drawing distinctions among various schools of thought in regard to rhetorical matters.[7]

Some scholars provided a rhetorical theory in the tradition of idealistic German philosophers and of historians such as Toynbee. They constructed cosmic accounts of all human behavior in terms of symbolic action, linguistic behavior, and the uses of symbols in the construction of society. Such cosmic theories tended to be grand panoramic depictions of human history and the human condition, portraying the basic unfolding of human action in dramatistic terms.[8]

Communication theory refers to the accumulated body of writings by experts studying communication from social scientific perspectives. Communication theorists have tended to develop accounts which were analogous to those of the natural scientists. They often seek to formulate their theories so that empirical studies can provide data to confirm or contradict their formulations.

Philosophical Clarification

Definitions of Communication   One important element of communication theory has been the attempt to characterize the essential nature of communication. Berlo's early influential book in communication theory was entitled *The Process of Communication* and characterized it as a dynamic process in which everything is related to every other thing in an infinite number of ways.[9] Subsequently he referred to that formulation as *process-as-mystery*.[10] Still the early attempts at philosophical clarification tended to define communication as a process and then go on to characterize the nature of that process. For example, Dance summarized some definitions of communication presented by the authors of an anthology that he edited and noted that it "is generally agreed upon . . . that communication in general and human communication in particular is a *process*." He saw the agreement about process as a substantial one and argued, "The means of examining something in a quiescent and immobile state are quite different [from] the means of examining something that is in a constant flux, motion, and process."[11]

One of the early philosophical controversies relating to the definition of communication as process was over the proper characterization of the process. Some scholars argued that too often the concept of process was explicated in a linear fashion in which a message source initiated purposive messages which were sent on to receivers. They preferred to emphasize the circular, reciprocal, constant flux and flow of process. The issue was forcibly presented by Smith in an essay titled "Communication Research and the Idea of Process." Smith argued that while scholars often defined communication as a process they seldom set up their research designs in such a way that they could get at the process nature of the phenomena.[12]

Dance and Larson examined 126 definitions of communication and concluded, "Although there are several points of difference in the many definitions of communication, upon at least one aspect the vast majority of scholars seem to be in relative agreement. Most students view communication as a *process*."[13] They noted that the major differences among the definitions related to the level of observation implied by the formulation, the question of intent, and the implication of a normative judgment. Certainly the question of whether or not one of the defining criteria for communication should be a conscious intent on the part of the initiator of messages has been basic to much philosphical analysis of the essence of communication. Linked to the question of intent is the notion that communication ought to be defined in terms of the successful achievement of intent. Dance and Larson concluded their survey and analysis of various definitions of communication with their own, which was "The production of symbolic content by an individual, according to a code, with anticipated consumption by other(s), according to the same code."[14]

In the controversy over the linear nature of the communicative process, a number of scholars suggested characteristics for communication that emphasized that it was, as Johannesen put it, "not a one-way transmission but a two-way dialogue,"[15] Stewart in a somewhat similar vein defined communication as "not simply an act or even an interaction. . . . The interpersonal approach we have developed stresses the idea that human communication is a transaction."[16]

Just as scholars in rhetorical theory have devoted great effort to formulating definitions of rhetoric, so have scholars in communication theory puzzled about the essence of their subject.

Philosophical Analysis of Speech and Language The tradition of doing philosophy by means of language analysis is an old and important one. In the history of America, John Locke's *Essay on Human Understanding* proved influential beginning in the colonial era. In early-twentieth-century western philosophy, language analysis once again became influential for such groups as logical positivists and the ordinary language philosophers who analyze existing nontechnical language to explore philosophical problems.

The relationship between rhetoric and philosophy has been particularly close in recent times. Indeed, an influential journal is entitled *Philosophy & Rhetoric*. Much rhetorical theorizing is philosophical in style. While communication theory has been less closely tied to philosophical systems, some important developments have been based on philosophical analysis. One philosophical tradition that has been important in communication theory is that of pragmatism as represented by such thinkers as Dewey, James, and Peirce. Berlo based some of his analysis of the process of communication on the work of Mead, and subsequent communication theorists in the symbolic interaction tradition often did the same. Dewey and Mead were both at the University of Chicago at one point in their careers and were close acquaintances. Morris, another pragmatist, made a philosophical analysis of language and meaning that distinguished three basic dimensions of language, the syntactical, the semantical, and the pragmatic.[17] Watzlawick, Beavin, and Jackson used Morris's framework as a basis for their study *Pragmatics of Human Communication*.[18]

Another line of philosophical analysis stemming from the ordinary language philosophers that has been influential in both rhetorical and communication theory is that of defining the nature of speech acts. The work of Searle has been particularly important for those interested in developing communication theory.

The philosophical analysis of speech acts is concerned with such questions as how words relate to things and why one string of words is meaningful and another is not, and with the general problem of meaning. To answer such questions, speech act philosophers posit that speaking a natural language is a human activity that can best be analyzed at the level of a unit they call a speech act. That is, they find the level of analysis that examines individual words too context-free for their purposes and the notion that the meaning of a word is its usage by people who speak the language too general for analysis.

They define the proper unit for analysis as the *illocutionary act*. Sentences are stipulated as the units for analysis in illocutionary acts. In addition, speech act philosophers often distinguish illocutionary acts from *perlocutionary acts*. An illocutionary act is essentially saying something and meaning it, while a perlocutionary act is the effect of an illocutionary act. Thus, if a speaker says something, means it, and intends an illocutionary effect and if the hearer understands the utterance, the result is an illocutionary act. A successful illocutionary act may result in the hearer being persuaded to action or being angry, sad, or bored. If a speaker says, "I promise to cut the price by 10 percent if you decide to buy within twenty-four hours," and means it, the result will be an illocutionary act if the hearer recognizes the speaker's intentions as getting him or her to know that the speaker is telling the hearer about the promise. In order to recognize the speaker's intentions, the hearer must know the language the speaker uses and the rules which govern the utterance of sentences in that language. If the hearer then agrees to buy the item, or refuses to buy it, that would be a perlocutionary act.

Searle argued that speaking a language is a rule-governed form of behavior. He was influenced in his analysis by some of the developments in linguistics following Chomsky. He pointed out that in the final analysis the proof that language was rule-governed "will have to come from showing that the hypothesis that human linguistic behavior is rule governed explains the data of speech behavior better than any alternative hypothesis." He went on to suggest that work by Chomsky indicated that "in certain areas, particularly syntax, we are well on the way to having explained a great deal of data on this hypothesis."[19] Searle distinguished two kinds of rules, *constitutive* and *regulatory*. He defined constitutive rules as those that create the possibility of new forms of behavior. Regulatory rules, on the other hand, are those that regulate something that is already happening. If people are already farming and have been doing so for a long time, a governmental agency might develop rules regulating how much acreage could be planted to what crops. Such rules would be regulatory in the sense that Searle used the term. Assume that a group of people decide to develop a new parlor game in which participants throw dice and the winner of each round then has the right to ask a question of any one of the losers. The person the winner questions would then have to answer the question truthfully. The laying down of such rules would *constitute* the game by providing the possibility for new social behavior. Observers who did not know the rules might well be mystified as to what was going on. Searle concluded, "It is important to emphasize the constitutive character of linguistic rules, for no set of purely regulative rules could account for linguistic behavior. . . . The possibility of speaking the language only exists within a system of constitutive rules."[20]

I have stressed the rule-governed analysis of speech acts because the philosophic tradition concerned with the analysis of rules and rule-conforming behavior has become increasingly important in communication theory. Later in the chapter I will examine in greater detail communication theorizing based upon philosophical perspectives about rules.

Guides to Communication Practice

Communication theory often includes rules of thumb to aid practitioners, descriptions of ideal or good communication events, and general criteria for evaluating communication as good or bad, effective or ineffective, ethical or unethical. Definitions of communication frequently relate to such questions as whether communication should be linear, manipulative, and effective in achieving the speaker's intent or whether it should be viewed as emergent, transcendent, and transactional. The rise of a humanistic approach to psychology was reflected in the development of interpersonal communication theory that stressed treating people in a nonmanipulative way.

Exemplar Communication Events   One component of communication theory is often a description of exemplar communication events. Theorists frequently will begin with a definition of communication and move next to an explication of the definition which involves characterizing the events to be studied in terms of a typical or ideal event. The procedure is illustrated by Thayer's comments in "Toward a Theory of Communication in Organizations: Some Speculations." After laying down some guiding assumptions and some basic propositions, Thayer went on to develop a conceptual perspective on organizational communication which saw it composed of an *operational information system,* a *regulatory information system,* and a *maintenance and development information system.* In discussing the interpersonal level of communication, Thayer described a typical or ideal communication practice in the following way:

> We must necessarily make a distinction between *systematic* human (or equipment biases) . . . and random aberrations. Neither can usefully be avoided or changed by enterprise managers, especially in view of the functional relevance to human behavior of human "noise" in the system. . . . One may increase the redundancy of either channel or message, but this widely practiced method for countervailing "noise" is inefficient and relatively ineffective. When message originators achieve an ability to construct messages that take into account systematic human errors in information processing, and at the same time protect against random "noise" through minimum channel or message redundancy, many of the so-called people-problems or communication problems will likely vanish.[21]

Dance and Larson also included ideal or typical communication events in their *The Functions of Human Communication.* They suggested that one important function was that of linking the individual to the social environment. Such linking requires communication, which typically involves self-disclosure. Self-disclosure is risky. The presentation of self may result in acceptance or rejection, and such responses will enhance or threaten the self-image. In discussing the notion of *decentering,* Dance and Larson suggested that it was present when "we focus our attention on the unique characteristics of other people and the likelihood that we will notice, rather than project, similarities is enhanced. Without decentering, our chances to verify similarities are diminished and our chances to discover differences virtually eliminated."[22] They portrayed two conditions which encourage decentering in communication events. One is that of threat and the other that of trust. Their discussion of trust reflected some of the typical interpersonal communication theory in the early 1970s:

> When the interpersonal responses of others signal acceptance of self, trust is the resulting condition. The self is safe. Not only safe, but it is confronted by circumstances that promise even greater levels of acceptance. . . . The basis for increased accuracy under conditions of trust is one's change in behavior as a source, rather than as a receiver.[23]

Thayer's depiction of organizational communication implies that good communicators ought to construct messages that take into account human errors in information processing and guard against random noise. The Dance-Larson analysis of the linking function implies that better social linkages will result from communicators who practice decentering and that one way to achieve such decentering and the resulting improved linkages is to develop trust through self-disclosure and acceptance.

Communication Models as Guides to Practice A prominent feature of communication theorizing has been the development of models of communication processes. In Chapter 4 I analyze the nature of communication models and their function in theorizing. Here I will simply note that starting with an early influential schema developed by Shannon and Weaver, a tradition of depicting descriptions of communication in terms of models flourished and continues to this day. Figure 1 presents some typical examples of communication models, including the original Shannon and Weaver model and the modifications of it by Schramm and Berlo. Figure 2 presents models aimed at overcoming what some theorists thought was a linear depiction of the process by the use of circular diagrams.

Social scientists used models for many different purposes in the 1950s and 1960s, including the depiction of individual choice in such matters as voting, consumer behavior, and the selection of mates; the depiction of collective choice in such matters as the exchange of economic goods, small-group formation, and political coalitions, adaptation, and change; and the diffusion of fads, rumors, political attitudes, and new products.[24] Communication models are thus one aspect of an extensive effort to depict human behavior by graphing, plotting, or diagraming the essential elements and fitting them into a structure.

A comparision of the many attempts to define the essence of communication with the variety of attempts to model the process reveals a number of important similarities. Like the definitions, models tend to abstract features of the process into a set of important elements and tend to differ on the question of whether an essential feature of a communication model should be the intent of the speaker. The concept of feedback in terms of a corrective mechanism implies an intent against which to judge the effect of messages. However, some subsequent model builders such as Barnlund in Figure 2 do not include the intentions of the persons taking part in the communication. Finally, both the models and the definitions often portray how communication should take place in order to be good, successful, or ethical rather than depicting what is generally the case when people communicate with one another.

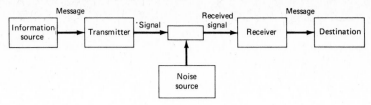

The Shannon and Weaver Model

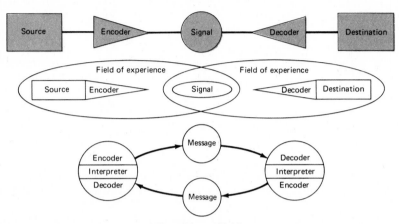

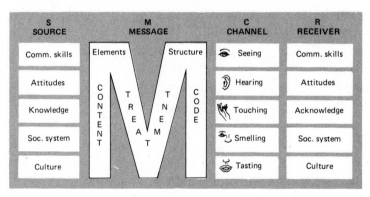

Three Schramm Models

S SOURCE	M MESSAGE		C CHANNEL	R RECEIVER
Comm. skills	Elements	Structure	Seeing	Comm. skills
Attitudes	CONTENT	TREATMENT	CODE	Hearing	Attitudes
Knowledge			Touching	Acknowledge
Soc. system			Smelling	Soc. system
Culture			Tasting	Culture

The SMCR Model of Berlo

Figure 1   Some typical linear communication models.
Shannon-Weaver model of communication (From Claude E. Shannon and Warren Weaver, *The Mathematical Theory of Communication,* Urbana, Ill.: University of Illinois Press, 1949, p. 98).
Schramm models (From Wilbur Schramm, "How Communication Works," in Schramm ed., *The Process and Effects of Mass Communication,* Urbana, Ill.: The University of Illinois Press, 1954, pp. 4–8).
The SMCR Model of Berlo (From David K. Berlo, *The Process of Communication: An Introduction to Theory and Practice,* New York: Holt, Rinehart and Winston, p. 72).

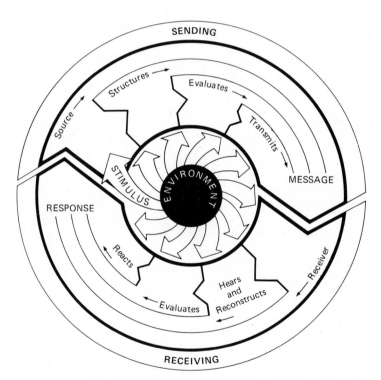

Barnlund's Interpersonal Communication Model

Andersch, Staats, and Bostrom Communication Model

Figure 2   Some typical transactional communication models.
Barnlund's Interpersonal Communication Model Adapted by Applbaum *et al* (From
Applbaum, Ronald, *et al, Fundamental Concepts in Human Communication,* San
Francisco: Canfield Press, p. 49).
Andersch, Staats, and Bostrom Communication Model (From Andersch, Elizabeth
G., Lorin C. Staats, and Robert N. Bostrom, *Communication in Everyday Use,* 3rd
ed. New York: Holt, Rinehart and Winston, 1969, p. 46).

Key Concepts as Guides to Practice   Both definitions of the essence of communication and models which depict the process in graphic form provide the basis for amplification by means of key concepts. A good deal of the communication theory relating to practical applications consists of the further definition and explication of important concepts implied by or associated with the definitions and models. Such concepts as *message source, encoding, decoding, channels, feedback, transmission, message, message structure, noise, redundancy, entropy, source credibility,* and *attitudes* may be implied by models such as those depicted in Figure 1. Concepts such as *openness, trust, self-disclosure, congruency,* and *authenticity* may be implied by a model such as Barnlund's in Figure 2. In Chapter 6 I examine the process of definition and the kind of knowledge that the definitions of communication, of rhetoric, and of such key concepts as those listed above can generate.

Descriptions of Rules and Norms as Guides to Practice   The practical applications of theoretical notions in textbooks and handbooks often specify a taxonomy of communication contexts and associated language games and then go on to specify the rules, norms, and customs associated with those contexts and games. The approach is illustrated by Miller's discussion of what he called the "situational approach" to conceptualizing interpersonal communication. He suggested that the typical taxonomy divides communication contexts into *intrapersonal, interpersonal, small group, public,* and *mass communication.* The defining criteria involve number of communicators, degrees of physical proximity, available sensory channels, and immediacy of feedback. Miller strongly criticized the taxonomy for its inadequacy as an assumptive system to guide research. He did note, "Despite these problems, its acceptance has been widespread and much of what presently passes for theory and research in interpersonal communication rests on a situational foundation."[25]

Miller's critique of such taxonomies as the basis for research was cogent and plausible. However, the popularity of taxonomies that distinguish communication contexts with their associated language games is a function of their usefulness as guides to practice rather than as assumptive systems for research. Successful practitioners of public speaking, for example, come to know the rules and norms for typical communication transactions within cultural groups. They can therefore give advice in terms of clearly specified communication transactions. They may take the category of public communication, for example, and further subdivide it into the typical ceremonial contexts, the typical lecture or briefing-session contexts, the typical persuasive or selling contexts. They may then specify some of the expected norms and rules of the game in terms of recommending the use of humor, the kinds of humor to use if appropriate, the use of evidence, the selection of language, the organization of messages, and so forth.

Standards of Criticism   Practice of the fine and practical arts requires criticism. Artistic forms and types evolve as practitioners try various ways of creating them and critics appreciate and praise some more than others. The forms which achieve critical acclaim then become standards and exemplars for future practitioners. In many communication settings, aesthetic concerns are joined by other standards of good communication, such as successful functioning or achieving desired effects. Criticism requires standards, and with highly developed communication contexts the specialists in criticism and those who coach newcomers to learn to communicate often spell out criteria, and these standards then take their place in the communication theory associated with practice. Statements like "Good interpersonal communication results in a growing awareness of self and others," "Never reveal your minimum disposition to your opponent in a negotiating session," "If you want to sell the product first make them like you as a person," and "To assure high-fidelity transmission of information be sure to encourage feedback from your listeners" are all examples of the implied criteria for evaluation.

Just as practical theorists develop taxonomies of situations, so too they often create taxonomies of functions, uses, and effects. An example of such a taxonomy would be the division of public communication into speeches to entertain, to inform, to convince, and to persuade. Dance and Larson divided communication functions into a linking function relating self to the environment and others, a mentation function, and a regulatory function regulating human behavior. [26] Such taxonomies imply standards for criticism. The speech designed to entertain can be praised for being very entertaining; the speech to persuade can be blamed for failing to persuade its target; the communication designed to link self to others can be praised for achieving satisfactory linkage. In Chapter 4 I examine some of the more academically popular special theories of communication and go into detail about their evaluative components.

Research Summaries and Related Concepts

In discussing communication theory, scholars often include summaries of the research literature. The notion that research ought to grow out of and feed back into theory implies that when investigators have completed an appreciable number of studies the results should begin to form integrated explanatory accounts of the phenomenon under investigation. By the 1950s an impulse developed to provide syntheses of research results which could be relevant to theory development.

Variable Analytic Studies and Related Concepts   Since the variable analytic research tradition in communication involved a strong commitment to theoretically based research, its proponents were actively involved in summarizing research results. A number of scholars made summaries of research in stage fright or communication apprehension, in ethos or source credibility, in message structure and content, and in audience variables. [27]

An example of the way the variable analytic research tradition furnished theoretical concepts in terms of research summaries is provided by Applbaum and his colleagues in *Fundamental Concepts in Human Communication*. The authors distill previous research summaries on *source variables* and delineate concepts such as *source credibility*, *credibility factors*, *credibility stages*, and *effects of source credibility*. They conclude that the research indicates a message's effect to be a function of the source's intentions, expertness, and trustworthiness; that the same message has a different effect depending upon the credibility of the source, and that it is not possible to separate the main factors relating to source credibility, since they interact. They also discuss the long-range impact of source credibility on attitude change and note that a "sleeper" effect seemed to erode the initial impact of source credibility.

In similar fashion Applbaum et al. discuss message variables and the concepts of *ordered* versus *disordered* messages, *primacy* and *recency* in terms of which portion of a message was likely to be remembered, *evidence* and attitude change, and *fear appeals* and the influence of *one-sided* and *two-sided* arguments. [28]

Cronkhite made a detailed summary of research into audience characteristics and their relationship of credulousness and persuadability. Such summaries tend to isolate as variables such concepts as *self-esteem*, *anxiety*, *authoritarianism*, *sex*, *dogmatism*, *cognitive needs*, and *commitment* or *ego-involvement*. [29]

Collins and Guetzkow summarized variable analytic studies in small group decision-making and isolated hypotheses that grow out of or are implied by the research. [30] Shaw followed a similar tack. In both instances, the authors culminated their summaries with hypotheses such as the following one from Shaw: *"Hypothesis 4 Groups usually require more time to complete a task than do individuals working alone* [Shaw's italics]." [31]

Media Surveys and Related Concepts The tradition of studying the mass media by means of surveys and polls has resulted in the development of a series of concepts which often are included in theoretical discussions. One of the first important concepts to grow out of the survey method was that of the *two-step flow* of communication, which was concerned with the impact of the media as mediated by opinion leaders. The two-step flow notion was part of the general approach of scholars examining media effects or asking what the media do to the audience. [32] Some subsequent investigators developed the *uses* and *gratification* approach, which portrays the audience as actively seeking out mass-media communication which fills the needs of the listeners. [33] The focus of the question shifted from what the media does to the audience to what the audience does with the media. Another notion arising from survey studies was the concept of the media as serving an *agenda-setting* function. [34] According to the agenda-setting formulation, the media tell the audience not so much what to think as what to think about.

Content Analysis and Related Concepts Scholars have applied the quantification procedures of content analysis to messages exchanged in two-person meetings, small group sessions, speaker-audience contexts, and the mass media. From content analysis of small group meetings, for example, Bales developed such concepts as the *task-dimension* and the *socio-emotional* dimension of group interaction. [35] In addition, Bales and his associates discovered a *three-*

phase pattern of problem-solving.[36] Fisher used a content analysis system to discover a *four-phase pattern*.[37] A number of other studies have examined the quantitative changes over time in communication interactions and sought patterns that characterize episodes, decisions, and idea development.[38]

Discourse Analysis and Related Concepts   Recently there has developed a growing impulse to study everyday conversations by naturalistic methods. A number of scholars have studied "everyday talk" in an attempt to find patterns that will lead to theory. Nofsinger draws an analogy between Darwinian investigations and conversational analysis. Only after the classifying and describing and the taxonomies are established does the "need for explanation arise."[39] Still, as in other methods of investigation the scholars doing discourse analysis have developed related concepts that assume a place in "communication theory" when this perspective governs a scholar's thinking. Among the more common concepts are *utterance, utterance pair sequencing, episodes, topical sequencing, turn-taking, enactment of episodes*, and *speech acts*. In addition to the concept of speech acts the students of discourse analysis often borrow philosophical notions about rules and rule-conforming behavior in developing their rationale for the study of everyday discourse.[40]

Nonverbal Communication Studies and Related Concepts   Scholars with a particular interest in the nonverbal elements in communication have studied the context of communication situations, the gestures, spatial geography, vocal intonations, facial expressions, eye contact, pauses, and the nonverbal give-and-take of communication transactions. They have developed such concepts as *paralinguistics, kinesics, proxemics*, and *double-edged communication*.[41]

My discussion of concepts related to and growing out of various historic lines of research is illustrative rather than exhaustive. My point is that scholars will often include some summaries and integrations of research results and use research-related concepts as important components in courses and essays concerned with communication theory. The nature and function of concept formation in communication theory are thus important considerations in the study of communication theory. In Chapters 5 and 6 I make extensive analyses of the uses of concepts in theorizing.

Explanatory Hypotheses

An important component in communication theory consists of structured and coherent sets of statements which taken together provide an explanation of a relatively well-defined domain of communication phenomena. Such explanations come closest in communication theory to the theories of the natural sciences. Their primary purpose is not to guide practice nor to provide criteria for evaluating good or bad, effective or ineffective, artistic or inartistic communication.

Information Theory   One of the earliest candidates for a scientific theory of communication was the mathematical theory of communication, also known as information theory. Communications engineers working on technical problems involved in designing efficient sending-and-receiving equipment and transmission lines developed the mathematical theory of communication as an explanation of information and its transmission.

The theory was constructed somewhat like a system of geometry. Shannon, for example, used the term *theorem* when he developed the mathematical structure of the theory in his paper "The Mathematical Theory of Communication."[42] The basic axiom of the geometry is that information is defined as uncertainty. In Warren Weaver's words, "Information is a measure of one's freedom of choice when one selects a message."[43] The theory specifies that uncertainty is measured in terms of the logarithm of the number of available choices. Shannon and Weaver defined a unit of measure of information called a *bit*, an abbreviation of "binary digit." Their decision to make *information* mean *uncertainty* implies that noise in the transmission system that causes uncertainty must also be considered as information. Thus, static becomes information and a distinction must be drawn between desirable and undesirable information.

When engineers adapt the axioms of the system to the mechanical construction of transmission systems or the electronic development of servomechanisms and computers, the theory provides a method of measuring information and of designing efficient transmission systems.

Information theory works best for the electronic and mechanical components in wired and wireless transmission systems. Technically the theory does not cover many of the semantic questions and psycholinguistic problems involved in human communication. One specialist in information theory noted that his book had been criticized by "an information theorist . . . for exploring . . . possible applications of information theory in fields of language, psychology, and art. To him, the relation between such subjects and information theory seems marginal or even dubious." The writer went on to say, "I have felt an obligation to the reader to discuss relations between information theory in its solid and narrow sense and various fields with which it has been connnected in the writing of others."[44]

A number of scholars have applied the concepts from information theory by analogy to the process of human communication.[45] Sometimes they were seeking a scientific model of communication and sometimes they were using the concepts and the general model of Shannon and Weaver as the basis for an artistic theory. In Chapter 4 I make an extended analysis of one important special theory that is related to what I call the message communication style and that is heavily indebted to the mathematical theory of communication for its general assumptive system.

Communication Models   Scholars may use models for several different theoretical functions. Earlier in the chapter I discussed the way models of communication can serve as ideal depictions of the way communication should take place. Scholars also develop models as a way to provide a scientific or social scientific explanation of phenomena.

Stogdill characterized the descriptive model as "an unpretentious name for a theory. Perhaps the term *model* also implies the probability of a somewhat shorter life span than that hoped for a theory."[46] He suggested that model-building involves the ability to observe events and determine the factors operating in the system, the ability to define each factor so others can identify the same dimension, and the ability to perceive the relationships among the different dimensions. Finally the model-builder should discover operational as well as structural characteristics of the system and find some way to represent these operations and characteristics in graphic form, in mathematical equations, or in clear descriptive language.[47]

My analysis of models useful for small group communication theory illustrates the difference between artistic and scientific models. The SMCR model of Figure 1 is often used as the basis for task-oriented small group communication. Barnlund's model depicted in Figure 2 can serve as the basis for growth groups or sensitivity groups. Another model can function as the ideal for consciousness-raising sessions. I have developed the emergent model of small group communication as a descriptive depiction of the natural unvarying dynamics of group process that applies to all groups regardless of the style in which the participants are communicating. Investigators developed the emergent model by intensive case studies of long-term leaderless group discussions. Studies of these groups revealed that communication became specialized, that some members talked more than others, and that the nonverbal communication, the message content, and the direction and flow of messages created and then reflected status differences among members.

The general dynamic by which an unorganized collection of individuals comes to be a structured and relatively stable system is a process of emergence. The members do not select a leader directly, but eliminate those who will not lead, and as others are gradually eliminated the leader role emerges. Instead of selecting a course of action or making a decision, the group eliminates the obviously unsuitable decisions until gradually a decision emerges. The emergent model of small group communication is a feature of all groups. The roles and decisions that emerge in a consciousness-raising session differ from those in a sensitivity group, and both differ from those in a task-oriented business meeting in a modern business corporation, but the norms, status arrangements, roles, and decisions in all three settings are negotiated by the same dynamic processes.[48]

Scholars have not always clearly differentiated the ideal models from the descriptive models when theorizing about communication, and the result has been some confusion about the function and usefulness of communication models. In the remainder of the book I will draw the distinctions and indicate how the two kinds of models function and to what purpose. Essentially the ideal models are part of the artistic special theories and the descriptive models are part of the general theories of communication.

Elevating Concepts to Theory Status   Sometimes scholars append the term *theory* to an important concept in communication. Fisher noted, "Our journals are replete with references to variables elevated to the status of theory—for example, 'self-disclosure theory,' 'ego-involvement theory,' 'source credibility theory,' 'leadership theory,' 'interpersonal attraction theory.' "[49]

Scholars are probably unwise in using the term *theory* in such an inappropriate fashion. Calling a concept a theory is often a rhetorical move to elevate, as Fisher implies, the results of a line of research to a higher status than it may deserve. Using the term in such an indiscriminate way also encourages the proliferation of terms and concepts. Fisher concludes, "The tendency to grant variables such omnipotent status, however, clouds the theoretical issues in favor of the variable. We rub our favorite variable(s) against other variables, singly or multiply, and thus confuse further the theoretical orientation in favor of an empirical orientation."[50]

Consistency Theories Among the early important *theories* in the sense of hunches or hypotheses that found their way into communication were a family of "balance" accounts. These explained persuasion in terms of an idealized consumer of messages. When the idealized communicator is comfortable, it is because of a consistent arrangement of meanings, cognitions, and attitudes that are in harmony. However, should new messages unsettle the balance, the individual becomes disturbed and the harmony becomes dissonant. The individual will feel constrained to regain a comfortable, consistent and harmonious state and will change some attitudes to achieve that condition.

Heider formulated an early balance or consistency account. Heider's system contained three basic elements: (1) a person who is the focus of the analysis, (2) a person who is a significant other to the first person, and (3) an impersonal factor that has a value or emotional valence for the focal person. The impersonal factor could include particular kinds of automobiles, schools of art, political positions, moral stands, and so forth. The three basic elements are connected by some important relationship term such as "liking" or "disliking." Heider assumed that the system was in balance if all of the relationships were positive or if two were negative and one was positive. Suppose the focal person likes the significant other and both dislike the anti-abortion movement; the system has one positive and two negative elements and is in balance. Likewise if the focal person likes the significant other and both like the anti-abortion movement the system is balanced. However, should the system contain two positives and one negative, it would be imbalanced and the focal individual would feel the strain for consistency. If the focal individual likes the other person and dislikes the anti-abortion movement while the other individual likes the anti-abortion movement, then the system is imbalanced. The focal individual will change to modify the positive attitude toward the other or the negative attitude toward the anti-abortion issue or both in order to bring the system back to equilibrium.[51]

Osgood and Tannenbaum developed another balance explanation, which they called a congruity hypothesis. In the Osgood and Tannanbaum account the focal individual receives a message in which the significant other is connected to a concept. The assertion linking the concept is assumed to be loaded positively or negatively. The focal person is assumed to have a prior attitude toward both the message source and the concept, and the attitude varies in either a positive or negative direction and in intensity. Thus, the assertion that the significant other has written a letter mildly attacking the anti-abortion movement would be a bit incongruent for the focal person who likes the significant other to a moderate extent but intensely dislikes the anti-abortion movement. [52]

Another and, perhaps, the most popular of the balance notions was formulated by Festinger and called "cognitive dissonance theory." Festinger's account focuses upon an idealized individual who has the piece of information that he or she smokes and the piece of information that smoking is likely to cause lung cancer. Such an individual would experience cognitive dissonance, according to Festinger's account, only if that individual also held strongly to the value of self-preservation. The account assumes that dissonance is psychologically uncomfortable and will create a strain which motivates the individual to bring about a situation which is more comfortable, by, for example, giving up smoking. [53]

Additional Hypotheses Accounting for Social Psychological Behavior Communication theorists often borrowed explanatory accounts and hypotheses from social psychology and included them in writings on communication theory in the 1960s. Since the borrowing was widespread, it would take a textbook in social psychology to do justice to all of the terms and concepts that found their way in a greater or lesser degree into conjecture about communication theory. I will simply mention some of the more important and briefly discuss the most influential of them.

In the 1950s and 1960s, Skinnerian psychology was popular and provided an assumptive system that was strongly biased in the direction of behaviorism for the study of organisms, including human beings. Communication theorists sometimes borrowed concepts and experimental approaches from behaviorism for the study of their concerns. The tendency was to study learning in terms of conditioned responses and to explain behavior in terms of more or less complicated combinations of a basic stimulus-response unit. When a stimulus was followed by a response and the response was reinforced, a conditioning process began that, if continued, would result in creating a learned behavior.

Communication theorists applied the behavioristic concepts by distinguishing between *empirical* and *hypothetical* constructs. Empirical constructs are operationally defined concepts. For example, if I define *habit strength* as the number of times a rat correctly runs a maze, the result would be an empirical construct. Assume, however, that a number of rats are subjected to stimulus and the responses to the stimulus are carefully indexed. If the investigators carefully control both the stimulus and the environment and discover considerable variability in the responses, they cannot account for the behavior on the basis of a simple stimulus-response relationship. They can, however, develop a *hypothetical construct,* which is a possible uncontrolled or unknown variable that cannot be observed which intervenes between the stimulus and the response. A set of hypothetical constructs would succeed if a theorist could account for the observable responses by assuming their intervention between the observable stimuli and responses.

Hull developed a system of empirical and hypothetical constructs to account for learning behavior of animals which became popularly known as part of "learning theory."[54] Osgood used hypothetical constructs to account for meaning in the communication process. Between the stimulus furnished by a word and the overt response to that stimulus, Osgood suggested the hypothetical construct of *representational mediation processes* to account for the observable variations in responses to the word from situation to situation for the same individual and from individual to individual. Osgood and his associates developed a research program to study representational mediation processes, and the result was the semantic differential procedure, which was designed to measure meaning.[55]

In recent years behaviorism has waned in popularity among communication theorists.[56] The balance theories assume complex psychological processes in human beings. A number of other more complicated formulations were suggested to account for social psychological behavior. McGuire, for example, developed an analogy based on the biological resistance to disease built up by inoculations to account for resistance to persuasion. Sometimes called "inoculation theory," the formulation suggested that to strengthen resistance to arguments against an attitude a person may strengthen that attitude with supportive arguments. Another way to strengthen resistance, however, would be to inoculate the individual with a dose of refuted arguments against the position.[57]

Somewhat similar to McGuire's "inoculation theory" is the notion that people who argue against an attitude that they hold will change it as a result. Some interpreted the effect of arguing for a point of view opposite from one's own as an instance of the cognitive dissonance hypothesis, since they assumed that a person who is induced to argue counter to a previously held attitude will experience a feeling of dissonance. Others accounted for the effect on the basis of the influence of role-playing. The notions about the effect of presenting an opinion counter to a held attitude are often called *counterattitudinal advocacy.*[58]

Some communication theorists adopted the idea from social psychology that people will attribute the causes of human action in systematic ways.[59] Often referred to as "attribution theory," the explanation suggested that human beings make judgments systematically and follow a process of inference-drawing and decision-making which is predictable. Insko and Schopler explained, "In a general sense, attribution processes refer to the perceiver's efforts at understanding the underlying stabilities in his environment."[60] More specifically, attribution explanations often dealt with the narrower question of how people attribute sufficient causes to account for the behavior of others and for their own actions. An important distinction relating to attribution accounts was whether or not the individuals attributed the cause of action to motives within the actors or to the influence of the situation. Another distinction was whether or not the individuals attributed the behavior to stable or momentary motives or situational constraints.

Kelman developed a typology of conditions to explain social influence on personal belief. According to the typology, people might be influenced to comply because they hoped to achieve a favorable reaction from others even though they did not believe the content of the behavior. A second social-influence situation was one in which people would identify with others by establishing or maintaining a desirable relationship. Since their identity or self-concept was closely tied to the others, they would be liable to social influence from the people they identified with. The final situation in which social influence was likely was when people internalized the behavior because they found the content of the belief underlying the behavior to be valid or correct. Some communication theorists adopted Kelman's "social influence theory" to provide an explanation of persuasion. [61]

Thibaut and Kelly developed an "exchange theory" to account for behavior in social groups, and it proved popular with a number of communication theorists. Based on an economic analogy, the exchange theory assumes that just as a customer gives a vendor money in return for goods, social interaction involves an explicit or implicit exchange of costs and rewards. The account also assumes that human beings will act so as to maximize rewards and minimize costs when interacting with others. [62]

Thibaut and Kelly formulated an explanation for judging whether outcomes are rewards or costs in terms of comparison levels. Outcomes above the comparison level are rewards, and those below it are costs. The comparison level is a generalized standard developed by an individual's past experience and information. In addition, Thibaut and Kelly provided a comparison level based on the next best social situation.

Elsewhere I have adapted and modified the social exchange explanation to the development of group cohesiveness and the attractiveness of a given group to an individual member. [63]

In general, communication scholars have often incorporated social psychological perspectives on such matters as equity, person perception, conflict, and interpersonal attractiveness into their discussions of communication theory.

Linguistic and Psycholinguistic Hypotheses The study of philology and linguistics has had a long tradition in western culture. In more contemporary times, scholars from a number of disciplines have concentrated their efforts on such questions as how children acquire language and how communities of people communicate with one another. Since the 1950s, communication theorists have become increasingly interested in developments in linguistics, psycholinguistics, and ethnographic approaches.

In terms of language acquisition, two early approaches suggested that children learned language (1) by imitating the utterance they hear or (2) by being conditioned to do so in a fashion compatible with a behavioristic position. The behavioristic approach saw language acquisition as a result of the reinforcement schedules provided by the environment that shaped the babblings of the infant into intelligible speech.

One of the first major attacks on the behavioristic approach to communication was launched by linguists who argued that the behavioristic assumptions could not account for the acquisition and use of speech. Chomsky is often cited as the leader of the movement, which argued that neither imitation nor operant conditioning could account for the ability of the child who has mastered a language to produce and understand novel utterances.

Those who attacked behaviorism as inadequate put forward another hypothesis to explain language acquisition. They first distinguished between language *competence* and *performance*. They saw competence as the latent ability to speak and understand a language and performance as the actual use of the language. According to their formulation, children might be competent to produce utterances that for some reason or another they never produced, but an adequate "theory" would have to account for those utterances as well as for the things the children did say.

They posited an innate language-acquisition device that enabled children to take a sample of natural language and infer from the sample the rules necessary for the creation and understanding of the sentences in their community.[64]

The study of the competence rules can be thought of as the study of the rules of a given language, but the study of performance requires an analysis of all that goes into natural talk, including such things as the intentions of the speakers, the situational constraints, the nonverbal elements, the physiology of speech, encoding, decoding, and the emotional evocations of speech, as well as linguistic competence. Williams and Lindsay suggested that one way to view psycholinguistics is "as the study of how competence enters into performance." They also suggested that sociolinguistics could be defined in terms of "how performance varies with the social factors of language behavior."[65]

Hymes, from an anthropological perspective, suggested that members of communities develop communication systems which are unique and that an ethnographic approach to communication is the best way to study them. Individuals may come to acquire communication competence within a community which functions much as does linguistic competence within a language community. Hymes argued that if anthropologists take as a starting point a linguistic code, they will leave out much that is important to understanding the use of that code in a given community. On the other hand, if the ethnographer makes a study of the culture of the community without examining the linguistic code, much that is important to understanding the communication is also lost. He suggested that an ethnolinguistic study would take as a starting place the structure of communication events. He concluded that from an ethnographic approach to communication, "It becomes a natural thing to consider the relations among the full range of communicative modalities and varieties of language, as selectively employed by persons and as variously deployed in a community."[66]

In the 1970s the influence of theoretical developments in the study of linguistics, psycholinguistics, sociolinguistics, and ethnolinguistics on communication scholars grew as the popularity of the variable analytic approach waned.

Mathematical Formulations   Although it was not a strong tendency, there was a marked impulse among communication theorists to develop mathematical theories. I have already noted the most well-developed such theory in my discussion of information theory. However, from time to time, scholars have made more modest attempts at mathematical modeling for communication events. Berger and Calabrese suggested an exploration of a developmental theory of interpersonal communication which included seven axioms and twenty-one theorems.[67] The axioms consisted of statements such as "*Similarities between persons reduce uncertainty, while dissimilarities produce increases in uncertainity.*" The Berger–Calabrese formulations were couched in mathematical terms such as axioms and theorems, but the theorems were not derived by computations and mathematical demonstration because they contained terms such as *reduce, increase,* and *are positively related* rather than quantities that could be interpreted mathematically.

Some, however, tried to use functions expressed in mathematical equations to express basic communication laws. One set of investigators presented the Woelfel–Saltiel theory in the following terms.[68]

At its simplest level, the theory suggests that an attitude is the joint effect of a set of messages, $x_1, x_2, \ldots, x_n$. The consequent attitude a is the linear sum of the messages divided by a number n of messages. Attitude a can be represented as:

$$a = \bar{x} = \frac{1}{n} x_1 + \frac{1}{n} x_2 + \ldots + \frac{1}{n} x_n = \sum_{i=1}^{n} \frac{xi}{n}$$

Hewes, Brazil, and Evans developed a "theory" relating to the interrelationships among messages, mediating variables, and behavior, The theory was formalized mathematically, based upon axioms expressed both verbally and in mathematical formulas, and interpreted as a stochastic model. The theory is based upon axioms and corollaries such as "*Axiom I* implies that the process being described is of the 'first order'; that is, predicting a future event is assumed to require no more information than that contained in the immediately prior event and the method of mapping one event onto the other."[69] I will not include the formulas in my brief review, since they tend to be matrixes which are cumbersome to portray and essentially meaningless out of context. The authors' approach is to develop the model from mathematical axioms and then test it empirically be setting up observational situations in which they fulfill the assumptions provided by the axioms. If the computations derived from the theory anticipate the results of studies designed to test it, the argument is that the theory has been supported. The authors conclude a study in the variable analytic form that examined the influence of persuasive messages on attitudes toward socialized medicine as follows: "The theory has also held up well under empirical test. The *worst* prediction of behavioral expectations failed to accurately predict only 6.6% of the subjects, while the best misclassified only 2.4%."[70]

Systems Accounts   The systems approach to the study and understanding of phenomena can be contrasted to the style of inquiry that analyzes events into parts and reduces their complexity into explanations based upon understanding their components. An example of the reductionist approach would be to explain consciousness in terms of physiological laws, to explain living matter in terms of physics and chemistry, and to explain physics and chemistry in terms of subatomic particles and wave motions. Thus, I might take a reductionist stance and argue that mental illness will eventually be explained in terms of some physical malfunction, that the physical malfunction will be explained in terms of chemical disturbances in the nerve cells, and thus that mental depression will at some point be cured by the taking of the proper pill. A systems approach would assume that important features of phenomena are emergent and based upon complex interrelationships among components such that the whole is greater than the sum of its parts.

Scholars in many different disciplines have taken the systems perspective as a basis for the study of living organisms and the universe itself. In the last several decades a number of communication theorists have applied it to their concerns. For a time the diversity of the literature served to confuse the issue for those communication theorists with an interest in moving to accounts which were not reductionist. Fisher, for example, reported attending a conference on systems theory and communication. He concluded:

> During two days of concentrated effort, we attempted valiantly, and ultimately futilely, to agree on recommendations for future systems research in communication. Moreover, we did not even agree on what constitutes systems approaches to communication inquiry.[71]

Fisher nevertheless went on to suggest some general characteristics of systems "theory" and to discuss research and "thinkpieces" in communication stemming from a systems perspective. Scholars with a systems viewpoint generally assume them to be holistic in the sense that the system is different from the sum of the component parts. They generally assume them to be either open or closed, although some theorists see degrees of openness. Open systems exchange energy and information with their environments and do not follow either the second law of thermodynamics or the principle of the conservation of energy. They generally assume that a system has a hierarchical structure. Thus, scholars with a systems perspective will often search for subsystems within a system and for the larger system in which the system they are studying is a subsystem.

The major scholarly work from a systems perspective has consisted of what Fisher termed "thinkpieces." He characterized them as "above all, models of inquiry. . . . That is, although the general properties of systems are common to all models, the suggested isomorphisms with empirical phenomena of communication vary widely, depending on the authors' emphases and interests."[72]

Typical of the "thinkpieces" which characterize contemporary scholarship relating to systems is one by Monge in which he examined the logical and empirical requirements for a systems perspective in the study of communication, discussed four alternative systems (open, closed, cybernetic, structural-functional), compared and contrasted the systems approach to competing philosophical positions, and concluded with a discussion of the epistemological nature of the perspective.

Monge argued that a systems explanation required the development of a mathematical model and further that "(1) the formal calculus entails expectations, (2) the terms of the calculus are loaded with empirical referents (by rules of correspondence), and (3) isomorphism is established between the logical system and empirical reality."[73] Monge's approach to theorizing was first to establish an explanatory model and then to check it against empirical data. He applied his approach to some concepts drawn from Watzlawick, Beavin, and Jackson.[74] The majority of the essay, however, examined causal explanations in contrast to teleological explanations, rules accounts of the practical syllogism in contrast to a systems perspective. The essay concluded by presenting the advantages of the systems approach to research and theorizing.

Monge's article is typical in that it contains a mixture of philosophical analysis, some suggested frameworks for possible research and theoretical development, and some argument in behalf of the advantages of using the frameworks.[75]

Generally, the scholars employing a systems perspective have not produced a great deal of research. Fisher noted that some network studies could be considered systems analyses but that the majority of the research had been in interaction sequences, and he referred to content analysis studies such as Bales's Interaction Process Analysis and his own work in interaction patterns through time in small group discussions. Some of the work, of course, was not governed by a systems perspective. However, Fisher pointed out that the use of stochastic probability models to analyze interaction data brought this line of research closer to a system approach.[76]

Farace, Monge, and Russell developed a structural-functional analysis of small groups in large organizations utilizing systems concepts and terms.[77] I have provided an account of the presidential political campaign as a communication system and traced the sharing of group fantasies through the various subsystems.[78]

Conceptualizing communication in systems terms is compatible with the emphasis on defining communication as a process and with the emphasis on nonlinear and transactional communication episodes. Several systems scholars have integrated information theory with systemic accounts.[79] For those searching for an alternative to the variable analytic research tradition, with its implied search for invariable relations and causal explanations, the systems perspective and the emphasis on interrelationships and holistic analysis is often attractive. At this point in the development of systems accounts, the emphasis has been upon philosophical and critical analysis of assumptions, possible approaches, and advantages and disadvantanges of systems research and theory.

Rules Theory   Much of the writing from the rules perspective consists of "thinkpieces" similar to the studies of systems approaches. I have noted earlier in this chapter that the speech act philosophers based their analysis upon an explication of constitutive and regulatory rules. The influence of linguistics and sociolinguistics and developments relating to the Chomsky approach to linguistic competence are interrelated with speech act philosophy and with the impulse to study communication from a rules perspective.

In addition to Searle, such philosophers as Toulmin, von Wright, and Harré have been influential on scholars in communication who are developing conceptualizations based upon rules.[80] Theorists and researchers who are using the rules perspective are searching for an account that incorporates gaming behavior and normative regularities that are not described by some iron law of nature but are in conformity with conventional, breakable rules.

An early seminal essay by Rosenfield examined communication as gaming activity and discussed rules, customs, and rituals associated with it.[81] A few years later, Cushman and Whiting expanded the analysis to define and explicate the nature of rules as related to communication.[82] Subsequently Cushman and a number of associates have published philosophical analyses of rules and their relationship to communication transactions in a variety of contexts. Much of the analysis has included comparative advantage arguments that contrast the rules perspective with the covering law perspective and with systems accounts.[83] However, recently Cushman has drawn together ideas from Searle, von Wright, Toulmin, Harré, Mead, and a number of lesser sources and developed a more detailed and less polemic perspective for viewing communication.

I will take the Cushman formulation as an example of a contemporary rules theory in communication. The Cushman account assumed that groups of people engaged in some task develop a system of rules to govern their information processing and coordinating. These systems of rules are persistent because they are functional. The term Cushman used for such persistent rule systems was *standardized usage*. Cushman argued that when people understand the standardized usage for a given community and context, they can communicate successfully with others who share that understanding. Scholars who discover the standard usage can then anticipate and explain the communicative behavior by referring it to the appropriate rules.

The application of the standardized usage to a particular communication event involves the understanding of *episodes:* "Episodes consist of the communicators' interpretation of the actual sequences of messages they jointly produce. . . ."[84] The nature of rules assures the possibility that people who understand the conventional usage may for a number of reasons fail to conform to them. People may be unconventional in order to win an advantage, for the shock value of breaking the rule, and so forth. An adequate account requires that we understand not only the standardized usage pertaining to an episode but also why people involved in a communication episode conform or fail to conform to the rules.

Cushman's answer to the problem of explaining comformity is von Wright's practical syllogism. The practical syllogism is an argument cast in the form of premises and conclusions. The premises are that an individual or a group of people want and intend to achieve a goal. They consider that in order to achieve the goal they must do certain things. Given these assumptions it follows that they set about doing the things they feel will achieve their goal. Thus, if the participants in a communication episode want and intend to achieve a goal and they consider that conforming to the standardized usage will achieve that goal, then they will conform.[85]

Cushman and associates have distinguished four levels of communication systems, each with a different sort of practical usage. The four levels are (1) mass communication, (2) organizational communication, (3) group communication, and (4) interpersonal communication. While the three more general levels require shared group and community rules, the fourth level, interpersonal communication, consists of the idiosyncratic rule systems of individuals. Cushman's formulation draws on Mead's analysis of the process of self-concept development through role-taking to account for the evolution of an individual's standardized usage. In Cushman's words, "The standardized usage employed is person specific." At the basic interpersonal level of analysis, "the content and procedural rules employed provide information regarding an individual's relationship to objects or persons and prescribe the communication patterns in regard to interpersonal roles."[86]

Conceptualizing communication in terms of conventional rules is compatible with an influential school of philosophy of language and with developments in linguistics, psycholinguistics, and sociolinguistics. In addition, it provides an alternative to the variable analytic tradition and the search for invariable relations that provide a causal explanation for communication events. The rules perspective opens the way for accounting for the intention of human actors and for the conventional nature of communicative activity.

It is an open question whether or not the systems approach and the rules perspective are different in kind. Some scholars have suggested that the trichotomy among laws, rules, and systems is not a useful one and that systems approaches can profitably be integrated with rules accounts.[87] Certainly the more popular formulations of rules accounts do assume that communication is a process and do emphasize the nonlinear and transactional nature of communication episodes.

At this point in the development of rules perspectives, the emphasis, as in systems approaches, has been upon constructing philosophical systems, making critical analyses of basic assumptions about the nature of being and knowledge assumed by various approaches, and providing a case for the comparative advantages of the rules accounts.

Summary

Communication theory is a confusing subject for study because the scholars formulating the ideas have used the term *theory* to refer to so many different kinds of thought structures. One important element in communication theories has been philosophical analysis and clarification such as explications of the term *communication* in definitional form, and philosophical analyses of such things as speech acts and communication rules. Another important element has been instructional: guides to communication practice such as exemplar communication events often presented as models, key concepts which aid in providing rule-of-thumb advice, descriptions of rules and norms, and standards of criticism.

Communication theory often includes research summaries and concepts growing out of research programs. Particularly important in this regard have been the variable analytic research, mass-media surveys, content analysis, discourse analysis, and research into nonverbal communication.

Among the important components of communication theory are structured and coherent sets of statements that have as a primary purpose not the guiding of practice but rather the providing of general explanations of communication events. Such explanations come closest in communication theory to the theories of the natural sciences. An important illustration of such material is information theory. Recently a number of theoreticians have provided mathematical formulations to account for communication in addition to the mathematical theory of communication.

Communication theorists often borrowed explanatory accounts from social psychology and adapted them to the communication contexts. Among the important social psychological accounts were behaviorist explanations of language acquisition and usage, consistency or balance theories, inoculation and counterattitudinal explanations of attitude change, Kelman's typology to explain social influence, and such other materials as exchange theory and attribution theory.

Communication theorists have often had an interest in the developments in linguistics, psycholinguistics, and sociolinguistics, and in the ethnographic approach to communication. Such concepts as language competence and performance and the study of language communities have had particular influence on explanations of communication episodes.

Systems accounts of communication have become increasingly popular as scholars from many different disciplines have taken the perspective that humans interact and communicate in hierarchical interrelated structures that function in a holistic fashion in which the totality amounts to more than the sum of its parts.

Also increasingly popular have been the rules approaches to formulating explanatory accounts of human communication. The rules perspective often focuses upon gaming behavior and normative regularities that are not necessarily described by some iron law of nature but are in conformity with conventional rules that can be broken.

Notes

1. For example, in 1967 Dance edited a volume of original essays in communication theory. The essays were written by Dell Hymes, anthropologist; George Gerbner, mass communication; Lee Thayer, psychologist and professor of business administration; John R. Searle, philosopher; Joost A. M. Meerloo, psychiatrist; Jerry A. Fodor, philosopher and linguist; James J. Jenkins, psycholinguist; Sol Saporta, linguist; Jack M. McLeod, journalism and mass communication; Hugh Dalziel Duncan, sociologist; Robert T. Oliver, speech communication; and Mary A. B. Brazier, neurophysiologist. Frank E. X. Dance, ed., *Human Communication Theory: Original Essays* (New York: Holt, Rinehart and Winston, 1967).
2. Among those who did provide such accounts were David K. Berlo, *The Process of Communication* (New York: Holt, Rinehart and Winston, 1960); Frank E. X. Dance and Carl E. Larson, *The Functions of Human Communication: A Theoretical Approach* (New York: Holt, Rinehart and Winston, 1976); B. Aubrey Fisher, *Perspectives on Human Communication* (New York: MacMillan, 1978).
3. For examples of anthologies, see Dance; also C. David Mortensen, ed., *Basic Readings in Communication Theory* 2nd ed. (New York: Harper &

Row, 1979). Essays sketching in theories or approaches to theories abound in the journals. Such essays are also featured in the yearbooks published annually since 1977 by the International Communication Association.

4. Most of the approaches have extensive bibliographies, and I will indicate in notes some typical sources for the reader who wishes greater detail and amplification.

5. See, for example, Lloyd F. Bitzer, "Aristotle's Enthymeme Revisited," *The Quarterly Journal of Speech* 45 (1959): 399–408; Wayne E. Brockriede, "Toward a Contemporary Aristotelian Theory of Rhetoric," *The Quarterly Journal of Speech* 52 (1966): 33–40; Gary L. Cronkhite, "The Enthymeme as Deductive Rhetorical Argument," *Western Speech* 30 (1966): 129–134; Lawrence W. Rosenfield, "Rhetorical Criticism and an Aristotelian Notion of Process," *Speech Monographs* 33 (1966): 1–16.

6. See, for example, William M. Sattler, "Some Platonic Influences in the Rhetorical Works of Cicero," *The Quarterly Journal of Speech* 35 (1949): 164–169; James Stephens, "Bacon's New English Rhetoric and the Debt to Aristotle," *Speech Monographs* 39 (1972): 248–259.

7. See, for example, Part I of Lester Thonssen and A. Craig Baird, *Speech Criticism: The Development of Standards for Rhetorical Appraisal*, 1st ed. (New York: Ronald Press, 1948).

8. Perhaps the foremost contemporary rhetorical theorist in this school is Kenneth Burke.

9. Berlo.

10. David K. Berlo, "Communication as Process: Review and Commentary," in Brent D. Ruben, ed., *Communication Yearbook I* (New Brunswick, N.J.: Transaction Books, 1977), p. 12. Berlo went on to write, "Fortunately for our intellectual future, the referent of *process-as-mystery* has diminished as our acceptance within the academy has risen. Process-as-mystery was not an intellectual position that could be translated into scholarly activity."

11. Dance, p. 293.

12. David H. Smith, "Communication Research and the Idea of Process," *Speech Monographs* 9 (1972): 174–182.

13. Dance and Larson, p. 28.

14. Ibid., p. 37.

15. Richard L. Johannesen, "The Emerging Concept of Communication as Dialogue," *The Quarterly Journal of Speech* 57 (1971): 373.

16. John Stewart, "An Interpersonal Approach to the Basic Course," *The Speech Teacher* 21 (1972): 9.

17. Charles W. Morris, *Foundations of the Theory of Signs* (Chicago: University of Chicago Press, 1938).

18. Paul Watzlawick, Janet Beavin, and Don D. Jackson, *Pragmatics of Human Communication* (New York: Norton & Co., 1967).

19. John R. Searle, "Human Communication Theory and the Philosophy of Language: Some Remarks," Dance, ed., p. 120. See also John R. Searle, *Speech Acts: An Essay in the Philosophy of Language* (London: Cambridge University Press, 1969).

20. Searle, "Human Communication Theory," p. 126.

21. Lee Thayer, "Communication and Organization Theory," in Dance, ed., p. 96.

22. Dance and Larson, p. 126.

23. Ibid., p. 122.

24. For a survey of model building in the behavioral sciences in the 1950s and

1960s, see Ralph M. Stogdill, ed., *The Process of Model-Building in the Behavioral Sciences* (Columbus, Ohio: Ohio State University Press, 1970).

25. Gerald R. Miller, "The Current Status of Theory and Research in Interpersonal Communication," *Human Communication Research* 4 (1978): 167. Donald Cushman and B. Thomas Florence do develop a conceptualization of interpersonal communication on the basis of the situational approach. They argue that at each level of communication system there are standarized usages consisting of "systems of rule governed symbol meaning associations." "The Development of Interpersonal Communication Theory," *Today's Speech* 22 (Fall 1974): 11–16.

26. Dance and Larson, pp. 41–49.

27. See, for example, Theodore Clevenger, Jr., "A Synthesis of Experimental Research in Stage Fright" *The Quarterly Journal of Speech* 45 (1959): 134–145; James C. McCroskey, "Oral Communication Apprehension: A Summary of Recent Theory and Research," *Human Communication Research* 4 (1977): 78–96; Kenneth Andersen and Theodore Clevenger, Jr., "A Summary of Experimental Research in Ethos," *Speech Monographs* 30 (1963): 59–78; Kim Giffin, "The Contribution of Studies in Source Credibility to a Theory of Interpersonal Trust in the Communication Process," *Psychological Bulletin* 68 (1967): 104–120; Herbert W. Simons, N. Berkowitz, and J. R. Moyer, "Similarity, Credibility, and Attitude Change: A Review and a Theory," *Psychological Bulletin* 73 (1970): 1–16; Erwin P. Bettinghaus, "Structure and Argument," in Gerald R. Miller and Thomas R. Nilsen, eds., *Perspectives on Argumentation* (Glenview, Ill.: Scott, Foresman, 1966), pp. 130–155; James C. McCroskey, "A Summary of Experimental Research on the Effects of Evidence in Persuasive Communication," *Quarterly Journal of Speech* 55 (1969): 169–176; C. David Mortensen, *Communication: The Study of Human Interaction* (New York: McGraw-Hill, 1972); Gary Cronkhite, *Persuasion and Behavioral Change* (Indianapolis: Bobbs-Merrill, 1969).

28. Ronald L. Applbaum, Karl W. E. Anatol, Ellis R. Hays, Owen O. Jenson, Richard E. Porter, and Jerry E. Mandel, *Fundamental Concepts in Human Communication* (San Francisco: Canfield Press, 1973), pp. 123–146.

29 Cronkhite.

30. Barry E. Collins and Harold Guetzkow, *A Social Psychology of Group Processes for Decision Making* (New York: Wiley, 1964).

31. Marvin E. Shaw, *The Psychology of Small Group Behavior,* 1st, ed. (New York: McGraw-Hill, 1971), p. 81.

32. See, for example, Elihu Katz, "The Two-Flow of Communication: An Up-to-Date Report on a Hypothesis," *Public Opinion Quarterly* 21 (1957): 61–78.

33. Jay Blumler and Elihu Katz, eds., *The Uses of Mass Communication* (Beverley Hills, Calif.: Sage, 1974).

34. Maxwell E. McCombs and Donald L. Shaw, "The Agenda-Setting Function of the Mass Media," *Public Opinion Quarterly* 36 (1972): 176–187.

35. Robert F. Bales, *Interaction Process Analysis: A Method for the Study of Small Groups* (Cambridge, Mass.: Addison-Wesley, 1950).

36. Robert F. Bales and Fred L. Strodtbeck, "Phases in Group Problem Solving," *Journal of Abnormal and Social Psychology* 46 (1951): 485–495.

37. B. Aubrey Fisher, "Decision Emergence: Phases in Group Decision-Making," *Speech Monographs* 37 (1970): 53–60.

38. See, for example, Laura Crowell and Thomas M. Scheidel, "Idea Devel-

opment in Small Discussion Groups," *Quarterly Journal of Speech* 50 (1964): 140–145: Kristin B. Valentine and B. Aubrey Fisher, "An Interaction Analysis of Verbal Innovative Deviance in Small Groups," *Speech Monographs* 41 (1974): 413–420; Donald G. Ellis and B. Aubrey Fisher, "Phases in Conflict in Small Group Development: A Markov Analysis," *Human Communication Research* 1 (1975): 195–212; Ernest L. Stech, "An Analysis of Interaction Structure in the Discussion of a Ranking Task," *Speech Monographs* 37 (1970): 249–256; Robert N. Bostrom, "Patterns of Communicative Interaction in Small Groups," *Speech Monographs* 37 (1970): 257–263.

39. Robert E. Nofsinger, Jr., "A Peek at Conversational Analysis," *Communication Quarterly* 25 (1977): 14.

40. See, for example, Elaine M. Litton-Hawes, "A Foundation for the Study of Everyday Talk," *Communication Quarterly* 25 (1977): 2–11.

41. See, for example, Mark L. Knapp, John M. Wiemann, and John A. Daly, "Nonverbal Communication: Issues and Appraisal," *Human Communication Research* 4 (1978): 271–280.

42. Claude E. Shannon and Warren Weaver, *The Mathematical Theory of Communication* (Urbana: University of Illinois Press, 1949).

43. "Recent Contributions to the Mathematical Theory of Communication," in Shannon and Weaver, p. 9.

44. J. R. Pierce, *Symbols, Signals and Noise: The Nature and Process of Communication* (New York: Harper and Row, 1961; rpt. Harper Torchbooks, 1965), p. 268.

45. See, for example, Dale D. Drum, "Change, Meaning, and Information," *Journal of Communication* 7 (1957): 161–170; R. Barry Fulton, "Information Theory and Linguistic Structuring," *Central States Speech Journal* 14 (1963): 247–257; Carl H. Weaver and Garry L. Weaver, "Information Theory and the Measurement of Meaning," *Speech Monographs* 32 (1965): 435–447; Allan R. Broadhurst and Donald K. Darnell, "Introduction to Cybernetics and Information Theory," *The Quarterly Journal of Speech* 51 (1965): 442–453.

46. Stogdill, p. 11.

47. Ibid., p. 4.

48. For a brief description of the model, see Ernest G. Bormann and Nancy C. Bormann, *Effective Small Group Communication,* 2nd ed. (Minneapolis: Burgess, 1976), pp. 15–21; see also Ernest G. Bormann, *Discussion and Group Methods: Theory and Practice,* 2nd ed. (New York: Harper & Row, 1975).

49. B. Aubrey Fisher, "Evidence Varies with Theoretical Perspective," *Western Journal of Speech Communication* 41 (1977): p. 9.

50. Ibid., pp. 9–10.

51. Fritz Heider, *The Psychology of Interpersonal Relations* (New York: Wiley, 1958).

52. Charles E. Osgood and Percy Tannenbaum, "The Principle of Congruity in the Prediction of Attitude Change," *Psychological Review* 62 (1955): 42–55.

53. Leon Festinger, *A Theory of Cognitive Dissonance* (Stanford: Stanford University Press, 1957).

54. For an analysis of Hull's learning theory, see Kenneth Spence, "The Postulates and Methods of 'Behaviorism,'" in Herbert Feigl and May Brodbeck,

eds., *Readings in the Philosophy of Science* (New York: Appleton-Century-Crofts, 1953); Gustav Bergmann and Kenneth Spence, "Operationism and Theory Construction," in Melvin H. Marx, ed., *Psychology Theory* (New York: Macmillan, 1951), pp. 264–270.

55. Osgood developed his theory in Charles E. Osgood, *Method and Theory in Experimental Psychology* (New York: Oxford University Press, 1953); see also Charles E. Osgood, George J. Suci, and Percy H. Tannenbaum, *The Measurement of Meaning* (Urbana: University of Illinois Press, 1957).

56. Indeed, Miller and Berger noted in a recent survey of the issue concerning behaviorism and its influence in communication research that if one defines behaviorism in terms of a "research posture which shuns recourse to intervening variables" then "We do not know of a single practicing researcher who is a committed methodological behaviorist." Gerald R. Miller and Charles R. Berger, "On Keeping the Faith in Matters Scientific," *Western Journal of Speech Communication*, 42 (1978), p. 48. They go on to argue that if one interprets philosophical behaviorism to include the notion that all we can ever know about mental states must be inferred from behavior then they see almost all communication researchers as philosophical behaviorists. My point here is that the Skinnerian approach to behaviorism which was once popular among communication theorists is now less popular. For a thorough critique of behavioristic theories of communication, see Frederic A. Gruber, "Why Empirical Methods Cannot Apply in Communication Research: The Case Against Behaviorism," in Fred L. Casmir, ed., *Intercultural and International Communication* (Washington, D.C.: University Press of America, 1978), pp. 7–41.

57. William J. McGuire, "Inducing Resistance to Persuasion," in Leonard Berkowitz, ed., *Advances in Experimental Social Psychology,* Vol. 1 (New York: Academic Press, 1964), pp. 191–229.

58. For a survey of counterattitudinal advocacy, see Gerald R. Miller, "Introduction: Counterattitudinal Advocacy: A Current Appraisal," in C. David Mortensen and Kenneth K. Sereno, eds., *Advances in Communication Research* (New York: Harper & Row, 1973), pp. 105–152.

59. See, for example, Charles R. Berger, "Attributional Communication, Situational Involvement, Self-Esteem and Interpersonal Attraction," *Journal of Communication* 23 (1973): 284–305.

60. Chester A. Insko and John Schopler, *Experimental Social Psychology* (New York: Academic Press, 1972), p. 227.

61. For an example of the adaptation of the Kelman scheme to communication, see Gerald R. Miller, *Speech Communication: A Behavioral Approach* (Indianapolis: Bobbs-Merrill, 1966), pp. 62–71.

62. John W. Thibaut and Harold H. Kelly, *The Social Psychology of Groups* (New York: Wiley, 1959).

63. Ernest G. Bormann, pp. 149–158.

64. For an essay which adapts these developments to communication, see Jerry A. Fodor, James J. Jenkins, and Sol Saporta, "Psycholinguistics and Communication Theory," in Dance, ed., pp. 160–201. For a representative attack on behaviorism from this perspective, see Gruber.

65. Frederick Williams and Howard Lindsay, "Introduction: Language, Communication, and Social Difference," in Mortensen and Sereno, eds. p. 364.

66. Dell Hymes, "The Anthropology of Communication," in Dance, ed., pp. 1–39.

53

Notes

67. Charles R. Berger and Richard J. Calabrese, "Some Explorations in Initial Interaction and Beyond: Toward a Developmental Theory of Interpersonal Communication," *Human Communication Research* 1 (1975): 99–112.

68. George A. Barnett, Kim B. Serota, and James A. Taylor, "Campaign Communication and Attitude Change: A Multidimensional Analysis," *Human Communication Research* 2 (1976): 227–244. For a fuller exposition of the mathematical formulations, see Joseph Woelfel and John Saltiel, "Cognitive Processes as Motions in a Multidimensional space: A General Lineal Model," in Casmir, ed., pp. 105–130.

69. Dean E. Hewes, Alan J. Brazil, and Dorcas E. Evans, "A Comparative Test of Two Stochastic Process Models of Message, Mediating Variables, and Behavioral Expectations," in Ruben, ed., p. 198.

70. Ibid., p. 212.

71. B. Aubrey Fisher, "Information Systems Theory and Research: An Overview," in Brent Ruben, ed., *Communication Yearbook 2* (New Brunswick, N.J.: Transaction Books, 1978), p. 81.

72. Ibid., p. 95.

73. Peter R. Monge, "The Systems Perspective as a Theoretical Basis for the Study of Human Communication," *Communication Quarterly* 25 (1977): 28.

74. Ibid., pp. 24–25.

75. For some other essays on the systems approach to communication, see B. Aubrey Fisher and Leonard C. Hawes, "An Interact System Model: Generating a Grounded Theory of Small Groups," *The Quarterly Journal of Speech* 57 (1971): 444–453, Peter R. Monge, "Theory Construction in the Study of Communication: The System Paradigm," *Journal of Communication* 23 (1973): 5–16; Brent D. Ruben and John Y. Kim, eds., *General Systems Theory and Human Communication* (Rochelle Park, N.J.: Hayden, 1975).

76. Fisher, "Information Systems Theory and Research," p. 96.

77. Richard V. Farace, Peter R. Monge, and Hamish M. Russell, *Communicating and Organizing* (Reading, Mass.: Addison-Wesley, 1977).

78. For research flowing from this perspective, see Ernest G. Bormann, "The Eagleton Affair: A Fantasy Theme Analysis," *The Quarterly Journal of Speech* 59 (1973): 143–159; Ernest G. Bormann, Jolene Koester, and Janet Bennett, "Political Cartoons and Salient Rhetorical Fantasies: An Empirical Analysis of the '76 Presidential Campaign," *Communication Monographs* 45 (1978): 317–329; David L. Rarick, Mary B. Duncan, David G. Lee, and Laurinda W. Porter, "The Carter Persona: An Empirical Analysis of the Rhetorical Visions of Campaign '76," *Quarterly Journal of Speech* 63 (1977): 258–273.

79. See, for example, Klaus Krippendorff, "Information Systems Theory and Research: An Overview," in Ruben, ed., *Communication Yearbook I,* pp. 149–171.

80. See, for example, Stephen Toulmin, "Concepts and the Explanation of Human Behavior," in Theodore Mischel, ed., *Human Action* (New York: Academic Press, 1969), pp. 71– 104; Stephen Toulmin, "Rules and Their Relevance to Human Behavior," in Theodore Mischel, ed., *Understanding Other Persons* (Oxford: Blackwell, 1974), pp. 9–30; George H. von Wright, *Explanation and Understanding* (Ithaca: Cornell University Press, 1971); Romano Harré, "Surrogates for Necessity," *Mind* 82 (1973): 358–380.

81. Lawrence Rosenfield, "A Game Model of Human Communication," in David H. Smith, ed., *What Rhetoric (Communication Theory) Is Appropriate for Contemporary Speech Communications?* (Minneapolis: Department of Speech-Communication, University of Minnesota, 1969), pp. 26–41.

82. Donald Cushman and Gordon C. Whiting, "An Approach to Communication Theory: Toward Consensus on Rules," *Journal of Communication* 22 (1972): 217–238.

83. For a typical essay including the comparative analysis of various approaches to accounting for communication with a case for the rules perspective, see Donald P. Cushman and W. Barnett Pearce, "Generality and Necessity in Three Types of Human Communication Theory—Special Attention to Rules Theory," in Ruben, ed., *Communication Yearbook I,* pp. 173–182.

84. Ibid., p. 178.

85. Ibid., pp. 177, 180.

86. Donald P. Cushman, "The Rules Perspective as a Theoretical Basis for the Study of Human Communication," *Communication Quarterly* 25 (1977): p. 39.

87. See, for example, Vernon E. Cronen and Leslie K. Davis, "Alternative Approaches for the Communication Theorist: Problems in the Laws-Rules-Systems Trichotomy," *Human Communication Research 4 (1978): 120–128.*

PART TWO

Special Communication Theories

3

Communication Styles and Special Theories

Chapter 2 presented a general survey of the sorts of statements and conceptualizations which characterize communication theories. In much of the remainder of this book I will be making a careful analysis of the nature of the knowledge we have about communication. I begin by drawing a distinction between the portion of our knowledge that is drawn from and closely related to the communication practices of people going about their daily affairs (special theories), and the portion of our knowledge that results from scholarly investigations designed to provide more universal understanding about communication (general theories). Since in our society scholars are also often teachers, they frequently theorize in a context that includes teaching and practice as well as research. They not only write essays that provide a general theoretical explanation of communication but also write handbooks and textbooks that provide how-to-do-it information about communicating. Frequently they mix the two kinds of knowledge together in their theoretical papers and in their handbooks to guide practice. As a result the material in Chapter 2 contains a mixture of the two kinds of theorizing.

Mixing special theories closely related to specific practices with accounts that purport to provide a general theory of human communication is sometimes useful, and when not useful is at least harmless. However, students of communication theory need to distinguish between the two kinds of theorizing, because they represent different kinds of knowledge and serve different functions.

My purpose in this chapter is to indicate the main features of the portion of the content of the material summarized in Chapter 2 that is closely tied to the way people communicate. What is the nature of the material found in textbooks on public speaking? on interpersonal communication? on small group communication? on organizational communication? What is the nature of knowledge composed of such concepts as *feedback, congruency, interpersonal trust, authenticity, noise, redundancy, logical proof*, and so forth?

In this chapter I examine theoretical developments from a perspective drawn from rhetorical history and criticism. Much as the historian Kuhn studied scientific theory and practice, I will report my studies of communication theory and practice in Colonial America and in the United States.[1] Later in the chapter I will compare my findings in the history of rhetoric with Kuhn's findings in the history of science. The comparison indicates that whereas there is one level of theorizing in the natural sciences (general theories), there are two levels for social scientists investigating communication (special and general theories). Both rhetorical and communication theory exhibit the two levels of theorizing, and both contrast with scientific investigations in that regard. I turn first to the nature of rhetorical and communication theories and then to the practice of normal science.

The Nature of Communication Styles

The basic concept for my analysis of the history of communication practices is that of *communication style*. By this term I mean that broad usage of a community of people engaged in significant discourse for which they understand the rules customs, and conventions. *Style* also has a much narrower sense of a strikingly different personal mode of expression unique to an individual. The aphorism "Style is the man" points to the idiosyncratic features of an individual's characteristic mode of communication. Those who would point to an individual speaker's deviations from the usual or the normal as evidence of style are using the term in the narrower sense. I view style from the broader perspective of the larger group, and in that perspective people who understand and appreciate the style conform to the norms and obey the rules. From the broader perspective the community usually has a style with rules, norms, and conventions that allow for tactical variations, and it is these tactical variations that result in individual stylists in the narrower sense.

Individual style and the style of a community are closely related, since people always practice communication within the assumptive system of a given rhetorical community. Communication is always artful in the sense that human beings are not born with natural instincts to communicate in the ways that have come to characterize the language games of the community. People always learn to communicate, and their instructors teach them according to the standards of the particular style.

Thus, communication critics cannot evaluate a given message or a communication episode *in vacuo*. The critic applies either the standards of a communication community of which he or she is a part, or the standards of the community that created the context for the event. A person with a striking style is practicing within the conventions of a larger community and stands out against that background. Daniel Webster, Edward Everett, and Abraham Lincoln were great stylists of the nineteenth century, but they were stylists according to the norms of oratory for rhetorical communities, which were much larger in that century than in the twentieth century. Similarly, Lowell Thomas, Edward Murrow, and Walter Cronkite as stylists of the twentieth century stand out against a background of communication standards quite different from those that guided the study and practice of the nineteenth-century stand-up orator.

I define *rhetorical community*, therefore, as the group of people who participate in a rhetorical style and share common rhetorical visions from within the perspective of that style.[2] The members of a rhetorical community will be able to speak or write (or in some way sense) a language system. Usually these language systems are the conventional natural languages, such as English, German, French, or Spanish. On some occasions the community may share a more arcane set of linguistic conventions, such as a Morse code, a sign language used by deaf mutes, or Fortran or Cobol (languages used in communicating with computers). Being able to use a common language is necessary but not sufficient to generate a rhetorical community. Many different rhetorical communities in many different cultures all use the English language.

The members of a rhetorical community will all understand the usual rites and rituals surrounding everyday communication *transactions*, as well as the conventions governing the more special and elaborate communication events. The Sheflens, approaching the study of communication from a perspective which emphasizes nonverbal elements, define transactions in terms of programs which participants in a given culture or community share. They write, "The program of the transaction specifies that certain actions are allowable, others are clearly not allowable. Still others are allowable by some definitions of the situation and not allowable by others." They note that in a conversation, for example, the programs that people share will authenticate certain speech and kinesic behavior as official. Within the rules of the programs, words and actions relating to serving the social bonds and assuring the participants that they are in agreement about the proper programs to follow are allowed. The Sheflens call these allowable enactments *contextuals* in that "they are appropriate to the formal context and tend to preserve the lawfulness of the transaction."[3] The Sheflen analysis also includes communication behavior that are inappropriate and the verbal and nonverbal messages that serve as monitors to keep the participants in a transaction on the proper program. Once the transactions common to a given rhetorical community are established, they are passed on to children and newcomers by their performance.[4]

In Chapter 2 I discussed Hymes' influential work in the ethnographic studies of speech communities and cultures. Hawes has discussed *speech communities*, which share not only the conventions of some language system but subsets of rules and norms that enable them to participate in communication transactions.[5] Frentz and Farrell set up a frame of analysis that borrows from Wittgenstein the concepts of *language games* associated with forms of life.[6] They go on to examine encounters and episodes within the rules of such language games. A number of other scholars have examined the rules for certain features of the transactions within a given rhetorical community.[7] The notion that rhetorical communities can be studied in much the same manner as ethnographers study cultural communities is one that is gaining acceptance among communication scholars.[8]

But a rhetorical community shares more than the ability to speak a common language and a tacit understanding of rules governing the common communication transactions of its members. A rhetorical community shares a common communication style and some common rhetorical visions. The requirement that a rhetorical community share a common style and some common visions limits the scope of such communities and means that within a given geographical area such as North America, a number of rhetorical communities will exist at any given time. In addition, a given individual may participate in several rhetorical communities at the same time. A person may communicate according to the conventions and rules of one communication style for a time and then shift to another in the same day.

How does a communication style come into being? Rhetorical practice furnishes the grounds for a style. A new style begins when small groups of people become disturbed by their here-and-now problems and meet together to discuss their difficulties, or when they associate to play with symbols, or when they communicate to create social bonds.[9]

If fantasies chain through their deliberations, they may start to communicate in ways which are unusual when compared to other current styles.[10] In the 1960s in North America, people began to participate in groups that celebrated authentic relationships and encouraged the overt expression of emotions. They established encounter groups and sensitivity sessions for the practice of authentic communication and for the instruction of newcomers. The result was a new communication style. In the last half of the sixteenth century in England, a number of ministers of the church began to meet together to discuss their difficulties. Their shared fantasies celebrated preaching and placed it as central in the church service. They came to appreciate a much plainer use of language from the pulpit than that of the majority of the ministers of the time. They established prophesying sessions for the practice of the new style and for the instruction of the newcomers.[11] Transported to America, the maturing of the style resulted in the New England Puritan sermon of the seventeenth century[12]

A new communication style thus begins with practices that violate the norms, customs, and rules of established styles. Because the new beginnings have no established criteria for evaluation or teaching, they are first propagated by modeling behavior. People drawn to the new practice try to emulate a sample of the communication with which they have come in contact. When radio was a new medium, people who talked over the air tried out different styles of speech. Some tried to orate in front of the microphone much as they would before a large crowd; others tried for some distinctive trademark such as speaking with exteme rapidity.[13] Some of the ways of speaking on radio proved popular, and neophytes interested in becoming radio personalities often imitated the popular announcers when practicing and when auditioning. When sufficient samples of the new style are available, some general rules of thumb evolve, which the initiated can use to teach neophytes and to evaluate communication practices. As a new style spreads more rapidly, partisans of the practice need to instruct more and more newcomers to appreciate and practice the style. They often set up special instructional facilities for that purpose. The devotees of the new authentic style of relationship communication in the 1960s set up sensitivity and encounter sessions to teach others how to communicate in the style just as the early Puritans set up prophesying sessions for the training of preachers in the new style.

Gradually, ideal and abstract models of communication emerge from the give and take of practice and teaching meetings. The natural specialization within interacting groups results in the emergence of some members as experts who can critically evaluate communication according to the ideal models and who can coach newcomers to improve practice and to encourage appreciation of "good" communication within the rules and customs of the style.[14]

With the rise of a group of communication experts comes a refinement of the concepts and a move to greater abstractness in the formulation of advice on how to communicate well. The experts come together to discuss their common interest in the communication style, and as they share the same assumptions about the general shape of the ideal communication events their discussion and arguments are largely focused on solving problems within the confines furnished by the assumptions. The analogy of a communication style with an athletic game is instructive, since people usually understand the conventional nature of a game and just as often assume that communication events are more analogous to natural phenomena than to rule-governed phenomena. Once the American game of football became popular, a group of experts arose to "coach" others in the proper way to both play and appreciate the game. Soon the experts began to hold clinics, write articles and textbooks, and generally discuss the finer points of the game. The experts developed plans and formations for offense and defense which were essentially of a puzzle-solving nature. Although the rules were changed from time to time, the great majority of the issues discussed by the experts related to playing the game within the rules. Similarly, the experts of a communication style tend to confine their theoretical discussions to solving puzzles such as whether the ideal model of a communication event should be depicted in graphic terms as a blueprint of an electronic circuit, as the flow chart for programing a computer, or as a circle or helix.[15]

The new communication style cannot flourish without criticism that modifies and refines its practice and helps instruct students to become better communicators according to the standards of the style. As critical standards become norms for the community and as they become explicit and abstract, they form part of the special rhetorical or communication theory that sustains and undergirds the practice and criticism of the style.

Such unique communicative types as the Puritan sermon and the Websterian commemorative address of the nineteenth century result from practice, criticism, and style-specific theories in a complex system of reciprocal relationships. Every unique communication type is artistic in the sense that it is artificial and the result of conventions that are not tied to situational constraints.

An ethnographic or historical or critical study of the style-specific special communication theories can provide answers to questions such as the following: Why do some rhetorical communities put such great emphasis upon informal two-person transactions? some upon emotional small group communication? some upon larger group meetings in which several people deliver long uninterrupted speeches? Why do some rhetorical communities put such emphasis upon music as a component of the transactions, such as the televised commercial message of the 1960s and 1970s or the Methodist camp meeting of the early nineteenth century, while others use very little music at all?

Even the most pragmatic of styles that evolve to meet practical needs, such as the business meeting so vital to corporate success in the developed countries in the twentieth century, always have a considerable element of consummatory appeal. That is, people who are connoisseurs of a style come to enjoy its practice when the communication approximates the ideal. I define a connoisseur as a person who is a participant in a human endeavor that includes the artistic design of social or material reality in order to achieve some ideal forms. For connoisseurs a good business meeting is enjoyable; a good sermon is an experience to talk about and savor afterward; a good sensitivity group or consciousness-raising session is an end in itself.[16]

The Development of Communication Styles

Both rhetoric and science are epistemic in their application.[17] That is, both rhetoric and science portray a vision of the world and provide an account of how things are and how they came to be. We can step back and examine the practice of normal science and the practice of communication from the viewpoint of a philosopher asking basic questions about the assumptions of each. We can also examine these phenomena from the viewpoint of a historian asking how scientific practices or communication in use have evolved. By stepping back and studying both science and communication we can gain a greater understanding of their similarities and differences.

In discussing these similarities and differences, I will use as a basic touchstone for comparison the interpretative structure of Thomas Kuhn in his provocative history *The Structure of Scientific Revolutions.*[18] The interpretative structure for the history of communication changes is from my work in the history of persuasion in the United States.[19]

Kuhn's work is controversial, and not all historians of science are in agreement with his central thesis that science does not move in an evolutionary direct line of progression to ever better understanding of some ultimate truth but rather that it proceeds by revolutionary shifts in which one explanatory framework is overthrown and replaced by another so different that participants in the two positions are actually living in two different worlds. But the section of his work that is most useful to me relates less to the broad frame of revolutionary change than to Kuhn's analysis of scientific *exemplars, paradigms,* and *disciplinary matrixes.*

In a reprinting of his book published seven years after the first edition, Kuhn added a postscript with this concluding section:

> Though scientific development may resemble that in other fields more closely than has often been supposed, it is also strikingly different. . . . One of the objects of the book was to examine such differences and begin accounting for them.[20]

The question of the similarities and differences between the practice of rhetoric and of science is an important one. What I will do is examine some of Kuhn's basic concepts that he uses for defining a scientific community and compare and contrast them with my concepts for explicating a rhetorical community. Basic to the comparison is the examination of what Kuhn discusses as the practice of "normal" science with the practice of a communication style.

Kuhn pointed out and corrected an important error in the first edition when he wrote his postscript to the Japanese edition. Kuhn noted that he used the term *paradigm* in two different senses in that he shifted ground from using it as an umbrella term for a total world view on some occasions to using it in a more restricted way on others. Kuhn characterizes the more restricted usage as "entirely appropriate, both philologically and autobiographically; this is the component of a group's shared commitment which first led me to the choice of the word. Because the term has assumed a life of its own, however, I shall here substitute 'exemplars.'" Kuhn's new term for the broader concept was *disciplinary matrix*. Kuhn used the term *disciplinary* to indicate that the perspective is the common possession of the participants in a particular discipline, and *matrix* because that term implies "ordered elements of various sorts." Kuhn included as one of the ordered elements in the disciplinary matrix the more restricted meaning of his original term *paradigm*. The exemplars are, thus, part of the disciplinary matrix of a given scientific community.[21]

The similarities between Kuhn's analysis of science and my analysis of communication styles and their practice is striking. My analysis derives from a study of the history of communication (rhetoric and public address) in North America; Kuhn's derives from a study of the natural sciences. That there are so many similarities is, I suppose, if one stops to think about it, not surprising. After all, Kuhn suggested that he was using tools of analysis borrowed from, among others, historians of art, and rhetoric and communication have an artistic dimension.

Kuhn describes the practice of "normal science" in a way that is analogous to my description of the practice of a "communication style." Kuhn argues that normal science is research activity firmly based on past scientific achievements which members of a scientific communication use as a foundation for further practice. Communication styles are artful creations of human beings that evolve as people go about their daily affairs talking to one another for many different reasons. Although one can discover commonalities that cut across communication styles, they are creations in the sense that they represent innovation, novelty, and unpredictability. One is never born a good communicator in a given style but must always be taught to appreciate it. Part of the communication theory associated with a style consists of the standards of excellence, models of exemplary communication events (similar to paradigms in the restricted sense which Kuhn subsequently called exemplar), and concepts to help newcomers learn about key features of the style.

Kuhn describes *paradigm* or *exemplar* in the restricted sense; he states that "some accepted examples of actual scientific practice—examples which include law, theory, application, and instrumentation together—provide models from which spring particular coherent traditions of scientific research."[22] In an analogous fashion I would argue that "some accepted examples or communication practice—examples which include application, criticism, and theory—provide models from which spring particular coherent communication styles and traditions."

Kuhn maintains, "Men whose research is based on shared paradigms are committed to the same rules and standards for scientific practice."[23] Likewise, I would argue, "People whose communication is based upon a shared rhetorical exemplar are committed to the same rules and standards of communication."

Kuhn further argues, "Acquisition of a paradigm and of the more esoteric type of research it permits is a sign of maturity in the development of any given scientific field."[24] In like fashion, I maintain, "Acquisition of a communication exemplar (model) and the more esoteric type of argumentation that it permits is a sign of maturity in the development of any given rhetorical community."

In a mature rhetorical style, the exemplar implies the sorts of argumentation that practitioners of normal communication within the rules of the style will use. Thus, not until the style reaches maturity will an observer discover highly developed esoteric argumentation and long patches of reasoned discourse without discussion of the basic assumptions underlying the argument.

According to Kuhn, a disciplinary matrix in a scientific community (the more general sense of *paradigm*) consists of a number of components. Kuhn suggests that among the most important are "symbolic generalizations" or low-level laws of nature. He uses as an illustration of symbolic generalizations the function that force equals mass times acceleration (F=ma). The second component is a shared commitment to models with heuristic power such as the notion that the molecules of a gas behave like tiny elastic billiard balls in random motion and to ontological beliefs such as that phenomena result from the interaction of qualitatively neutral atoms. The third component includes common values such that predictions should be accurate, that quantitative predictions are preferable to qualitative, and that there be shared standards regarding the admissible margins of error in measurements. Finally, the disciplinary matrix includes exemplars (*paradigm* in the restricted sense). Exemplars are the concrete problem-solving activity of the discipline.[25]

The equivalent of Kuhn's disciplinary matrix is the rhetorical vision of a communication community. A rhetorical vision consists of a number of components similar to the parts of the disciplinary matrix. Where the matrix has low-level laws of nature, the rhetorical vision has "rules of thumb" which serve to guide practice and anticipate the production of a good or effective communication transaction. Where the matrix has a shared commitment to models with heuristic power, the vision has a shared commitment to models that serve as ideal types or standards for practitioners to strive to emulate. Like the matrix, the vision will include common values and ontological beliefs. However, one of the crucial differences between science and rhetoric is that the scientific values are empirical; predictions are tested against observations. Historically, rhetorical visions have varied in their values. Some are "scientific" in that they are very similar to those Kuhn outlined for science, but many have been anti-scientific, romantic, transcendent, intuitive, or Platonic in their philosophical cast. Thus, a rhetorical vision may share common values such that miracles are a likely occurrence, God is the ultimate source of true knowledge, the super-natural makes its presence felt in visible fashion and communicates directly with human beings, and the only true avenue to knowledge is the direct experience of communion with God.

Finally, the rhetorical vision includes exemplars (*paradigm* in the restricted sense). Exemplars are concrete communication transactions. Exemplars include the way participants invent, construct, and exchange verbal and non-verbal messages in the varied contexts which the vision emphasizes for communication. Among the main components of exemplars are the programs for transactions which the participants share and which children or newcomers must learn before they can participate in communication according to the rules of the style. These programs include the contextual requirements and the norms that monitor transcontextual behavior. The accepted exemplars also include the rules and norms that regulate the communication games of the community.

Kuhn's major contribution is his concept of paradigm. He argues that the paradigm (exemplar) concept emphasizes the overriding importance of participating in problem-solving or puzzle-solving activity according to the model of the ideal or exemplar research in order to participate in the scientific community.[26]

According to Kuhn, many philosophers of science are mistaken because they assume that students in laboratories or solving end-of-text problems are simply applying theories and rules they have learned by reading the text material. Rather, the student begins an initiation into a scientific community and continues for some time thereafter by doing problems.[27] He notes, "All physicists . . . begin by learning the same exemplars: problems such as the inclined plane, the conical pendulum, and Keplerian orbits; instruments such as the vernier, the calorimeter, and the Wheatstone bridge."[28] The end result of actually participating in puzzle-solving according to the rules of the exemplar, or rehearsing model experiments, is to see the world through the matrix of that paradigm. Such an individual only has language to talk about certain kinds of problems and to construct certain sorts of experiments. A paradigm shift is impossible without the conversion process familar to students of religious rhetoric.

How do scientists convert from one paradigm to another at the crucial point in history when a scientific paradigm shift takes place? Kuhn argues that communication across paradigms is almost impossible. What is required is that the "participants in a communication breakdown . . . recognize each other as members of different language communities and then become translators." Kuhn continues:

> To translate a theory or worldview into one's own language is not enough to make it one's own. For that one must go native, discover that one is thinking and

working in, not simply translating out of, a language that was previously foreign. That transition is not, however, one that an individual may make or refrain from making by deliberation and choice, however good his reasons for wishing to do so. Instead, at some point in the process of learning to translate, he finds that the transition has occurred, that he has slipped into the new language without the decision having been made.[29]

People come to participate in a new rhetorical style in much the same way that scientists come to share a new paradigm in science. They appropriate the norms and rules by taking part in communication transactions, by becoming aware of the monitoring messages, verbal and nonverbal, that condition them to the norms, and by inferring the rules from participation. They learn the vision by participating in the dramatization of the basic scenarios which provide the fabric of its social reality, much as the neophyte physicists participate in the classical experiments such as the inclined plane.

Kuhn's book proved popular in the intellectual community of the 1960s and 1970s. The wave of romanticism that swept through the intellectual communities in the United States during the 1960s tended to emphasize subjectivity and intuition (the rhetorical vision which evolved shared a set of values different from those Kuhn outlined for the scientific community). The book's popularity may be partly a reflection of Kuhn's emphasis upon the subjective nature of science as opposed to the objective analysis of some prior historical accounts. In addition, he presented the novel and prestigious activity of the most esoteric of the natural sciences as falling into the familiar patterns of the thinking in the humanities and social sciences. How nice to know that the physicists are like the psychologists or scholars in communication and that their vaunted "theories" resemble other patterns of thinking as represented in other disciplines. No wonder that many who tried to apply Kuhn's explanatory structure to their interests neglected what was to him the important theme of the book, namely, "Though scientific development may resemble that in other fields more closely than has often been supposed, it is also strikingly different."[30]

To this point I have drawn some of the resemblances. The differences, however, are substantial and important to any student of communication and rhetorical theory. Rhetoric is not the same as science; communication theories are not the same as the theories in the physical sciences. I turn now to an examination of the differences between science and communication, with an examination of the artistic elements in rhetoric and communication.

The Art of Communication

By the *communication arts* I mean the intervention of human beings into the shaping and forming of communication transactions. When human beings intervene into any material or social reality with the conscious intent of rearranging either or both to some ideal form the result is the artificial as opposed to the natural. The artistry may be dedicated to achieving some exemplar drawn from "nature," and thus the "more natural the better" the communication event. But the natural styles of communication are as artificial as the more obviously stylized transactions. Among the historic disputes as various communication styles contended for adherents in the past has been the question of whether or not communication transactions should be natural. Should an actor portraying a part do so by deeply feeling the emotion from "inside out," thus allowing the unstudied gestures and intonations of deep feeling to communicate the interpretation of the character, or should the actor plan and present the interpretation by thinking through and practicing gestures and vocal intonations? Should the good speaker try to be natural in manner and concentrate on the ideas he or she is trying to communicate to the audience, or should the speaker rehearse the gestures? Should the personae in televised commercial messages be common ordinary people acting in a natural manner, or should they be idealized, trained actors?

As soon as human beings intervene in the unfolding of material or social realities, they introduce art and artificiality. People may develop human artifacts for primarily aesthetic or primarily pragmatic purposes, but the aesthetic dimension is always part of the activity. Weapons for hunting and war are marked and shaped for decoration and display. Tools for farming and woodworking vary in shape and style from culture to culture.

Until human beings introduced artistry into animal husbandry and gardening, one could say that the various forms of flora and fauna were the result of *natural* forces of evolution. Theoreticians could provide a number of natural, causative factors which would account for the course of evolution. Darwin, for example, suggested that natural selection accounted for most of the diversity of form and color. The principle suggests that if form was functional in a way adapted to survival in a given context, then it was selected out by nature to flourish. Darwin suggested another principle, which was that of sexual selection. The principle suggests that if a form was sexually attractive it would be genetically transmitted from parent to offspring and thus selected out by nature to flourish.

Theoreticians might have posited forces governing the universe that were less preoccupied with sex and survival and more artistic in their preferences. Such theoreticians could have posited that an aesthetic force was governing the universe and using the mechanism of sexual selection to create ever more beautiful creatures and plants.

At any rate, once human beings entered the picture and began to systematically change the appearance, form, and function of domesticated animals and plants the aesthetic dimension became important. Indeed, in some instances the aesthetic dimension becomes overriding, as in the case of certain show dogs whose practical uses for hunting or herding other animals becomes unimportant.

With the introduction of artistic factors in any human activity comes the necessity to learn the practice and criticism of the art. In the process of designing more attractive forms, the specialists develop a special theory consisting of scientific and artistic components. As the specialists discuss and refine theoretical questions, they often come to solve smaller and smaller points of difference and to raise more and more technical and minute matters to be central issues in the art. An uninitiated person thus often cannot understand, much less appreciate, the finer points of a given endeavor. For example, I find certain very fine show dogs to be ugly to my untrained eye and certain very fine wines to be distasteful to my untrained palate. To appreciate the beauty of the dog or the taste of the wine I would have to study the theory, practice the art, and criticize some specimens in discussions with people who were familiar with the practice.

The connoisseur is competent to pass judgment on matters of art or taste in a given field of endeavor. Individuals may become connoisseurs in a large variety of activities. People become dog breeders, pigeon fanciers, rose enthusiasts, or opera buffs. Take the case of the gourmet who must undergo a period of study and practice in some style of cooking and wine tasting to develop his or her palate and achieve the ability to judge food and drink according to given standards. Human beings have been taking natural food stuffs and artfully changing them by baking, basting, boiling, broiling, seasoning, mixing, and decorating them for thousands of years. In the process, different styles of cooking have emerged, just as in the process of communication, human beings have artfully created distinctive communication styles.

Without the artificial changing of foodstuffs there would be no need for, and indeed no point in, criticism, beyond the judgment "This tastes good" or "This isn't any good." There would be no need for a theory of cooking, in the sense of principles and methods which grow out of practice. What connoisseurs do is set standards on the basis of tastes that are sometimes not even naturally attractive, so that it is not possible for an unschooled person to make critical judgments. The people who set standards need models of excellence and ways to criticize practice.

In one of the dialogues of Plato, rhetoric was compared to cookery, and scholars devoted to the importance of communication have been irked by what seems to them to have been a demeaning comparison ever since. To make my point about the importance of models of excellence, therefore, I will turn to a more fanciful comparison. The dog breeder must have a model of the ideal dog in mind in order to select an individual animal to train for dog shows, at which the judges will supposedly have a similar ideal type in mind in making their decision. The model of what is good and bad and the critical standards related to the models come to be an important part of the theory of the art of breeding show dogs. When a person learns to become a dog fancier, the process is similar to the way a physicist learns a paradigm or an individual learns a communication style. Namely, individuals attend dog shows, discuss the results, and breed and train their own dogs.

When a particular breed of dog is judged primarily on aesthetic grounds, the possibilities for imaginative variations of form and color are increased when compared to breeds that also have some pragmatic function. For instance, hunting dogs, which compete in field trials, tend to have ideal forms related more to function than do nonworking breeds, which are evaluated largely on the basis of form and color.

There are obvious functional bases for communication. Communication can have pragmatic purposes such as decision-making, coordinating the efforts of groups of people to achieve a common goal, negotiating sales of merchandise, and so forth. But communication always has an aesthetic dimension, and in some instances the joy of wordplay and the attractiveness of expression become the major focus for the connoisseurs.

There are scientific theories that relate to dog breeding. Fanciers can utilize the Mendelian theory of dominant and recessive characteristics in the genetic material to breed certain forms into the offspring and assure that certain undesirable features drop out of the breed. The laws of heredity as well as the laws which govern crossbreeding and hybridization set some limits for the art of dog breeding.

There are also scientific theories that relate to communication. The energy in a sound wave can be measured, and the effect of the amount of energy on the human ear can be explained scientifically. A community is not likely to develop a style of communication that restricts the amount of power in a sound wave to the point where people cannot hear one another when communicating face to face. Before the invention of electronic amplifying equipment, speakers talking to large groups of people often developed styles of communication that included a careful, slow formation of consonant sounds and the bellowing of vowels. Often these speakers spoke very slowly to increase the likelihood of being heard and understood. The eighteenth-century British evangelist George Whitefield, for example, spoke to thousands in the open air and developed a style of clear articulation and great physical force in projecting his voice to his listeners.[31]

General Versus Style-Specific Special Theories of Communication

Theoreticians working to develop a coherent theory to explain a class of communication events have tended to confuse style-specific theories with the more general propositions which cover all or many rhetorical communities. Figure 3 depicts the additional level of analysis required for the study of communication when contrasted with the scientific study of natural phenomena.

Figure 3 indicates that at the first level of theory and research in the natural sciences is the basic stuff of the study, the natural phenomenon itself. The first level of theory and research in communication, by contrast, consists of human beings discussing natural phenomena *and* their social realities.

At the second level we have scientists practicing normal sciences and discovering solutions to puzzles relating to the general theories they develop. The comparable activity in theory and research in communication at the second level is the practice of a communication style in which communication theorists discover style-specific theories to guide practice and criticism.

At the third level in natural science is the philosophical and historical study of the practice of normal science to discover how it evolves, what its theories consist of, and what values it implies. The crucial distinction between theory and research in science and in communication is that the third level for communication research is analogous to the second level for scientific study. That is, scholars studying the practice of communication styles at the third level are analogous to the scientists practicing normal science at the second level.

Figure 3   Levels of analysis for the study of natural phenomenon contrasted with levels of analysis for the study of communication.

Level of Analysis	Theory and Research in Natural Science	Theory and Research in Communication
Level IV		Philosophical and historical study of communication theory and practice.
Level III	Philosophical and historical study of the practice of normal science.	Scholars analyzing the practice of communication styles to discover knowledge about communication.
Level II	Scientists practicing normal science to discover theories about natural phenomenon.	Connoisseurs studying communication practices to develop theories to guide practice and criticism.
Level I	Natural phenomenon.	People practicing a communications style.

The third level of investigation in theory and research in the natural sciences consists of the work of philosophers and historians, while that activity is reached only at the fourth level of analysis in theory and research in communication. Much of this book deals with theory and research from philosophical and historical perspectives, which means that it is viewing communication from the perspective of the fourth level. The remainder of this chapter will concentrate on clarifying the distinction between the second (special style-specific) and third (general) levels of theorizing in communication. In addition, it will indicate how investigators who have confused the two levels have raised research questions that were, in principle, unanswerable.

At the second level of communication theorizing, specialists within the perspective of a rhetorical community discuss and develop special theories that contain (1) rules of thumb as to how best to create artistic and effective communication transaction, (2) basic assumptions or values which guide the communication practices, and (3) descriptions of the exemplars of good communication for that community. Communication theory within the framework of rhetorical communities (second-level theory) is analogous to the scientific theories (second-level theories) that are part of the disciplinary matrix of a scientific community, in the sense that it influences the practice of rhetoric much as scientific theories influence the practice of science.

The special communication theories at the second level, however, are style-specific, and that is an important difference between them and scientific theories at the same level. When a scientific paradigm, including the heuristic models and laws of nature, comes to prominence it has, historically, swept almost all practitioners before it. That is, the new paradigm comes to be the matrix through which all members of the scientific community view the world.

Artistic communication theories that are part of rhetorical styles do not have this all-or-nothing feature. Many different communication styles exist side by side in any given geographical location and any given historical period. In short, the student who learns the current disciplinary matrix in subatomic physics can move to any other group of subatomic physicists and begin discussing common puzzles because they all share the same theories. The person who learns how to communicate in the style of intercollegiate debate cannot, however, without further training deliver a good revival sermon in the style of a contemporary religious camp meeting. (To be sure, since the two styles have similarities the debater might well learn the revival style more rapidly than a person whose previous training had been confined to conversational styles.) The person who learns to communicate in a business meeting at a large corporate banking institution cannot go to consciousness-raising sessions and apply the same communication theories to the different style.

The communication theories developed at the third level of analysis are more likely to be analogous to the general theories of the physical sciences at the second level in the sense that they provide a scientific account of human behavior based upon either lawfulness or strong generalizable regularities. That is, the scholars who study communication across styles may discover general explanations that relate to the way in which people communicate rather than the details of how people communicate in one specific style.

Katz has suggested that one way to develop a general theory about language is to have linguists make detailed scientific studies of different natural languages such as Iroquois, French, and German. With the preliminary descriptive work out of the way, theorists could then make comparative studies and develop a theory composed of features common to a number of languages.[32] In much the same way, scholars might make essentially ethnographic studies of various rhetorical communities. Theorists could use such studies to discover the common features shared by a number of rhetorical communities and styles, and such commonalities might lead the way to a communication theory similar in scope and generality to the theories of the natural sciences.

To sum up, communication theoreticians at the second level are refining the formulations which guide actual practice and criticism within a specific communication style. They may refine concepts such as *openness, trust*, and *self-disclosure* when theorizing about one style and concepts such as *concealing minimum disposition, bluff,* and *hard line* when theorizing about another. Theoreticians at the third level are developing generalized explanatory accounts of the various theories, practices, and critical evaluations involved in the communication taking place at the second level.

Throughout the book I will emphasize the notion that the subject matter of the social sciences includes the self-conscious action of individual human beings. The distinction between human motion and human action makes a similar point. Because human beings are fascinated by communication, they self-consciously discuss, criticize, and plan their communicative behavior. In short, they theorize about their communication, and that theorizing takes place at the second level. The kind of special communication theory developed at the second level becomes the subject matter for a social scientific approach to a general communication theory at the third level.

As a student of communication you may well study special theories from the second level such as the SMCR model of communication and general theories from the third level such as the dissonance theory. The central point of my analysis is that artistic theories from the second level cannot yield explanations such as those provided by accounts formulated at the third level. For example, investigators searching for covering laws ought not take theoretical formulations from special theories at the second level as the hypotheses of their studies. Investigators might take a more fruitful approach by studying a wide range of communication styles and discovering that every style involves a number of rule-governed communication games. After such a survey they might formulate a suitable question for social scientific investigation, which would be something like "What are the processes which govern the inception, rise, maintenance, and decay of rules which constitute and regulate communication games?"

Style-Specific Communication and Rhetorical Theory   Communication and rhetorical theory at the second level of analysis consists of codified rules, models of ideal communication, advice on how to practice good communication according to the ideal, and so forth. Thus, Aristotle's *Rhetoric* is a handbook by one of the experts in a style of communication common to Greece in a certain historical period. Much of the book consists of descriptions of the typical contexts for communication transactions and discussions of the ideal messages for such contexts. The contexts all contain programs for transactions that include relatively formal messages delivered by one rhetor for a judge or an audience. Aristotle does not deal with other communication transactions, probably because the style he was discussing was not appropriate to them. We know from Plato's dramatization of it in the dialogues that another important communication context saw a group of people in a relatively informal setting at a meal or under a plane tree in which one person questioned another according to the conventions of a quite different style. Haggling in the marketplace might well have created yet a different communication style in Aristotle's Greece. Indeed, the ancient conflict over the Asian and Attic style illustrates the point. Gorgias was a practitioner of quite a different style of speaking than were the speakers of Athens. When he came to Athens he aroused controversy but won over some partisans to his style of communication.[33]

When a new style is introduced into a rhetorical community and attracts converts, the result is a controversy, and among the leading issues of that controversy will be questions relating to the proper way to communicate: What are good reasons? How can we prove a point in debate? Should a good sermon contain stories drawn from the common experiences of the audience? In a good communication transaction do participants exhibit strong emotion? Do they break down and weep? For example, William Ellery Channing was a spokesman for a new style of preaching when he delivered his famous sermon "Unitarian Christianity," and he devoted roughly the first half of that speech to the question of the proper way to use the Bible to prove a theological position.[34] The Puritan preachers in the two centuries preceding Channing's sermon had seldom discussed such questions of proof, because they shared a common set of assumptions about the nature of the Bible and the proper way to use the scriptures to make a theological point.

The Puritans had divided in the 1740s, however, over the question of whether or not a good communication transaction included highly emotional responses on the part of the participants. Was it a work of God or a work of the devil when people began to moan or weep or fall into dead faints during services, and was it appropriate for preachers to exhibit verbal and nonverbal evidences of great emotional frenzy during their speeches? Charles Chauncy and Jonathan Edwards conducted a learned discussion over such communication issues in the 1740s, and the debate itself is evidence of a change in the rhetorical style of part of what had before that time been a cohesive rhetorical community.[35]

In the 1960s a new rhetorical style arose in academic communities in North America, a style that taunted the traditional community with epithets and obscenities, and a furor arose over the issue of how one negotiates with communicators who present nonnegotiable demands.[36]

Few scholars have argued that rhetorical theory is like scientific theory. To be sure, few have tried to unravel exactly what rhetorical theory consists of and how it functions as explanation and as knowledge. The matter often rested upon precedent. As a result, scholars have emphasized two major features of the rhetorical tradition: (1) they have written the history of rhetorical theory, and (2) they have treated rhetorical theory as though historical principles and rules were applicable to contemporary communication.

Scholars who write of the history of rhetorical thought tend to be concerned with questions of the source of classical ideas. Who wrote the fragment on rhetoric entitled *Rhetorica ad Herennium*? Is the manuscript on rhetoric attributed to Aristotle the work of the master? Or is it the notes of students studying with Aristotle? Was the writer of a medieval rhetoric heavily influenced by Cicero? Was the writer of a British eighteenth-century rhetoric heavily influenced by Aristotle? Scholars writing the intellectual history of thinking about communication thus map the various schools and the reactions to them down through the years.

On the other hand, scholars who treat rhetorical theory as though it consisted of general principles applicable to contemporaneous communication problems, often write exegetical works in which they try to discover the meaning and usefulness of Aristotle's definition of rhetoric. Or they may examine the concept of the *enthymeme* and how it relates to the practice of argumentation and debate, or the meaning of *ethos* in classical Greek rhetoric and how the concept might be used in twentieth-century America. Some scholars, therefore, have studied the writings of classical figures in rhetorical theory as though they were similar to scientific theories such as Newton's. That is, they have studied the historical writings on rhetoric as though they expressed, if not invariable relations similar to the law of gravity, at least important principles which were applicable across time, geography, and culture. The study of general rhetorical theory presumably provides insights into rhetorical practice and is a way to understand communication.

The analysis of communication styles reveals, however, that rhetorical theory is often not a coherent, homogeneous body of principles discovered in classical times and handed down through the centuries as human universals which explain communication. Rather it is a collection of style-specific theoretical formulations developed at the second level to guide the practice of a time-specific and culture-bound rhetorical community. Much of what is included in communication theory is analogous to rhetorical theory in that it is the style-bound theory which guides teaching, criticism, and practice.

General Communication and Rhetorical Theory   Scholars have taken the historical traces of rhetorical theory and collected, codified, and commented upon them. Insofar as the scholarship makes comparative studies that clearly delineate the theory associated with one rhetorical community from the theory associated with another and discovers the similarities and differences, it is moving in the direction of providing a general rhetorical theory at the third level. However, rhetorical scholarship has provided few comparative studies that have resulted in a general rhetorical theory.

But a number of communication theorists, have put forward accounts at the third level. For example, consistency accounts purport to explain changing attitudes no matter what the style of communication involved in the transaction. The Puritan preacher who aroused cognitive dissonance in an auditor using the Puritan rhetorical style would have achieved an important part of the conversion process, just as would the consciousness-raising session that created dissonance in a participant.

Summary

A comparison of scientific investigations and theorizing with communication studies indicates that while there is one level of theorizing in the natural sciences, there are two levels for social scientists investigating communication. The natural scientists develop general theories, whereas the study of communication results in both special and general theories.

The broad and common communication usage of a community of people constitutes their communication style. A rhetorical community is a group of people who participate in a communication style and have common rhetorical visions. The members of a rhetorical community understand the common language usages and the usual rites and rituals surrounding communication contexts and episodes.

Rhetorical practice furnishes the grounds for a communication style and generates rhetorical communities. A new style begins when small groups of people become disturbed by their here-and-now problems, meet and discuss them, and begin to share fantasies. A new style begins with communication practices that violate the norms, customs, and rules of established styles. As experts emerge, they develop a rhetorical rationale to aid in teaching and evaluation of the communication.

Kuhn's analysis of the practice of normal science parallels in many respects the way people practice a communication style. There are some crucial differences between communication and science, however, including the fact that the theoretical material relating to communication contains a strong artistic component, including exemplar communication models. There are often functional purposes for communication episodes within the standard contexts of a rhetorical community, but in all instances communication also has an aesthetic component.

The first level of theory and research in the natural sciences is the natural phenomena under study. The first level of theory and research in communication, by contrast, consists of human beings discussing natural phenomena and their social realities with one another.

At the second level we have scientists practicing normal science and discovering *general theories* about material reality. The comparable activity in theory and research in communication at the second level is the development of *special style-specific theories* to guide practice and criticism.

At the third level we have the philosophical and historical study of the practice of normal science on the one hand, and the search for general theories of communication by the researchers in communication on the other.

Both communication theory and rhetorical theory on the second level consist of similar style-specific materials. At the third level of analysis, the generalizations of historical and critical scholars stem from the search for recurring patterns that explain families of rhetorical styles and communication. Social scientific investigations of an ethnographic nature may search for patterns in a fashion similar to humanistic investigations. Many social scientific investigations, however, have aimed for general theories that would apply across styles and account for communication in terms of lawful regularities or strongly probable tendencies.

Notes

1. Thomas Kuhn, *The Structure of Scientific Revolutions*, 2nd ed. (Chicago: University of Chicago Press, 1970). I have integrated some of my findings from 1620 to 1860 in an unpublished book manuscript entitled *The Force of Fantasy: The Restoration of the American Dream*. The general shape of my analysis is apparent in the following essays: "The Rhetoric of Abolition," in Ernest G. Bormann, ed., *Forerunners of Black Power: The Rhetoric of Abolition* (Englewood Cliffs, N. J.: Prentice-Hall, 1971), pp. 1–36; "The Abolitionist Rhetorical Tradition in Contemporary America," ibid., pp. 231–241; "The Rhetorical Theory of William Henry Milburn," *Speech Monographs* 36 (1969): 28–37; "Fetching Good Out of Evil: The Rhetorical Uses of Calamity," *Quarterly Journal of Speech* 63 (1977): 130–139.

2. The concept of *rhetorical vision* is part of a symbolic convergence account of communication based upon the process of sharing group fantasies. A *rhetorical vision* is a coherent interpretation of various shared fantasies which presents a broader view of important human concerns. The fantasy themes and types which compose the vision are often pulled together and integrated by a master analogy. The *dynamic sharing of group fantasies* is a communication episode in which messages contain a rhetorical narrative or drama in a setting other than the here-and-now of the group. The dramatizing messages catch the participants' attention and begin to chain through the others; the tempo of the conversation picks up, members grow

excited, interrupt one another, laugh, show other emotions, and identify with the sympathetic characters in the narratives. The members who share the fantasy participate with the appropriate responses, so if the story is funny they laugh; if serious, their verbal and nonverbal participation is in a suitable tone. The symbolic convergence account is a general theory in that it is based upon evidence that groups of people have a universal tendency to share fantasies in their communication.

3. Albert E. Sheflen and Alice Sheflen, *Body Language and Social Order: Communication as Behavioral Control* (Englewood Cliffs, N. J.: Prentice-Hall, 1972), p. 75.
4. Sheflen and Sheflen, p. 124.
5. Leonard C. Hawes, "How Writing is Used in Talk: A Study of Communicative Logic-in-Use," *Quarterly Journal of Speech* 62 (1976): 350–360.
6. Thomas S. Frentz and Thomas B. Farrell, "Language-action: A Paradigm for Communication," *Quarterly Journal of Speech* 62 (1976): 333–349.
7. See, for example, Robert E. Nofsinger, Jr., "The Demand Ticket: A Conversational Device for Getting the Floor," *Speech Monographs* 42 (1975): 1–19; Robert E. Nofsinger, Jr., "On Answering Questions Indirectly: Some Rules in the Grammar of Doing Conversation," *Human Communication Research* 2 (1976): 172–181; Charles R. Berger and Richard J. Calabrese, "Some Explorations in Initial Interaction and Beyond: Toward a Developmental Theory of Interpersonal Communication," *Human Communication Research* 1 (1975): 99-112; Mark L. Knapp, Roderick P. Hart, Gustav W. Friedrich, Gary M. Shulman, "The Rhetoric of Goodbye: Verbal and Nonverbal Correlates of Human Leave-Taking," *Speech Monographs* 40 (1973): 182–198.
8. See, for example, Gerry Philipsen, "Navajo World View and Culture Patterns of Speech: A Case Study in Ethnorhetoric," *Speech Monographs* 39 (1972) 132–139; Gerry Philipsen, "Speaking 'Like a Man' in Teamsterville: Culture Patterns of Role Enactment in an Urban Neighborhood," *Quarterly Journal of Speech* 61 (1975): 13–22; Jack L. Daniel and Geneva Smitherman, "How I Got Over: Communication Dynamics in the Black Community," *Quarterly Journal of Speech* 62 (1976): 26–39. For a theoretical discussion of an ethnographic approach to communication, see Dell Hymes, "An Anthropology of Communication," in Frank E. X. Dance, ed., *Human Communication Theory: Original Essays* (New York: Holt, Rinehart and Winston, 1967), pp. 1–39.
9. For a survey of the uses of communication, see Frank E. X. Dance and Carl E. Larson, *The Functions of Human Communication: A Theoretical Approach* (New York: Holt, Rinehart and Winston, 1976).
10. For an explanation of fantasy chaining, see Ernest G. Bormann, "Fantasy and Rhetorical Vision," *Quarterly Journal of Speech* 58 (1972): 396–407.
11. For a survey of the prophesying sessions and their role in the establishment of the new style of preaching, see Irvonwy Morgan, *The Godly Preachers of the Elizabethan Church* (London: Epworth Press, 1965)
12. For a history of the New England Puritan sermon, see Babette May Levy, *Preaching in the First Half Century of New England History* (Hartford, Conn.: American Society of Church History, 1945).
13. Among those who spoke with extreme rapidity were "Hoot" Gibson, Bill Sterne, and Walter Winchell.
14. My thinking here owes a debt to Lawrence Rosenfield's provocative papers, "The Anatomy of Critical Discourse," *Speech Monographs* 35 (1968):

50–69; and "A Game Model of Human Communication," in David H. Smith, ed., *What Rhetoric (Communication Theory) is Appropriate for Contemporary Speech Communication?* (Minneapolis: Department of Speech-Communication, University of Minnesota, 1969), pp. 26–41. For a discussion of communication rules and their analysis, see Donald P. Cushman and W. Barnett Pearce, "Generality and Necessity in Three Types of Human Communication Theory—Special Attention to Rules Theory," in Brent D. Ruben, ed., *Communication Yearbook I* (New Brunswick, N. J.: Transaction Books, 1977), pp. 173–181.

15. For an essay which illustrates the puzzle-solving features of theorizing within a communication style see Frank E. X. Dance, "Toward a Theory of Human Communication," Frank E. X. Dance, ed., *Human Communication Theory: Original Essays* (New York: Holt, Rinehart and Winston, 1967), pp. 288–309.

16. For a discussion of pragmatic and consummatory group styles, see Ernest. G. Bormann, *Discussion and Group Methods: Theory and Practice*, 2nd ed. (New York: Harper and Row, 1975), pp. 27–51.

17. That science is epistemic is a given. For communication as epistemic, see Robert L. Scott, "On Viewing Rhetoric as Epistemic," *Central States Speech Journal* 18 (1967): 9–17; "On Viewing Rhetoric as Epistemic: Ten Years Later," *Central States Speech Journal* 27 (1976): 258–266.

18. Thomas Kuhn, *The Structure of Scientific Revolutions*, 2nd ed. (Chicago: University of Chicago Press, 1970).

19. Ernest G. Bormann, *The Force of Fantasy: The Restoration of the American Dream*, unpublished book manuscript.

20. Kuhn, p. 209.

21. Ibid., pp. 186–187. Kuhn's modifications of the ideas in the first edition may well have come from extensive critiques of such concepts as *normal science and paradigm.* See Imre Lakatos and Alan Musgrave, eds., *Criticism and the Growth of Knowledge* (Cambridge, Mass.: Cambridge University Press, 1970).

22. Ibid., p. 10.

23. Ibid., p. 11.

24. Ibid., p. 11.

25. Ibid., p. 181–187.

26. Kuhn notes in the postscript to the book in which he comments some years after its original publication that the paradigm as a shared example was the central, most novel, and least understood aspect of the book. p. 187.

27. Kuhn, p. 187.

28. Ibid., p. 187.

29. Ibid., pp. 202, 204.

30. Ibid., p. 209.

31. See, for example, C. Harold King, "George Whitefield: Dramatic Evangelist," *Quarterly Journal of Speech* 19 (1933): 165–175; Eugene E. White, "The Preaching of George Whitefield During the Great Awakening," *Speech Monographs* 15 (1948): 33–43.

32. Jerrold J. Katz, *The Philosophy of Language* (New York: Harper and Row, 1966).

33. Bromley Smith, "Gorgias: A Study of Oratorical Style," *Quarterly Journal of Speech* 7 (1921): 335–359; Bruce E. Gronbeck, "Gorgias on Rhetoric and Poetic: A Rehabilitation," *Southern Speech Journal* 38 (1972): 27–38.

34. William Ellery Channing, "Unitarian Christianity," in Wayland Maxfield Par-

rish and Marie Hochmuth, eds., *American Speeches* (New York: Long-mans, Green and Co., 1954), pp. 230–263.

35. For an analysis of the controversy, see Edward M. Collins, Jr., "The Rhetoric of Sensation Challenges the Rhetoric of the Intellect: An Eighteenth-Century Controversy," in DeWitte Holland, ed., *Preaching in American History: Selected Issues in the American Pulpit, 1630–1967* (Nashville: Abingdon Press, 1969), pp. 98–117.

36. Robert L. Scott and Donald K. Smith, "The Rhetoric of Confrontation," *Quarterly Journal of Speech* 55 (1969): 1–8.

80

4

Contemporary Special Communication Theories

In this chapter I examine the way much contemporary communication theory turns out to be style-specific and closely related to teaching and practice of communication styles. The purpose of the analysis is to clear up misconceptions about the nature of style-specific special communication theories and indicate how they consist of the same sorts of linguistic statements as special rhetorical theories.

Three Communication Styles and Their Theories

The people of the United States are currently practicing a number of different communication styles. Some of the popular styles relate to a limited number of transactional contexts, and thus some styles relate primarily to conversation, some to communicating on the electronic media, some to negotiating buying and selling agreements and other contracts, some to religious conversion, some to task-oriented group and organizational communication. I will examine the three distinct styles that are currently receiving considerable attention from North American scholars. When useful I shall make less detailed references to other styles, historical as well as contemporary. The three styles are commonly known as "public speaking," "interpersonal communication," and "communication theory." The common labels imply that public speaking is clearly a study of stylistic concerns relating to a specific transactional context and that communication theory is something more akin to learning theory in psychology or to the general theories in the natural sciences. Thus, at first glance I may seem to be comparing apples and oranges. The mislabeling of rhetorical styles is one of the factors in the current state of confusion relating to communication theory. I will analyze the similarities and differences among the theories associated with each of the three styles in some detail, but to eliminate the confusion stemming from the labels I will refer to the three styles as *the public speaking communication style*, *the relationship communication style*, and *the message communication style*.

The Public Speaking Communication Style Nineteenth-century scholars of communication tended to neglect the communication theory associated with informal transactions and emphasized occasions for oratory in the pulpit, in deliberative assemblies, and before the bar. They taught their students rhetoric and elocution in order to achieve an exemplar of communication which was called *eloquence*. For much of the theory which undergirded the stately and involved style of their oratory they drew upon classical rhetorical styles such as those employed by Cicero. Just as nineteenth-century architects often returned to classical Greece and Rome for the style of public buildings, communication theorists often returned to classical times for the style of their communication. However, the elaborate and involved style of nineteenth-century oratory was replaced at the turn of the twentieth century by a more direct form of address. Scholars turned their attention from oral eloquence and oratory to literature and composition. Elocution fell into disrepute.

Of course, communication is too central to human culture and behavior to be ignored for long by scholars. When the reaction came, it came in part from within departments of rhetoric or English literature and composition. The style the new impulse developed and propagated was one which its proponents called "public speaking," and when they formed a professional association to aid them in restoring oral communication to what they thought was its rightful place in the academic environment they called themselves the National Association of Academic Teachers of Public Speaking. The public speaking style drew heavily on the rhetorical tradition, going back to classical times for its theoretical developments. Aristotle defined *rhetoric* as the art of finding the available means of persuasion. Many writers in the public speaking style have provided definitions after Aristotle, but they have done so by formulating variations on the theme of intentional persuasive communication.[1]

The public speaking communication style itself was given coherent expression largely in the basic public speaking courses organized by the participants in the new style in order to teach newcomers how to practice the style and in the textbooks they wrote for these courses, beginning in the first decades of the twentieth century. The current public speaking style is supported by criticism and theory that have evolved gradually over the last sixty years. An early and important textbook containing the theory was written by James A. Winans in 1915 and is entitled *Public Speaking*.[2] By the time Winans wrote his book, the practice and criticism of the communication style had reached a point where he could provide a model of the ideal communication events and include detailed discussion for the student who wanted to approximate the ideal in practice. Reflecting the new styles reaction against the lofty "purple passages" of the Ciceronian eloquence of the nineteenth century, Winans recommended that conversation furnish the standards for the new style.

The basic model or exemplar of the public speaking style is essentially a situation in which the central character is the *speaker*. Other parts of the transaction include an *audience* and an *occasion*. The speaker is the motivating force in the communication transaction; while taking the occasion into account and adapting to the audience, the speaker sets the whole thing in motion and the audience then *responds* to the speaker. The speaker selects or is furnished a *topic* (another element of the model), and after carefully analyzing the audience, the speaker skillfully fashions supporting material to adapt the topic and ideas to the specific audience. The final and most important element in the model is the *speech*, which emerges from the dynamic interplay of the other parts of the model. The audience is not passive but responds moment by moment as the speaker talks and may provide complications to which the speaker must then adapt. If the audience is hostile to the speaker, to the speaker's position on the topic, or to both, the drama is heightened. The speaker who succeeds against high odds—that is, against a hostile audience or on an unfavorable occasion—is generally evaluated as having done a better job and produced a better speech than one who gains a favorable response under more favorable conditions.[3]

The speaker in the exemplar communication transaction is alert to the audience's responses and adjusts to the unfolding situation. In the final analysis the speaker succeeds or fails on the basis of native ability, trained artistry, and the capacity to take initiative and act in such a way that he or she achieves consciously thought-out objectives and purposes.

To summarize, a good public speaking communication transaction is one in which a skillful speaker with a clear purpose analyzes the audience and occasion carefully and wisely, selects a suitable topic, develops an organizational pattern, fills in the outline with suitable amplifying material, delivers the speech with appropriate nonverbal gestures and vocal intonations, phrases the ideas in suitable language for the hearers, carefully observes the audience's reaction, and achieves his or her purpose by gaining a suitable audience response.

As the neophyte physicist learns the paradigm of Newtonian mechanics by doing experiments such as the inclined plane and the pendulum, so the beginning public speaker learns the exemplar by giving speeches. The student learns the rules and norms as well as the standards of good speaking by the process of giving speeches to audiences according to the expectations and rules of the various programs for speeches to inform, to convince, to persuade, to entertain, and so forth.

The theory associated with a good public speaking communication transaction is related to the basic parts of the exemplar. The theory deals with the communicative behavior that are both allowed and not allowed within a given context. In addition, the finer points of the theory consider those communications that may or may not be performed. In short, the theory spells out the rules that provide the boundaries of approved behavior within the context as well as the area of freedom within which people can vary tactics and still play the language games. Usually the theory considers contextual rules in terms of *types* of speeches, so discussions of the nature of informative speeches and occasions appropriate for such discourse becomes an important part of the theory. The theory discusses the nature of the ideal speaker and ways in which neophytes can learn to project a suitable persona from the platform. The theory will include generalizations about the nature of audiences and deal with such matters as the characteristics of audiences composed of people of diverse or similar ages, of diverse or similar socioeconomic and educational backgrounds, of diverse or similar interests and attitudes.

Since the speech itself is perhaps the most important feature of the exemplar of public speaking communication, the theory deals with many aspects of the speech. Much of the theoretical discussion concerns ways for individuals to research a given topic area, select a central idea, analyze the collected information in order to find the logical connections which exist among the various subissues, and finally to come to some structured explanation of the main theme. Another aspect of theory relates to organizing the material to adapt it to the audience. Such audience adaptation requires a thorough analysis of the specific audience for a given speech. Additional theoretical material will include such things as phrasing the ideas in suitable language and the use of gesture and voice to deliver the speech in a successful way.

The Relationship Communication Style   The most recent of the three academic styles emerged in the 1960s. Whereas the public speaking communication style and the message communication style both emphasize communication as a tool to achieve other ends, for the most part the new style emphasizes communication as the most important relationship among people, as a positive value in and of itself.

The 1960s saw a reaction against science, not throughout the entire society, but on the part of substantial groups of people. The participation of the United States in the Vietnam War was divisive; science's contribution to the war made it suspect. Many became disenchanted with the "establishment." Anything hinting at the control of one human being over another was anathema to those caught up in the new impulse. Certainly the communication styles that emphasized intentional communication aimed at achieving persuasion or behavioral change in others was undesirable and came to be a focus of attack and conflict as the new style emerged. The rise of humanistic psychology, the human potential movement, and interpersonal communication all came together to form the new style.

The relationship communication style developed its theory in the latter part of the 1960s and early 1970s.[4] The model of good communication in the theory of interpersonal communication differs substantially from the exemplar of the other styles. The theorists for the relationship style disliked mathematically expressed formulas, schema, and blueprints. They rejected the model of communication based upon the cybernetic analogy with feedback as a crucial principle for information transmission and control instruments. They rejected a paradigm that saw human beings communicating like machines and celebrated instead the uniqueness of people and their potential to be different from machines.

The theorists for the new style used the term *feedback* to refer to all the verbal and nonverbal responses that express reaction to another, or feelings, or a response to another person's communication behavior. One of the aphorisms of the style is "You cannot not communicate."[5] The point of the principle is that all responses to a participant in a communication transaction can be interpreted in terms of relationships, feelings, and attitudes.

The principle "You cannot not communicate" points up the central rejection of purposive, intentional communication aimed at control of others in a communication transaction. Unintentional behavior communicate feelings, or at least others are stimulated to feel and respond and infer meanings from the entire context of communication. The relationship style broadens the concern of communication theorists considerably by the assumption that you cannot not communicate. As a result, the theory associated with the relationship style contains much material about nonverbal communication.

The public speaking style devotes considerable theory to the occasion and to the contextual influence on the programs governing certain transactions within its purview. The relationship communication style features context as part of its concern with nonverbal communication. The theoretical formulations deal with such contextual features of communication transactions as where people sit or stand in relationship to one another, what sorts of clothes they wear, what their hair styles are, how they walk, how they gesture, how close are they to one another when they speak, whether they touch, and how they communicate through senses such as touch and smell.

The model or exemplar of good communication in the relationship style is couched much more in the language of the philosopher, the psychiatrist, and the theologian than the engineer. Indeed, certain theologians such as Buber and Kierkegaard, and philosophers such as Sartre, have provided some of the sanctions as well as some of the more important technical words and concepts for the theory.

The model of the relationship style, as one might expect given the nature of the impulse which resulted in its formulation, is difficult to explain in clear and simple language with precise definitions of basic concepts. The style celebrates feelings and experiences and puts much less value on cognitive activity designed to structure and explain experience.

Like the public speaking style, the transactional model of the relationship style is dramatistic, but it features not one central person but several cooperative participants who cease to play games with one another and who are real and honest, who take risks and disclose their authentic selves. Their basic attitude is that they should deal with others as authentic human beings and not as things or machines. They are no longer wearing masks and playing the roles that made them less than human and shielded them from contact with others. As authentic communicators, they are open and they welcome human relationships. They disclose their feelings to one another. Self-disclosure is risky, and they begin communicating with one another in authentic ways only when a climate of mutual trust is established by active and empathetic listening and by demonstrated honesty on the part of all. Evaluative feedback by the listeners is evidence of such honesty. People often have trouble talking about themselves honestly, but once risked, the self-disclosing communication tends to open up others, and they in turn disclose. The emotional tone of the communication is warmed by congruent, honest, and open communication as people take more and more risks and are accepted for themselves.

In the warm and trusting climate of a good communication transaction, people can reveal their innermost feelings and discuss their hopes and fears. The participants can discover their authentic selves, grow in awareness, raise their consciousness to higher levels. They can express their feelings, cry, and laugh without worry of acceptance or rejection. As the climate builds to ever more intimate and significant communication, important relationships evolve among the participants.

A good self-image is an important ingredient in the ideal relationship transaction. One way to build a good self-image is by participating in communication according to the standards and norms of the style. A person opens up to others and receives frank and honest evaluative feedback (i.e., response to an evaluation of oneself as exposed), and then by acceptance of the meaning of the response the person learns how to change in order to improve the self.

The process of communication, the transactions in which all participate and create meanings, results in the participants' discovering their potential and becoming aware of their authentic selves. In the ideal situation the result for the individual is a stronger self-image, a greater sensitivity to others as people, and a higher consciousness of the human condition.

Kuhn's insight that the scientist appropriates a paradigm by doing the classical experiments in order to give the theory and concepts empirical meaning is illustrated most strongly in an analogous fashion by the way people learn to communicate in the relationship style. The public speaking and message communication styles are older and more mature and thus some steps removed in time from the gestation period when they were controversial and when many people were drawn to them and had to learn quickly the programs required for the transactional forms. The student of relationship communication learns the style by participating in discussions which approximate the exemplar. The learning sessions in the 1960s and early 1970s were almost always conducted by a "trainer" or "facilitator" or "leader" who coached the participants and tried to model their communication until it approximated the ideal.

The Message Communication Style I have saved the presentation of the theory of the message communication style for last because while few scholars have argued that rhetorical theory or interpersonal communication is scientific, a good many have argued that communication theory is analogous to scientific theory.

The message communication style evolved historically after the public speaking style and before the relationship style. While the liberal arts and humanities were providing a hospitable environment for the growth and practice of the public speaking style, a number of the people involved in its study were searching about for appropriate theory and research for their new emphasis on communication. Some of them suggested that a more scientific approach modeled after developments in psychology would be an appropriate mode of investigation.[6]

While more and more scholars of public speaking were moving to study speech events by scientific methods, engineers were applying scientific methods to the study of communication. The early efforts of both speech scholars and engineers tended in the direction of the study of the acoustics of sound, voice production, and voice disorders.[7] Some of the engineers, however, were involved in the transmission of information, particularly by sending messages by telephone and radio. Out of the impulse for a scientific approach to communication and specifically out of the work of the engineers, there emerged in the 1940s a new way of practicing and criticizing communication. The result of this new exemplar was what I call the message communication style.

By the 1940s, engineers working at such places as the Bell Telephone Laboratories, the Massachusetts Institute of Technology, Harvard University, and the Pennsylvania State University were beginning the development of electronic thinking machines. They tended to blueprint their plans for electronic circuits in message-transmission systems, and when they came to explain the exemplar of their communication style they used a schematic drawing similar to a blueprint. One of the first important descriptions of the ideal communication event in the new style was Shannon and Weaver's schema presented in their study *The Mathematical Theory of Communication*.[8]

Schramm, who was more interested in mass communication than in the technology of its transmission, adapted the Shannon–Weaver blueprint for his purposes, and Berlo, who had studied with Schramm at Illinois, made further modifications, which resulted in a description of the ideal communication event that was abstract enough to include both human and machine communication.[9]

The basic idea of the theory was that of human beings communicating with a machine. *Cybernetics* is the study of the way humans set goals and control behavior to achieve them, and the way machines can come to serve the same function. The study of cybernetics is based upon the ability of organisms and machines to provide and use feedback. The term *feedback* refers to information about the output of a machine or the behavior of an organism that is continuously fed back to a control device and changes the operation or behavior in order to correct errors and achieve predetermined goals. (*Feedback* in the message communication style is quite different from the concept as used in the relationship style. Feedback in the relationship style is essentially a response of any sort whatsoever and often is evaluative.)

The new theory included a set of critical standards to guide practice and enable the initiated to coach or teach neophytes how to practice the style. Good communication transmitted information with high fidelity. That is, the more information the system transmitted from source to receiver without distortion or loss, the higher the fidelity of transmission and the better the communication event. *Noise* in a communication system cuts down on fidelity and is therefore undesirable. To combat noise such as static, the engineers discovered that repetition of message elements increased a receiver's ability to decipher the appropriate information. The theorists called the repetition of message elements *redundancy*. However, redundancy was costly in terms of time and energy, and since the new style valued the conservation of energy, they judged that good communication should also be efficient in terms of energy output (costs). The exemplar of the style, therefore, was one in which noise was minimized and the redundancy level adjusted to a rate that resulted in high-fidelity transmission of information with no unnecessary repetitions.

Finally, the theorists were interested in the speed of transmission. Messages traveling across telephone or telegraph wires or through radio waves moved with great rapidity. Nonetheless, if more messages could be transmitted in less time by shortening the time for a given message or by transmitting several messages simultaneously, that was considered a virtue as well.

The exemplar communication transaction in the message communication style is an abstracted schema drawn from the model of man talking to machine. Assume that a person wants to talk to a computer. The first step is to decide what the machine is to do. The programmer then plans a message to cause the machine to perform the task, puts the message into symbols the computer can understand, punches the message in machine language onto cards, and feeds the cards into the computer. The machine reads the cards until it comes to something it cannot understand. Perhaps the card has a word on it that is not in the machine's vocabulary, or the card may contain a sentence with improper grammar (a comma may be missing). The computer stops and prints out a sentence which explains that there is an error of a certain kind on the incomprehensible card. The programmer finds the offending card, discovers the improper sentence, corrects it, and replaces the card in the computer. Now the machine understands and continues to process message cards until it cannot understand something else. Thus, the human being communicates with the machine to achieve understanding and to transmit information back and forth.

The computer either understands the messages completely or does not understand them at all. When the computer indicates that it does not understand a message it aids the programmer in the debugging process. The corrective mechanism in the system of communication between programmer and computer is called *feedback*. When communication engineers found ways to teach machines to indicate the source of a communication difficulty they discovered a powerful principle with many practical applications. Although the principle has always operated in goal-directed behavior, it had not drawn much attention until the development of automation and computers elevated it to a key position in the theory of the message communication style.

Feedback functions in two major ways within the theory. In the first instance, feedback provides the initiator of the communication with a mechanism to assure fidelity of transmission or understanding. The computer fails to understand and indicates the source of the decoding problem. The programmer

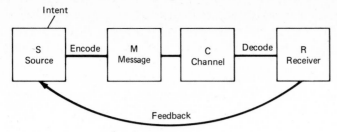

Figure 4   A typical schematic description of the exemplar communication in the message communication style.

redrafts the message to make it clearer, and the machine then understands. In the second instance, feedback provides evidence of the extent to which the initiator of the communication has reached a control objective and thus provides a bearing so the new messages or adjustments can achieve the desired control. The machine equivalents of information transmission and control in human communication are informative and persuasive communication transactions.

Figure 4 presents a typical schematic description of the exemplar communication transaction in the message communication style. I am using essentially the same model Berlo presented, although many others operating within the framework of the exemplar and working primarily as puzzle solvers have suggested different pictorial layouts and have changed some of the labels for the elements of the model.[10] The exemplar of the communication style portrays an initiator and controller of the communication transaction in the form of a *source*. The source begins with a goal for the transaction, encodes messages to achieve the goal, selects proper channels, transmits the message to the receiver, and awaits feedback to discover whether or not the communication was successful in achieving the goal. Notice that in the message communication style the concept of feedback is closely related to the notion that the message source has a clear goal against which to test the responses of the receiver. The feedback loop does not help the machine achieve its intent when communicating with a programmer—rather the feedback is designed by the programmer and is reactive to the active communication efforts of the source.

To summarize, the exemplar of message communication envisions a transaction in which a message source designs a message to achieve a clearly specified purpose or goal, encodes the message into an appropriate linguistic system, and transmits the message through appropriate channels, where it impinges upon some sensory device or organ and is decoded by the receiver. The information contained in the message is decoded by the receiver in such a way that it reflects the information encoded by the source with high fidelity. Thus, if the message is transmitted by Morse code over a telegraph line, the letters of the English alphabet which form the words are encoded into Morse dots, spaces, and dashes, sent across the wire, and decoded into the same Morse code dots, spaces, and dashes as were originally put into the line by the message source. In turn the receiver translates the Morse dots, spaces, and dashes into the same letters of the English alphabet as the receiver used to start the encoding process. Should the message fail in some way, the receiver emits cues that the source can interpret as aids to draft new or revised messages in order to achieve the desired information transmission and control of outcomes.

As with all communication styles, the message communication style is appropriated or learned by participating in transactions conducted according to its precepts. One common instructional exercise, the equivalent of the physics student doing the experiment involving the inclined plane, is to have a member of a class play the role of message source and inform the rest of the class (who are instructed to play the role of message receivers) how to make a geometric pattern with paper and pencil, or how to fold a piece of paper into a boat, or a bird, or how to do some other relatively complicated piece of origami. In one popular variation, the instructor gives the message source some patterns made by tracing around the edges of a domino. The instructor gives each person playing the receiver role a domino and several sheets of paper. The source's intent is to get each receiver to duplicate a given pattern.

The instructor will often repeat the exercise using a new pattern in each repetition and increasing the number of channels and the opportunity for feedback from replication to replication. For example, in the first treatment, the instructor might place the student behind a screen so that the receivers cannot see the source, who must explain how to form the pattern by verbal descriptions. Screening the message source also eliminates nonverbal feedback, and the instructor cautions the receivers to give no verbal feedback. In the second condition the source might be allowed to see the receivers, to receive nonverbal feedback, and so forth. In the third condition the source might be allowed to see the receivers and they might be allowed to see the source's gestures and provide verbal as well as nonverbal feedback. The instructor thus creates an ever closer approximation of the exemplar model of a communication transaction in the message communication style. After each replication the fidelity of information transmission is checked by comparing the replication of the pattern drawn by the receivers with the pattern the source was seeking to get them to replicate.

Communication styles also have an associated rhetorical vision or view of social reality. Influential figures in the early development of communication theory saw the universe as winding down.[11] They saw this winding-down process as a tendency to disorganization. They used the word *entropy* to refer to the general tendency of things to grow disorganized. In their view, information was the opposite of entropy or negative entropy, and they saw the creation and transmission of information as requiring energy to combat the natural tendency toward disorganization. Left alone, information would decay under the natural entropic forces. Energy was a value to be protected, and the organization and transmission of information was a goal to be sought. Norbert Wiener reflected the general ethos of the style when he referred to speech as "a joint game by the talker and listener against the forces of confusion."[12] In the game against confusion the computer was always cooperative. Models of the message communication style are prescriptive and not scientific, because of the fact that people often fail to cooperate in the joint game against confusion. They bluff, lie, and try to mislead. If the model were scientific, then all or an appreciable subset of communication would fall into the pattern the model describes. Yet,

Wiener points to a number of contexts in society in which people indulge in communication transactions that are very different from joint games of talkers and listeners against the forces of confusion. Wiener notes about the legal system, for example:

> It is a game . . . in which the litigants try by methods which are limited by the code of law to obtain the judge and the jury as their partners. In such a game the opposing lawyer, unlike nature itself, can and deliberately does try to introduce confusion in the messages of the side he is opposing. He tries to reduce their statements to nonsense, and he deliberately jams the messages between his antagonist and the judge and jury. In this jamming, it is inevitable that bluff should occasionally be at a premium.[13]

The prescriptive nature of the communication theory is also apparent in the way criticism grows out of it. Using a scientific theory like Newton's does not yield criticism such as "That is a bad free fall by that cannon ball, for it failed to travel the distance prescribed by the formula $S = 1/2gt^2$." Suppose, however, that an instructor who understands the theory of the message communication style observes a videotape of a two-person conference conducted according to the norms and rules of the style. Assume further that both the instructor and the people observed share an appreciation and understanding of the exemplar transactions. The instructor comments, "You are confused because you are not providing one another with adequate feedback." In the context of a message communication transaction the evaluation is both sensible and helpful. The participants can then work on their feedback skills according to the standards for good feedback spelled out in the theory.

The Uses and Abuses of Special Theories

The Fallacy of Deriving Hypotheses for General Theories from Special Theories   The communication theory that grows out of and relates back to the practice and criticism of a communication style always consists of artistic elements as well as scientific components. The scientific method of investigation that aims at discovering laws similar to the laws of physics or chemistry is appropriate to those features of communication styles which are common to many styles. If the investigator applies the scientific method designed to discover causal relationships to the artistic features that are conventional, customary, and rule-governed but style specific, the result is always trivial. Questions of causality about the communication practices of a rhetorical community that are specific and unique to that community are in principle unanswerable. A scholarly community that attempts to answer unaswerable questions is like the legendary community of medieval scholars who devoted their time to learned discussions of how many angels can dance on the head of a pin. An immense amount of "scientific" research in communication has been misguided in that the investigators have tried to find causal connections that allow for prediction and control among elements of communication transactions that were style-specific.

A major task of the philosophy of communication, therefore, is to sort out those questions from past research that were answerable and that appear useful as guides for scientific investigations aimed at developing general theories from those questions that when answered will explain a special theory and the communication style of a community of limited size and duration.

Significant forms, patterns, correlations, and invariable relations all imply a regularity beyond the arbitrary choices of communicators. Thus, thunder follows lightening and can be said to be a sign of or to mean lightning. However, we cannot choose to change thunder from meaning lightning to meaning the coming of a rainbow. Sometimes lightning is followed by a rainbow and sometimes it is not, but lightning is causally connected to thunder; the sparking phenomenon that characterizes the movement of electricity through the air also vibrates the air to create a sound wave. On the other hand, the artistic features of a communication style are rule-governed to some extent. The participants lay down quite arbitrary rules for their communication games. If they decide to refer to a certain meteorological phenomenon with the word *lightning* or the word *Blitzen* they are dealing not with a lawfulness like that which characterizes the relationship between lightning and thunder but with a rule-established conventional relationship that is subject to their whims. Similarly, if a rhetorical community establishes a communication transaction such that when lightning strikes a tree and causes it to burn they form a circle of people around it while a predetermined spokesperson chants in rhyme and makes broad jerking gestures and the members of the group interrupt at customary places to make rhythmic shouts, such events will be idiosyncratic, conventional, and arbitrary. The spokesperson may produce messages which take a recurring form from ritual to ritual so that an anthropologist might recognize a video or audio tape recording as being one of the type, but the form of the message would be style-specific

Suppose a researcher in search of a general law of communication drew a sample of subjects from a rhetorical community who worship the fire god that comes from the sky to rest in a tree, and then varies the sex of the spokesperson and the amount of chanting and rhyming as independent variables in order to discover the amount of attitude change measured by semantic differential scales. Such an effort would be doomed to failure. On the other hand, the ethnographer who studied the rhetorical community in order to find the rules and customs by which they communicate would be asking questions for which field-study data would be appropriate. The ethnographer would end with a case study or rhetorical criticism of the communication of the community. The ethnographic study would, primarily, provide insight into the special communication theories which related to communication practices of that particular rhetorical community.

The Puritan preachers spoke for an hourglass, divided their sermons into two major parts, and peppered their sermons with "firstly" and "secondly" and other devices to aid the audience's memory; these practices were part of the artistic side of the Puritans' special rhetorical (communication) theory. Computer programmers write their messages to the machines on specially prepared forms with great care and precision in a carefully constructed grammar; this is part of the artistic side of their special communication theory.

As I have indicated previously, communication theory is a particularly confusing field of study because experts have sometimes referred to special and general theories with the common term *theory*. Thus some have included the model of the message communication style as an important component in communication theory. Sometimes they have used *theory* in the sense of a scientific causative account at the third level of analysis. Sometimes they have used the term to refer to theory in the artistic sense.

Confusing Exemplar Models with Descriptive Models A good many communication theorists have been confused over the nature of models. As Kuhn pointed out, a disciplinary matrix in a science often includes heuristic models as well as the exemplar of the research. Since some scientific theories have heuristic models as important parts of their theory and since some communication theorists wished to provide similar accounts, they concluded that the models of the message communication style were in some way more analogous to the models of science than to the exemplars of the public speaking style.

A brief analysis of the construction and use of heuristic models in the natural sciences will provide a basis for comparison with the models of communication styles. I will use a relatively simple and yet historically important example to illustrate the nature of scientific models. As often happened in the development of science, a number of low-level laws expressing invariable relationships among the properties of gases preceded the formulation of the model that was an important part of the dynamic theory of gases. Boyle's law, for example, states that the pressure of a gas varies with the volume and temperature so that pressure is inversely proportional to volume. Gay-Lussac's law states that there is a proportional relation between pressure and temperature. A number of additional laws dealing with such things as the relationship between the pressure and the conduction of heat also preceded the discovery of the model.

Early in the nineteenth century, theorists formulated the dynamic theory of gases to explain the laws governing functional relationships among pressure, volume, heat, and so forth. An important part of the theory was a hypothetical construction of a dynamic system composed of rigid particles in random and rapid motion moving in accordance with the laws of mechanics. In a sense, the theoreticians were playing a game—they were constructing a mechanical system that operated according to known laws of Newtonian mechanics, and seeing if their observation of phenomena related to gaseous substances indicated that gases behaved as if they were constructed in the same way as the hypothetical system. The theoreticians called the rigid particles *molecules*. Gases, according to the hypothetical system, consist of a large number of molecules moving randomly and colliding in haphazard fashion with each other and with the walls of any containing vessel. The velocity of the molecules varies with the temperature of the gas, and the pressure on the walls of a container results from the impact of a very large number of molecules on the walls of the vessel. To increase the pressure on the walls of a vessel the molecules must increase their velocity, which requires energy. Adding heat to the system should, then, provide additional energy to increase the velocity of the molecules, and thus their impact on the walls will be greater and the pressure will increase.

A mathematician can deductively derive other laws relating to the behavior of gaseous materials from the translation of the model into functional relationships. The model is deductive because mathematicians can use observable relationships to compute the number, mass, and velocity of particles in the model such that the observed behavior would result. Particles such as those computed on the basis of observations can then be used to compute further relationships, which can be checked against other laws or other experiments. The theory allows for the deduction of both Boyle's law and Gay-Lussac's law by mathematical computation.

Notice that the scientists did not directly observe little particles flying about in containers of gas. What they did observe were samples of gas acting as if they were composed of molecules moving randomly and speeding up with increases in temperature.

The positing of a set of constructs that are not directly verifiable introduces a new dimension to scientific theories. As the natural sciences grew more and more complex and as more and more was learned about electromagnetic wave motion and about particles in subatomic physics, this sort of theory became quite common. In a sense the molecule construct is a fiction in this theory, but it is a very important kind of fiction. Not just any hypothetical construct would do. The construct of a system composed of a container filled with space and little particles in constant motion is called a heuristic model, because it is not the same as the gas but it acts in the same way in some very crucial regards and allows for prediction of results.

The dynamic theory of gases yielded all the then known laws governing properties of gases by deduction; but it yielded some hitherto unknown laws by mathematical computations in the same way that it implied the known ones. If the assumption was made that the molecules had some mass, the theory yielded laws that predicted the effect of great pressure on the gases. With the molecules tightly restricted, as they would be under great pressure, the theory predicted much different effects than when the gas was under little pressure. Experiments designed to test these mathematically inferred laws became *critical* experiments because so much was at stake. An experiment that tests a mathematically inferred relationship can, if the results are negative, seriously restrict the scope of the theory or even cast some doubt upon its usefulness. If a critical experiment is positive it provides dramatic support for the theory itself. Thus, in the value system of the natural scientists the discovery by mathematical computation of a hypothesis for experimental testing came to be highly valued. The value came to be generalized in terms of the desirability of deriving hypotheses for investigation from theory.

Early investigators trying to apply the scientific method to communication events often tried to derive their hypotheses from theory. Unfortunately they had no heuristic models such as the dynamic theory of gases to provide them with mathematically derived hypotheses for their laboratories. In the absence of scientific models, the investigators often took elements of the exemplars of various communication styles as the basis for their investigations.

Interestingly enough, in the middle decades of the twentieth century a communication style evolved among intellectual communities studying the social sciences that celebrated "model-building" as a desirable form of theorizing. Kaplan, writing in the 1960s, noted:

> To be sure every culture, every period of science, exhibits some style or other, and is subject to the norms of its own fashions. It is impossible to wear clothing of no style at all. If the current fashion dictates the building of models, and perhaps even the kind of models to be constructed, it is not for that reason alone to be condemned. I have nothing against the current mode, but I trust that it is not shamefully old-fashioned to be interested still in what lies underneath; glamor isn't everything. What I object to is both the blanket condemnation and the indiscriminate enthusiasm that are evoked by models. As with abstract expressionism in painting, I am afraid that model building is made too much a matter of principle, pro or con, and not enough a matter of the values, esthetic or scientific, achieved in the specific instance. [14]

Indeed, many scholars in speech communication who were developing theories in the period when model-building was fashionable tried to work out models in the style of other behavioral scientists. Thus, they tended to take the exemplar of the message communication style, since it was already portrayed in graphic form, and make it the basis for model-building. By taking models from special artistic theories and applying them as scientific constructs to explain and account for communication behavior, they introduced a confusion into theory and research that plagues us to some extent to this day.

Miller, writing in the 1960s, provided a typical analysis. He suggested that "most models of the speech communication process serve three major functions: an organizational, or communicative, function; a heuristic, or research-generating, function; and an anticipatory, or predictive, function." He defined models "as a kind of classificatory system that enables one to abstract and to categorize potentially relevant parts of the process." [15]

Miller saw models similar to the one in Figure 4 as serving a heuristic function. He uses as an example of the kind of hypothesis suggested by the model the functional relationship between the source's encoding skills and the receiver's attitude toward the speaker and the position that the speaker advocates. More specifically, he suggests that the number of mispronunciations in a message is functionally related to the credibility of the source and the attitude toward the proposition. Miller also saw the model as having if not predictive power at least the ability to anticipate events. [16]

Most important to our concerns, Miller argued, "It is useful to think of models as arbitrary constructs, as judgments made by the person who creates the model. By adopting this view, one avoids the pitfall of assuming that there is a *correct* model of speech communication; he discards one common meaning for the term 'model,' i.e., 'something eminently worthy of imitation, an exemplar or ideal.' "[17] Miller's position was that no current model of speech communication was worth such a laudatory evaluation, thereby implying that he saw an exemplar or ideal in the Platonic sense as an ideal type for all times and all places. The models of communication theories associated with specific styles are exemplars for the members of a rhetorical community limited in time and space who practice communication in a specific and idiosyncratic style.

Ironically, while Miller argues against the notion that any "present model of speech communication is worthy of such lofty praise" as to be an exemplar he does infer that the models he discusses, including Berlo's, are able to generate scientific research. Certainly a heuristic model in the scientific sense must have wide scope across time and place. My argument is that the models of communication theorists in the 1960s and 1970s were exemplars in the sense that they were something eminently worthy of imitation for the communication styles which employed them. None of the models so far put forward in communication theory have been analogous to the heuristic models Kuhn discovered in the disciplinary matrices of the natural sciences.

Because the models are artistic, the practitioners of various communication styles have considerable freedom for improvisation and for variations of form. Thus, human communication exhibits a diversity among various cultures and in various historical times as varied and interesting as the forms and styles of the fine arts. Let us consider for a moment Miller's example of a research hypothesis derived from the model that included the functional relationships among a speaker mispronouncing words and the effect of such speech upon audience attitudes toward the credibility of the source and toward the position the speaker advocates. Historically in North America, several communication styles have flourished which included mispronunciations in terms of dictionary standards of English as aids to credibility.

Foster, writing from a wide background as a speaker and teacher of public speaking, recalled a successful speech by H. G. Wells that "blithely violated some of the traditional rules of oratory." Foster then judges:

> Again the truth was forced upon me that nobody can find out what moves audiences today merely by studying the classic utterances of other days. Some speakers who faithfully follow the models in the old textbooks leave the audiences cold—even when the audiences do not leave the speakers. The speeches are rhetorically correct but oratorically soporific. Teachers of speech may as well admit it. On the other hand, some of the best speakers of our time violate rules which were memorized by the old-time students of 'oratory.' These speakers do not respect even the right of a verb to agree with its subject, or the right of an antecedent to have something to antecede. [18]

Populist and neo-Populist speakers of the late nineteenth and early twentieth century spoke in a style that emphasized their common origins, and they used mispronunciations and ungrammatical expressions as part of their appeal to identify themselves as just plain folks. Huey Long consciously varied his pronunciation and grammar depending upon the style of the audiences to which he spoke. [19]

A given rhetorical community could well make of mispronunciations a game much like the game of "dozens" practiced by some rhetorical communities in black ghettos of large northern cities or like punning games played in certain intellectual communities. Such a community might reward the speaker who exhibits the most humor and creativity in breaking the rules of upper-middle-class white pronunciation. Of course, some rhetorical styles focus on correct pronunciation; in them a mispronunciation becomes a major flaw not only in communication but in professional ability. Radio announcers who host classical music programs participate in a communication style that makes a fetish of the correct pronunciation of names of composers and titles of musical works. My point is that Miller's research question is style-specific in that for some rhetorical communities mispronunciations would detract from a speaker's credibility while for other groups violating norms of pronunciation would add to a person's credibility.

I have distinguished two levels of communication theory (the second and third levels of Figure 3, p. 72). The second level is the style-specific theory that is an integral part of the practice of a communication style and is to be found in handbooks and textbooks designed to aid in indoctrinating children and newcomers to the practices of communication. The third level provides an explanation of communication in general. Scholars may study communication theory and practice at the third level of Figure 3 in order to provide interpretative structures, to explain historical developments, to make critical evaluations of communication styles, to make scientific descriptions of communication styles, or to provide generalizations which explain theory and practice at the second level.

The Dynamic and Developmental Nature of Communication Styles

The world is seldom as neatly divided and categorized as our structured interpretative accounts of it. I have described the main features of the three communication styles in somewhat static terms in order to portray their essentials. My intention is not to characterize the special theories as unchanging ideal types. Communication styles evolve and develop in dynamic fashion over time. Circumstances change, and the specialists in the style puzzle over problems and modify the exemplars. I have indicated some of the historical factors involved in the rise of the three styles discussed in this chapter. The interpersonal communication style was by 1980 apparently waning in popularity. Indeed, some writers were shifting their usage of the term *interpersonal communication* to encompass both the interpersonal and the message communication styles. Some theorists were attempting to create amalgam theories that integrated elements of the interpersonal and message communication style. Some were substituting the term *public communication* for *public speaking*. I have not traced the evolving modifications and mutations in the styles. To keep up to date with the current state of any special communication theory, scholars must continually monitor the changing formulations as they appear in textbooks, handbooks, convention papers, and journal essays.

Often theorists who are drawn to several communication styles will try to integrate the special theories associated with each. Conceivably an amalgam of some elements of the message communication style with elements of the relationship style could create a new third style that would serve useful functions and achieve, for instance, high-fidelity communication of information and trusting relationships among communicators. Theorists attempting such integration would have to be careful not to mix incommensurable elements. For example, the message communication's model of intentional communication on the part of a source using a test cycle based on feedback and concluding an episode after achieving intent is incompatible with the relationship communication tenet that you cannot not communicate.

Theorists interested in improving special communication theories and their associated practices would be wise to first untangle the special theories one from another and then from general theories as well before proceeding to modify their exemplars.

Summary

The people of the United States are pluralistic in their communication practices. They participate in a variety of rhetorical communities. North American scholars are currently giving considerable attention to three communication styles. They are the public speaking, relationship, and message communication styles. These three receive the bulk of the attention in textbooks, classrooms, and scholarly journals, although there are a number of other styles which are of concern, including such things as negotiating, consciousness raising, conversion, and assertiveness training.

The public speaking communication style came into prominence in the early decades of the twentieth century with the formation of the National Association of Academic Teachers of Public Speaking and the proliferation of courses in public speaking in the years from 1915 to 1935. The special theory associated with public speaking is related to the exemplar communication transactions in which the skillful speaker with a clear purpose analyzes the audience and occasion, selects a suitable topic, develops an organizational pattern, fills in the outline with amplifying material, delivers the speech with appropriate gestures and vocal intonations, phrases the ideas in clear and interesting language, observes audience reaction, and achieves his or her purpose by gaining a suitable auidence response.

The theory deals with context in terms of a taxonomy of types of situations that includes the special characteristics of each audience types. Much theoretical discussion in the style relates to selecting a central idea, collecting and analyzing information, organizing the speech, and adapting the material to the audience. The theory also deals with ways to establish the speaker's ethos.

The relationship communication style is the most recent to emerge; it came to prominence in the 1960s and 1970s. The model of exemplar communication in the special theory associated with relationship communication involves two or more people in communication transactions in which they deal with one another in authentic terms. They are open, accepting, and self-disclosing. The communication episodes develop feelings of trust among the participants. They develop strong self-images and good deep interpersonal relationships, which are facilitated by the congruent expression of evaluative feedback.

The special theory emphasizes that people cannot not communicate and thus includes much material on nonverbal gestures, cues, vocal intonations, and the communicative implications of nonverbal context.

The message communication style came to prominence in the period of World War II and is based upon a special theory that grew out of information-processing computer systems, electronic transmission of information, and servomechanisms.

The exemplar model of the message communication style involves a source with an intent who encodes a message, selects appropriate channels, and transmits the message to a receiver. The receiver decodes the message and provides feedback to the source. The source then checks the extent to which the original message succeeded in achieving high-fidelity transmission of information or control. If the original message was successful, the episode concludes. If not, the source encodes another message and tests for success, and so the process proceeds until the source achieves the intent.

The special theory of the message communication style saw information as the opposite of entropy (negative entropy) and the transmission of information as requiring energy. The theory viewed communication as a joint game against confusion.

The point in deriving research hypotheses from theory in the variable analytic research tradition is to discover a general theory of communication. Investigators have sometimes assumed that the exemplar model of the message communication style was a heuristic model and part of a general theory. They then drew hypotheses for social scientific investigation from that model. When investigators drew their research hypotheses from any of the special theories, they set themselves an impossible task. At best they provided statistical evidence about regularities within the rhetorical communities practicing that particular style of communication. At worst they sampled a population that contained some people who practiced a particular style and a number of other people who did not, and the results were misinterpreted.

The heuristic models of the natural sciences serve as basic elements of general theories which had wide scope. The exemplar models of special communication theory have a bearing only on the communication of the community of people who try to achieve the exemplar in practice. Even within the rhetorical community, however, people may choose not to emulate the model or they may be too inept to achieve good communication according to its precepts. Heuristic models of the natural sciences relate to physical processes, which differ from the conventional and arbitrary exemplars of style-specific communication theories in that they are invariable.

People may not like what they feel to be the manipulative implications of the message communication style and may choose not to participate. They might not like the law of gravity or the model of the dynamic theory of gases or the double-helix model of DNA, but when they trip they fall and when a nail punctures their tires the air escapes.

Artistic models are not as closely tied to material reality and thus can take more varied forms than the models of general theories. Human communication exhibits a wide intercultural and historical diversity because artistic models are not closely tied to the stubbornness of experience. Even within the same historical period and culture, various people will be members of communities which have divergent styles of communication.

Notes

1. For a detailed history of the developments summarized here, see the following essays in Karl Wallace, ed., *History of Speech Education in America* (New York: Appleton-Century-Crofts, 1954): Giles Wilkeson Gray, "Some Teachers and the Transition to Twentieth-Century Speech Education," pp. 422–426; Marie Hochmuth and Richard Murphy, "Rhetorical and Elocutionary Training in Nineteenth-Century Colleges," pp. 153–177; Frank M. Rarig and Halbert S. Greaves, "National Speech Organizations and Speech Education," pp. 490–517; Mary Margaret Robb, "The Elocutionary Movement and Its Chief Figures," pp. 178–201; Donald K. Smith, "Origin and Development of Departments of Speech," pp. 447–470.
2. James A. Winans, *Public Speaking, Principles and Practice,* (Ithaca, N.Y.: Sewall Publishing Co., 1915).
3. Among some of the models of excellence according to the criterion of "winning the day" against difficult odds were Wendell Phillips speaking on the mobbing and killing of the abolitionist Owen Lovejoy before an unruly audience in Faneuil Hall, Boston; Henry Ward Beecher facing the hostile audiences in British textile milling towns during the Civil War; and, Henry Grady speaking on the "New South" before a Northern audience after the Civil War.
4. By the early 1970s the style was mature enough so articles reflecting the emerging theory began to appear in publications such as *The Quarterly Journal of Speech* and the *Speech Teacher*. See, for example, Richard L. Johannesen, "The Emerging Concept of Communication as Dialogue," *Quarterly Journal of Speech* 57 (1971): 373–382; Theodore F. Nelson, "Recapturing Enthusiasm for the Fundamentals Course," *Speech Teacher* 19 (1970): 289–295; Joseph P. Zima, "Self-Analysis Inventory: An Interpersonal Communication Exercise," *Speech Teacher* 20 (1971): 108–114; Joseph A. Ilardo, "Why Interpersonal Communication?" *Speech Teacher* 21 (1972): 1–6; John Stewart, "An Interpersonal Approach to the Basic Course," *Speech Teacher* 21 (1972): 7–14. The November 1974 issue of *Speech Teacher* (23:279–324) carried a symposium titled "Interpersonal Communication Instruction: Theory and Practice" which consisted of four articles.
5. Popularized by the book by Paul Watzlawick, Janet H. Beavin, and Don D. Jackson, *Pragmatics of Human Communication: A Study of Interactional Patterns, Pathologies, and Paradoxes* (New York: Norton, 1967).
6. *Quarterly Journal of Speech* 1 (1915): 195.
7. James Curtis, "The Rise of Experimental Phonetics," in Karl Wallace, ed., *History of Speech Education in America* (New York: Appleton-Century-Crofts, 1954), pp. 348–369; Andrew T. Weaver, "Experimental Studies in Vocal Expression," *Quarterly Journal of Speech* 10 (1924): 199–204.
8. Claude E. Shannon and Warren Weaver, *The Mathematical Theory of Communication* (Urbana, Ill.: University of Illinois Press, 1949).

9. Schramm presented his model in "How Communication Works," in Wilbur L. Schramm, ed., *The Processes and Effects of Communication* (Urbana, Ill.: University of Illinois Press, 1954), pp. 3–26; Berlo developed his model in David K. Berlo, *The Process of Communication* (New York: Holt, Rinehart and Winston, 1960). From the perspective of almost two decades Berlo commented upon his model as follows: "It could be argued that S-M-C-R was not intended as a 'model' of communication, that it met none of the tests of theoretic modelling, and that it was developed as an audio-visual aid to stimulate recall of the components of a communication relationship; however, the defense exceeds the benefits. The fact of the matter is that, like many of my colleagues, I simply did not understand the underlying assumptions and the theoretic consequences of what I believed, and had not grasped the limited fertility of the research tradition in which I had been trained." David K. Berlo, "Communication as Process: Review and Commentary," in Brent D. Ruben, ed., *Communication Yearbook I* (New Brunswick, N. J.: Transaction Books, 1977), p. 12.
10. For a survey of such models, see C. David Mortensen, *Communication, the Study of Human Interaction* (New York: McGraw-Hill, 1972).
11. An excellent presentation of the rhetorical vision of the message theory of communication is to be found in Norbert Wiener, *The Human Use of Human Beings: Cybernetics and Society* (Garden City, N.Y.: Doubleday Anchor Books, 1954).
12. Ibid., p. 42.
13. Ibid., p. 111.
14. Abraham Kaplan, *The Conduct of Inquiry: Methodology for Behavioral Science* (San Francisco: Chandler, 1964), pp. 276–277.
15. Gerald R. Miller, *Speech Communication: A Behavioral Approach* (Indianapolis: Bobbs-Merrill, 1966), p. 53.
16. Ibid., pp. 57–58.
17. Ibid., p. 53.
18. William Trufant Foster, "Random Notes on Public Speaking," *Quarterly Journal of Speech* 33 (1947): 139–140.
19. Ernest G. Bormann, "A Rhetorical Analysis of the National Radio Broadcasts of Senator Huey Pierce Long," *Speech Monographs* 24 (1957): 244–257.

PART THREE

General Communication Theories

5

The Analysis
of General Theories
of Communication

In earlier chapters I drew a distinction between style-specific or special theories of communication and theories that purport to provide a general account which explains communication events across styles. In Chapters 3 and 4 I analyzed the special theories. In this chapter and in Chapters 6 and 7 I turn to an examination of knowledge about communication developed at the third level of analysis.

My first task is to set up a framework for philosophical analysis. To do so I draw heavily on the precedent provided by the philosophy of science. I begin by providing a framework of analysis drawn from the study of the language of science and then apply that framework to the language of general theories, which contain knowledge about communication across styles.

The Philosophy of Science

An important group of twentieth-century philosophers have had a common interest in the systematic investigation of the language of science. This group incorporates scientists with a philosophical bent and philosophers trained in mathematics, logic, and the theoretical aspects of science. P.W. Bridgman is an example of a scientist with an interest in examining the basic assumptions of the scientific method. His work in developing the notion of operational definitions was an important contribution to the philosophy of science. Bertrand Russell is representative of the philosophers who are also mathematicians and logicians. The philosophical analysis of the language of science draws from the work of such groups as the Cambridge analysts, the Vienna Circle of logical positivists, and some of the pragmatists in this country. In addition to Bridgman and Russell, some of the important figures in this movement are Rudolph Carnap, Ludwig Wittgenstein, A. J. Ayer, Gustav Bergmann, Herbert Feigl, Hans Reichenbach, Charles Morris, and Otto Neurath.[1] This list is by no means exhaustive, but it does contain the names of some of the representative individuals in this movement. The various "schools" that have participated in this strain of philosophizing differ as to style and method, but their common emphasis on the study of the basic assumptions of science through the analysis of language justifies calling their work the philosophy of science.

The philosophers of science have used language analysis to clarify the nature of scientific knowledge and method. An interesting result of this analysis is that some statements that seemed to say something about the world turned out, upon careful investigation, to be empty of such content. These statements could not be verified scientifically, either because they were logical statements or because there was no way to gather empirical evidence for their verfication.

The members of the movement have generally used the philosophy of language to analyze the natural sciences. In the 1960s, however, they turned their attention to analyzing the language of the social sciences. Scholars at the Minnesota Center for the Philosophy of Science, for example, worked extensively in clarifying and critiquing research and theory in the social sciences. A number of psychologists became conversant with the tools of the philosophy of science and applied them to psychological theory and research. Stevens' work in the application of the philosophy of science to experimental psychology is of particular interest in that regard.[2]

Although the philosophers of science have analyzed the language of the natural and social sciences, they have not studied the language of the humanities and fine arts extensively. Certainly, scholars can apply the same analytic methods to the theoretical structures in communication as have been used to study the natual sciences and many of the social sciences. Such analysis has proved useful to research and theory in the natural and social sciences, and properly used it could prove to be equally valuable in communication.

Communication Research and the Philosophy of Science

What are the uses of a philosophy of communication? The bearing of a philosophy of communication on research practice and method may not be immediately apparent. Nevertheless, a careful analysis of the nature of knowledge is a prerequisite to sensible research programs and projects. Applying the techniques of the philosophy of science to general communication theories would yield direct applications to the problems faced by research workers. Such clarifications as the following would be possible: this question is suitable for investigation by the scientific method; this question cannot be answered on observational grounds; this is a pseudo-question in the sense that it cannot be answered at all; this theory is not at all like a theory in physics, nor is it like a theory in experimental psychology, and therefore it cannot lead to questions for research in the same way; this is a special theory suitable as a guide to practice and an aid in developing appreciation for the arts of communication, but it cannot yield predictions as theories in the physical sciences often do.

If research workers understand these matters they will know how to take the advice that questions for research should grow out of and modify theory. In addition to such direct applications to research problems in communication, the analysis of general theory will give the student some understanding of the nature of deduction and mathematics and the role of statistics in communication research and theory.

The Analysis of Language

Before we can apply the tools of the philosophy of science to the analysis of communication theories, we must understand these tools and how they can be used. I will begin with techniques developed by one of the projects of the philosophers of science—the attempt to develop a unified basis for science. The project sponsored an important series of monographs titled the *International Encyclopedia of Unified Science,* under the editorship of Otto Neurath. Charles W. Morris wrote the second number of the first volume of the series for the purpose of supplying "a language in which to talk about, and in so doing to improve, the language of science."[3] In the monograph entitled *Foundations of the Theory of Signs* Morris succeeded in developing an approach to language analysis which scholars in a number of disciplines have used to clarify the foundations of their fields. A popular book in the field of communication by Watzlawick, Beavin, and Jackson adapted Morris' division to the study of human communication. They entitled their book *Pragmatics of Human Communication.*[4]

I begin with the language of investigators at the third level studying such things as the gestures of two people involved in an interpersonal communication episode, the paralinguistic elements accompanying talk, the sharing of group fantasies, and the experience of communication anxiety. When investigators talk of these events they may use the words of a natural language such as English or German, or they may use the symbols of mathematical procedures such as an analysis of variance or the integral calculus. Such talk may be complicated enough, but it is confined to the basic observational level. In these cases the investigators' language will be concerned with describing observable behavior of human beings and the surrounding context. The investigators will require a more complex language to discuss their observations adequately and to develop theoretical accounts to explain them. I can simplify the explanations of the basic dimensions of language by confining my discussion to the object-language level. Once the nature of the object-language is clear, I can clarify the more complex languages by replicating essentially the same lines of analysis.

Morris used the term *semiotic* for his study of the general theory of signs and languages, and he subdivided semiotic into three major areas of emphasis. Morris defined the dimensions of language as the *syntactical,* the *semantical,* and the *pragmatical.*

The Syntactical Dimension   Whatever symbol system (language) the researchers use, one part of the process involves the relationship of the symbols to one another. Morris named the formal relationships among signs the *syntactical dimension* of language. The syntactical dimension requires a group of symbols which form the elements of the language plus the formation rules which govern the correct way to place the elements into proper statements. The disciplines of grammar, symbolic logic, and mathematics study this dimension of semiotic abstracted from the other elements of language usage. The syntactical dimension of language is rule-governed in the sense that in order to use the language members of the language-using community must agree upon some conventional norms as to which formal combinations are correct and which are incorrect. Some of the rules may be broken and the participants in the communication episode may still share meanings. Certain rules, however, must be followed or efforts at communication will be unsuccessful. Scholars studying the syntactical dimension often direct their attention to determining what the syntactical rules of a language are.

The Semantical Dimension   Another aspect of the investigators' language involves the relationships between the objects under study and the symbols for them. In commonsense terms, the semantical dimension involves meanings. Morris labeled the symbol-object relationships the *semantical dimension.* The semantical dimension includes the rules which specify how the symbols denote objects. Members of a language-using community must agree which symbols will denote which features of their common experience in order for them to communicate. Again, these rules are conventional and arbitrary in that we can name the objects of our experience in an infinite variety of ways but we cannot violate the semantical rules of a community for long without destroying the basis for communication.

Semantics may be both a science and a tool of science. A sociologist, anthropologist, or linguist might study how a community of people use their language. The investigator in this instance observes the way the people talk and tries to infer the semantical rules which govern their communication from observational descriptions of their linguistic behavior. Scholars conducting a scientific study of the semantic dimension of the language might summarize their investigation by compiling a dictionary.

When philosophers use the study of semantics as a tool of science, they do so by making a critical analysis of the semantical rules in order to keep the language of a discipline free of ambiguities and to discover statements which are meaningful, in the sense that they have observational denotations as contrasted to sentences which have no observational interpretations. Since the scientific method is based upon observation, the philosopher of science who clarifies whether or not a group of descriptive statements has an observational base provides an important service. My use of the tools of language analysis to examine the theoretical structures in communication will concentrate on matters of ambiguity and observational validity.

Morris' analysis of the semantical dimension of semiotic should not be confused with "General Semantics." General Semantics as popularly conceived by the followers of Korzybski such as Wendell Johnson and S.I. Hayakawa is much broader in its scope than the semantical dimension of language; like semiotic, with which it roughly corresponds in scope, it involves all aspects of communication.

The Pragmatical Dimension The third dimension of semiotic deals with language in use. Morris labeled the behavioral effects of communication the *pragmatical dimension*. Watzlawick, Beavin, and Jackson characterize pragmatics as *"the sender-receiver relation, as mediated by communication* [emphasis the author's]."[5]

In the United States the word *chicken* relates syntactically to other symbols in English according to certain grammatical rules such as those applying to the general category of nouns, and semantically it denotes a certain kind of observable fowl. But when people respond to the word as they use the language, they may become physically and emotionally aroused by the pejorative use of the term. If several young males interpret the word as an insult, they may respond with increased heartbeats, sweaty palms, and faster respiration. The sender-receiver relation as mediated by the message *chicken* may develop into physical combat.

A View of Language

From this viewpoint, language is seen as the sum of all three dimensions of semiotic. If I abstract out one dimension for further analysis, I am focusing on an element of a complex process and need to be aware of the dynamic interrelationships which characterize language use.

When I discuss a given dimension of semiotic, certain terms are implied by the feature under study. For example, *implicates* is a term relating to the study of the syntactical dimension. Thus, if I say that a set of statements implicates a conclusion I am making a statement about the syntactical dimension. *Denotes* is a term in the semantical dimension, and if I say that according to the rules of English usage a certain symbol denotes an object such as a chair, I am saying something about the semantical dimension. *Expresses* is a feature of the pragmatical dimension, and if I say a communication expresses a person's feelings or emotions I am saying something about the pragmatical dimension.

Although philosophers of language use the terms more precisely, the three dimensions of semiotic are roughly equivalent to some of the more common concepts we use in everyday discussions of language. The syntactical dimension is similar to what we usually have in mind when we talk of grammar, the semantical is similar to denotation, and the pragmatical is similar to connotation.

I can abstract the syntactical dimension of a language for study without taking the other aspects of semiotic into much account. For example, I can study the logical implications of language and ignore the semantical dimension by substituting symbols for meaningful propositions. The fact that I can study logic and mathematics symbolically illustrates the way syntactics is the foundation for a complete analysis of a language. I can abstract the semantical dimension from the pragmatical for the purposes of analysis if I take the syntactical into account. However, for an analysis of the pragmatical dimension I must make a prior study of the syntactical and the semantical.

The Language of Science   When a community of people use words according to the rules of their language, they may do so for many purposes and may arouse diverse responses; but one important purpose will be to talk about the world. Talk about observational features of material reality is the distinguishing feature of the work of the natural sciences. Communication scholars as well will discuss observational features of material reality and, perhaps more important, of the social realities of rhetorical communities. Investigators of communication episodes will express some of their important findings in statements that have a clear semantical relationship to observables. Insofar as possible the natural scientists try to emphasize the denotative (semantical) features of their language and keep the connotative aspects of the pragmatical dimension to a minimum.

Robert Oppenheimer states the viewpoint of the atomic physicist when he writes:

> Common-sense language is inherently ambiguous; when the poet uses it, or the rhetorician, he exploits the ambiguity, and even when we talk in ordinary life we almost need ambiguity in order to get by. But in science we try to get rid of that, we try to talk in such simple terms and match our talk with deeds in such a way that we may differ as to facts, but we can resolve the differences.[6]

Statements of Fact   The way scientists go about talking in simple terms and matching their talk with deeds can be explained by examining a subclass of statements which I call statements of fact. I distinguish statements of fact from other well-formed sentences by the way they stand in relation to objects. When Oppenheimer writes of matching word to deed, he is dealing with the semantical dimension and the rules by which grammatically sound sentences may be related to observations. I define *statements of fact* as that subclass of syntactically sound sentences for which we can make a truth decision on the basis of observations. Statements of fact are empirical expressions in that they say something about the world.

Let's take a representative statement of fact from the research notebook of an investigator in small group communication. The investigator notes, "Member A sat between members F and D at the second meeting of the group." The sentence is syntactically sound. The writer followed the formation rules of the English language and expressed a proposition. Had the investigator been distracted or been doodling and written a jumble of words such as "Over above meeting in between plus," the string of symbols would not conform to the syntactical rules of English and would not have been a statement of fact. The first defining criterion for a statement of fact is, thus, the requirement that the sentence be syntactically sound.

The second criterion is that the sentence have empirical content. "Member A sat between members F and D at the second meeting of the group" has empirical content in the sense that the investigators can specify the semantical rules required to assure that the statement denotes something about the events that took place in the small group communication laboratory. Oppenheimer suggested that the quest for objectivity, in a practical sense, eventually comes to the two requirements that researchers understand one another and that all qualified practitioners mean essentially the same thing.[7] The minimum requirement for scientific communication is community agreement about the rules governing the semantical relations of the discipline's language. The second criterion brings with it the possibility of falsehood. Or, put another way, empirical content of sentences implies potential truthfulness. The fact that scientists can tell their colleagues something about their findings means that they can tell them something false about the events they are studying. Unless I am understood, I cannot be objective and nor can I lie.

Operational Definitions The operationalism of P. W. Bridgman is a sophisticated attempt to deal with the problem of matching word to deed or of specifying semantical rules for the rigorous investigation of phenomena. I can define *communication anxiety* operationally. That is, I can specify in a research report that what I mean by the notion of communication anxiety is the set of operations that I went through to have subject A fill in a paper-and-pencil inventory reporting her feelings of anxiety when communicating. The concept can mean the further operations I went through to score the test and assign it a quantified value as an index of the anxiety. Bergmann and Spence in their article "Operationism and Theory Construction" suggest that if we trace the terms of the researcher's language back to "the immediately observable," then we "know what he means," and that is sufficient for "*operational definition of constructs* [emphasis the authors']."[8]

In recent years, operational definitions have become a point of contention for philosophers. Some have argued that the early claim that operational definitions exhaust the meaning of theoretical concepts is untenable. The argument is that theoretical terms have prior meanings and that a finite set of operations does not provide an adequate sense of what they mean. Others have pointed out that in an absolute sense it is impossible for an individual investigator, let alone another investigator, to replicate a set of operations at a different time.[9]

Nonetheless, operational definitions provide one of the best methods for social scientific investigators to achieve the reliability of quantification which is important for the intersubjective nature of the scientific enterprise. Unless theoretical conclusions demonstrated in one setting by one team of investigators can be supported or falsified by other investigators in other settings, their evaluation by the scholarly community is impossible.

Reliability in this context refers to the ability of investigators to assign the same descriptions to repeated observations under conditions assumed to be constant. Usually these descriptions are quantified. If a given investigator assigns the same numerical value to the observation from one time to another or if other investigators assign the same numerical value to observations under conditions assumed to be constant, the test or measure is reliable.

Validity in this context refers to the usefulness of an investigator's observations in terms of providing results bearing on the question under investigation. Does the procedure measure what it is supposed to measure? The validity of an operational definition is an important question for social scientific investigators of communication processes. To what extent do the operational definitions of concepts exhaust their meaning, and to what extent are additional meanings implied or expressed in the terms of the study?

If the people who read my research report know the operations that I went through in making my *observations*, they can understand what I mean when I write about communication anxiety. The question "What do you mean by *communication anxiety?*" becomes an important one in the case of statements of fact. We may well be confused, because *communication anxiety*, like most concepts in communication, carries with it a large freight of the commonsense ambiguity so important to everyday communication. Usually investigators set out to study the phenomenon we normally have in mind when we use terms like *speech anxiety* or *communication anxiety* in our everyday commonsensical discourse. For example, if I attempt to study communication anxiety rigorously in the laboratory, I must purge my language of the commonsense ambiguities, and in the process I may develop a set of operations to make observations and quantify those observations, which I now fit to my words in such a way that my language is clear. My gain in clarity as a result of operational definitions is often at the expense of much of the original meaning of the term. In retracing my steps at the end of the study I must exercise great care to provide an argument that the evidence gathered by my use of the operational definitions provides support for my conclusions about what we normally mean when we say someone suffers from a high level of communication anxiety.

Often communication research has suffered because the investigators have tacitly shifted ground from the ordinary usage of terms to operational definitions and back again to commonsense meaning. They may have assumed the usual meaning of such terms as *attitude, opinion, anxiety, cohesiveness, ambiguity, authoritarianism,* and *dogmatism* in their opening discussion of the theoretical rationale for their hypothesis. They then may have used operational definitions such as administering paper-and-pencil tests or scales in their description of method. They then shifted back to the ordinary usage in their discussion of the results and their drawings of conclusions. Since they used the same words for the two very different semantical meanings, the unwary investigator and the reader alike were often mislead.

When I define *communication anxiety* in terms of my administering a test to a subject, the concept no longer means "mental distress, worry, uneasiness brought about by the apprehension of punishment or misfortune as a result of communication."[10] I hope the data I gather by means of my operational definition will be related to the communication phenomenon I set up to study, but simply calling such operations by a term of importance in our everyday discussion and analysis of communication will not assure such connections.[11]

The scientist rids commonsense language of as much ambiguity as possible by means of operational definitions. When I define *communication anxiety* operationally, the concept simply means the observations that I made and the conditions under which I made them. When I spell these operations out carefully in my study, other investigators should be able to replicate the observations and thus replicate my study.

Truth and Falsity   When I define the concepts in a statement operationally, I can make observations so that I can judge the statement to be true or false. Scientists try, in principle, to find universal agreement as to truth or falsity of such judgments, or, in Oppenheimer's words, "We may differ as to facts but we can resolve the differences." That is, should other competent observers make the same observations under the same conditions, they would make the same judgment as to the truth or falsity of the statement "Subject A scored 52 on the communication anxiety index." In practice, of course, the ideal is seldom reached.

Statements such as "Member A sat between members F and D at the second meeting of the group" and "Subject A scored 52 on the communication anxiety index" qualify according to my criteria as statements of fact. They are well-formed (syntactically), meaningful (semantically), and either true or false. I make the decision as to truth or falsity by observation. I place myself in the position specified by my operational definition and view the meeting from that angle. I observe the three individuals I have named A, F, and D. I look at the relationship among them and examine that relationship in terms of my operational definition of *sitting between*. If the member named A is sitting between two members but they are those we have named E and F rather than F and D, I judge that the statement of fact is false. Since I must make an observation to make a truth decision, the statement has empirical content.

Directly Verifiable Statements of Fact   If I have observed carefully and reported the observations about the seating arrangement in the experimental group accurately, then the statement is true. It is true because of the semantical relationship between the statement and the observables. The semantical rules which I specify clearly so that others can understand and apply them are expressed as *definitions*. The definitions are arbitrary—that is, the semantical rules are not given but may be changed by the mutual agreement of the people using the terms to communicate with one another. When I apply the semantical rules to the observables, however, I cannot arbitrarily change the truth or falsity of the statement by convention. I find a stubbornness to my observations which is not reflected in the malleability of the symbol systems I arbitrarily create. The observables in this case include the members named A, F, and D and their postures and the spatial relationships among them. As in all scientific research I make my final decision about the truth or falsity of the statement on the basis of my direct observation of some selected elements of my environment. For my study of the seating arrangement of the group discussion, the statement of fact was *directly verifiable*.

That is, I could personally look and see the facts described by the statement and make my own judgment as to its truth or falsity. Let us say that in this instance the observation of the group reveals that A is sitting between F ad D and the statement of fact is true.

Let us assume another instance when an investigator has recorded on her work sheets, "Subject A scored 52 on the communication anxiety index." The researcher is careful and she rechecks her coding before making her final computations. When she rechecks the communication anxiety index filled in by Subject A she computes it to be 51. She scores the index a third and fourth time and still computes it to be 51. She decides that her first notation was an error. The record in her work sheet was a *false* statement of fact. Again it was a directly verifiable statement of fact for the investigator, because she could make a truth decision on the basis of her direct observation of the facts. Thus, a statement of fact may be false as well as true. The commonsense ambiguity which allows us to talk of "true friends" and "true facts" confuses the issue and must be avoided in a technical analysis. Facts are not true or false; they simply are or are not the case. Only *statements* about facts can be true or false. *Truth* refers to a semantical relationship among symbols and objects or facts. The notion that facts are true and truth is factual makes the age-old identification of the word with the thing. In order to facilitate my analysis I must draw a clear distinction between observables and the language that I use in discussing those observables. The notion of statement of fact, therefore, refers to sentences about facts that are syntactically sound and have clearly spelled out semantical rules so that they may be judged to be either true or false.

Indirectly Verifiable Statements of Fact   Not all statements of fact are directly verifiable. The statement "Subject A has less communication anxiety after taking a course in speech communication than he had before taking such a course" is not directly verifiable. Of course, we could give an operational definition to the concept *communication anxiety*, and the statement then would be directly verifiable. We could define communication anxiety as the set of operations involved in giving and scoring the Personal Report of Communication Anxiety Test, or the operations involved in measuring a person's heartbeat. [12] But often we are not as interested in these matters as we are in studying the inner feelings and perceptions of subject A. Let us say that what we have in mind when we say that subject A has less communication anxiety after taking the course than before is that he has less mental distress, worry, and uneasiness brought about by the anticipation of punishment as a result of communicating with others. Now, subject A either has or does not have such inner states, so the statement about them is a statement of fact, but we cannot verify the statement directly because we cannot observe A's mental distress, worry, and uneasiness. If we define the concept of communication anxiety as referring to the inner states, then the statement is an *indirectly verifiable statement of fact*.

Investigators will have to make their decisions about the truth and falsity of such statements on the basis of observation of the effects of the inner states. They may infer inner states from the observation of such behavior as A's shaking knees, quivering voice, scoring of a self-report index, introspective accounts describing inner feelings, measurement of bodily functions, and so forth.

Humanistic scholars deal for the most part with indirectly verifiable statements of fact. Statements like "Longinus wrote the essay *On the Sublime*" are examples of indirectly verifiable statements of fact. We cannot, at least until a suitable time machine is invented, journey back to watch the writing of the essay in order to see who is doing the writing. We can, however, examine directly certain historical traces such a reports of eyewitnesses recorded in diaries, letters, and other documents concerning the essay. On the basis of such *evidence* we may decide that the statement "Longinus wrote the essay *On the Sublime*" is false.

When scholars make a decision as to the truth or falsity of an indirectly verifiable statement of fact, the statement is, for them, conclusively demonstrated as either true or false. The statement "Abraham Lincoln debated Stephen Douglas at Ottawa, Illinois, in the senatorial capaign of 1858" is an indirectly verifiable statement of fact that has been *conclusively* demonstrated as true to the satisfaction of most scholars.

Some indirectly verifiable statements of fact have so little directly observable evidence bearing on their truth or falsity, or the evidence that is available is so ambiguous, that a decision as to their truth or falsity is nearly impossible. In such an instance the statement is said to be *inconclusively verified*. The remark about Longinus writing *On the Sublime* is such a statement for some scholars in rhetoric.

When researchers feel that they have a good case for establishing the truth or falsity of an indirectly verifiable statement of fact, such as a statement about the measurement of meaning, or of communication anxiety, or of attitudes, or about the author of *On the Sublime*, they may publish their findings. Readers will then examine their arguments. Typically such interpretations consist of the statement of fact that were directly verifiable for the investigator and which he asserts to have been true or false, plus his inferences from these directly verifiable statements to the truth or falsity of the indirectly verifiable statement of fact. The readers will examine the arguments and will decide whether they are convinced or not. If they are not convinced and remain undecided, then, for them, the statement is an *indirectly verifiable inconclusive statement of fact*. For those who are convinced, the statement becomes an *indirectly verifiable conclusively demonstrated true* statement of fact. For those who conclude from his evidence and his argument that the statement is false, it becomes an *indirectly verifiable conclusively demonstrated false* statement of fact.

Since much research in communication is concerned with indirectly verifiable statements of fact, there is a chance for bias, gullibility, personal dislike, and politics to intrude into the question of whether such statements have been conclusively demonstrated as true or false. The way is thus open for scholarly controversy and for contradictory findings in empirical research.

Object-language and Metalanguage   My discussion of statements of fact has, so far, been confined to the simplest cases in which the researcher is discussing objects such as historical documents or the positioning of discussion group members. At this level of direct decription of observables the researchers are using an *object-language*. Since the object-language is used to discuss facts and only facts, it does not contain the words *true* and *false* because these words are not applicable to facts. They describe certain features of the semantical dimension of language.

Of course, we must have a richer language which contains important terms like *truth*. Such a language I call a *metalanguage*. The object-language is the more primitive in the sense that its vocabulary is confined to words describing objects. I cannot discuss the processes of communication in an object- language, since it contains no words that refer to language symbols, speakers, or listeners. Metalanguage, however, is richer than object-language. It contains all the words of the object-language. Thus, objects like chairs and chickens can be discussed in both object-language and meta-language. In addition, metalanguage contains words that refer to symbols in object-language and terms for important features of the syntactical, semantical, and pragmatical dimensions of language. The metalanguage must have a vocabulary large enough to talk about language, objects, and speakers. For example, if we engage in a discussion of the syntactical dimension of the object-language we need a metalanguage with words that refer not to objects but to the symbols of the object-language. Metalanguage sentences such as "*Chair* is a five-letter word," or "*Chair* is a noun" are about the syntactical dimension of the object language. Statements about the object language may be statements of fact, but in these cases I must depend upon observations of linguistic occurrences in order to determine their truth or falsity.

If we wish to discuss the semantical dimension of an object-language such as the one employed by an instructor in a communication class, we have to develop a metalanguage with some words that denote things and with other terms that refer to the symbols in the object-language itself. If we use a metalanguage largely based upon the natural language of English and the teacher's object-language is German, we can usually distinguish the two levels of language without much trouble. However, if both our object-language and our metalanguage are based upon English, then there is a strong possibility of confusion. We can avoid some of the confusion by employing a linguistic convention to index those metalanguage words which refer to object-language symbols. The index can serve to distinguish the words we use in the metalanguage that refer to objects from those that refer to words. Often scholars who study object-languages use single or double quotation marks as indicators of metalanguage symbols that denote object-language words. In this chapter I will use single quotation marks for that purpose. Thus, when I use *'chair'* I mean it to denote the word *chair*. When I use *chair* in the metalanguage I mean it to denote the piece of furniture.

If I were explaining the semantical rules of English to someone who spoke only German, I would have to specify or point to the class of objects denoted by the English word 'chair.' I could do this quite simply if I also spoke German by asserting that *"Auf English Stuhl heisst* 'chair.' " If you keep in mind that we are communicating in a metalanguage, then the statement " 'Chair' denotes chair" is not the nonsense it may at first seem. The statement is not a tautology of the order of "A is A" either. Rather, when I assert " 'Chair' denotes chair" in a metalanguage I am making a statement of fact about a semantic relationship in an object-language between the five-letter word 'chair' and a class of objects which are pieces of furniture.

The sentence " 'Chair' denotes chair" is similar to the assertion " *'Stuhl'* denotes chair." If you find the statement trivial or confusing, you should reread this section, because the crucial distinction between metalanguage and object-language is exemplified by the statement.

Metalanguage statements may be statements of fact in the same fashion as object-language sentences. Thus, if a critic within the public speaking style uses a metalanguage to describe a given speaker's object-language, the critic may assert, "When the president said X to the American people in a nationally televised broadcast, the speaker lied." The Rhetorical critic's assertion is, in turn, true or false depending upon whether or not the president's statement of fact was false. Statements of fact about speakers may be either directly or indirectly verifiable, and we may make the same analysis of a critic's metalanguage statements that we made of object-language statements.

Notice, however, that while I can use a metalanguage to specify semantical and syntactical rules for an object-language and be arbitrary and creative, I cannot excercise the same control over the objects to which the language applies. I can rather easily change my semantical rule so that the symbol which referred to the class of objects which are furniture used for sitting is changed from 'chair' to *'stuhl,'* and I can change the syntactical rules which characterize the sentence "I ain't going" from incorrect to correct. But I cannot with the same ease and arbitrariness change the objects from furniture that is useful for sitting to objects that fly about and carry passengers from place to place.

Laws of Nature   To this point all my examples of statements of fact have been particular statements dealing with a single subject or a single group setting. Not all statements that refer to observables deal with particulars. Of crucial scientific importance are general statements such as "Water when heated boils." Although the comment about water boiling fulfills most of my requirements for a statement of fact in that it is well formed and meaningful, the question as to the truth or falsity of this generalization is a difficult one to answer. Certainly the statement refers to facts and is based upon observation. In addition, the observation of relevant facts has so far supported the statement. All the water that has been heated sufficiently has boiled. Readers with an empirical bent might feel some uneasiness at this point because of the vague way I specified the concepts *heated* and *boils* in my formulation of the statement. Their desire for precision may cause them to say that water has sometimes been heated and has not boiled. I can make the generalization more precise by including all *relevant variables*. For example, I could rewrite the statement as "H_2O, 99.9 percent pure, heated to 100° centigrade at a pressure of 15 pounds to the square inch, will boil."

When we cook our eggs in the morning, all we need to know is that if we heat tap water sufficiently, it will boil. In the laboratory we often need the more precise formulation, particularly if we want to quantify our measurements. Before we can assign numbers to the boiling point,—that is, predict at what number on the scale of the thermometer the water will begin to bubble,—we must isolate the invariable relationships between heat and boiling. This requires that we take into account all other factors important enough to influence these relationships.

The generalization about water boiling is based upon observation. It takes a functional relationship between the heating of water and the boiling point, and, to this point, the relationship has been invariate. The statement makes the claim that, without exception, every sample of water that has been heated, is now being heated, and will be heated will boil. The claim is a bold one, but by risking much the generalization gains much. If the statement were "Heating is correlated with boiling by a coefficient of .90," it would claim much less and gain much less. If the latter generalization were the best available, then the water would have to be watched each morning to see if it would boil for coffee.

Scientists who study natural phenomena (objects) at the second level of scientific analysis phrase their findings in object-language statements. People participating in the practice of a communication style at the second level phrase their comments about material reality in object-language statements, but they often shift into a metalanguage when they discuss usage. When they talk about grammatical or ungrammatical statements, logical or illogical arguments, they move to metalanguage analysis of the syntactical dimension. When they talk about fidelity of information or misrepresentation of the facts, they speak in the metalanguage about the semantical dimension. When they discuss audience response or the ability of language appeals to arouse emotions or establish relationships among people, they discuss the pragmatic dimension of language. Special communication theories at the second level require a metalanguage for their development.

Implied in a theory of types such as this one is an infinite regression of linguistic levels. Thus social scientific investigators seeking general theories of communication at the third level of analysis will require a metalanguage to discuss the communication theory, criticism, and practice at the second level. Those who find infinite regressions cognitively unsettling can take comfort from the fact that for most practical purposes, theory and research in communication require an understanding of only three levels of analysis: object-language, metalanguage, and meta-metalanguage.

Prediction, Postdiction, and Control   Because of the generality of the law of nature, it covers *every instance*, and so long as it works it enables prediction about every instance of water that is heated. Prediction allows control. In addition to prediction and control of future events, such a statement allows inference about past events. Given suitable heating in the past, the boiling water can be inferred. The determination of the historical age of a given object by determining the state of decay of carbon 14 in the object and the use of the laws of astronomy to determine the date of a historical eclipse are examples of the use of laws of nature to postdict.

When cave dwellers discovered the law of nature that "Water when heated boils," they no longer had to depend upon an anthropomorphic explanation for the phenomenon of water bubbling and vapor rising and the water biting their fingers when they touched it. They could simple say, "Whenever water is heated, it boils." Before this discovery the bubbling water may have seemed capricious, the work of spirits and gods; afterward it had a natural cause. The cave dweller equipped with a law of nature could arrange to bring water close to fire and make it boil. From that point on he or she could control the environment to some extent. The cave dweller could eat soup instead of raw saber-tooth tiger, for example. The *technological* improvement in the life of the cave dweller is analogous to the more sophisticated technology of an engineer drawing up a blueprint for a machine and taking it to the shop and saying, "Build this machine, and I predict that putting tobacco in this hopper and cigarette paper here and cellophane here and turning on the motor will result in tailor-made cigarettes wrapped in cellophane coming out of this end of the machine." Such a machine may never have existed before, but because of laws of nature such an innovation or invention is possible. Technology with its resultant modification and control of our environment rests upon laws of nature.

Universal Agreement About Invariable Relations   One of the important features of the scientific method is that it searches for universal agreement about invariable relations such as those expressed in laws of nature. Replication of experiments must result in agreement among the researchers as to the nature and extent of these relations. Since this is the case there is a universality to the statement of scientific laws. Specific statements of fact cannot, ever in principle, be universally agreed upon. Only those having actually had an opportunity to observe the facts involved in a specific statement can agree about its truth or falsity. Scientific laws are stated in such a fashion that, in principle, everyone could replicate the conditions described by the law, observe the results, and agree that the promised invariable relations held. The beginning chemistry student goes through these steps when he or she replicates an experiment in the laboratory. The student may produce oxygen by certain combinations of chemicals brought to reaction. The laws of chemistry are so firmly established that if the experiment fails to produce oxygen, the instructor instead of questioning the laws examines the student's laboratory procedure. When students do the experiment properly then, like thousands of beginning chemistry students before them, they agree that oxygen is invariably produced under these conditions.

Induction

With the rise of empirical observation as a way of knowing and with the development of modern science in the Renaissance, such philosophers as Francis Bacon (1561–1626), John Locke (1632–1704), and David Hume (1711–1776) examined the notion of *cause* as used in the sense that boiling water had a natural cause, and with this analysis of the method of science came the analysis of *induction*.[13]

Laws of Nature and Generalization by Complete Enumeration   David Hume's analysis of causation is the culmination of this line of philosophy. it is one of the most important treatments of the problem of induction. Hume directed his attention to the relationship between the notions of cause and of induction. A law of nature, as opposed to generalization by complete enumeration of a class, requires an act of faith, according to Hume. The generalization "All members of this seminar in communication theory are graduate students" could be based on an examination of the records of the five students enrolled. If such investigation revealed that students, *A*, *B*, *C*, *D*, and *E* were all graduate students and all enrolled in the seminar, the generalization is true. This generalization is by complete enumeration of a class and is a shorthand way of expressing the same thing as the five particular statements of fact that assert of each student that the student is both a member of the seminar and a graduate student. Such a generalization, while often useful, is much different from a law of nature. Hume pointed out that arriving at a law of nature inductively required an act of faith because it covered many more instances than could be observed in making the generalization and, indeed, covered many more instances than ever *could* be observed. Thus, inductively arriving at a law of nature involved making the assumption that the regularities observed in the past would continue in the future. Hume maintained that there was no logical ground for such an assumption.

Falsifying a Law of Nature   Hume's analysis points up one of the essential differences between a law of nature and a statement of a particular fact. "Water when heated boils" is a statement that has many features in common with the other statements of fact analyzed in this chapter, and yet it is impossible to conceive of sufficient observations to judge its truth. Judgments about its falsity, however, can be made because only one negative instance is evidence enough to make the statement false. Even one thimbleful of H_2O of sufficient purity heated to 100° centigrade at 15 pounds per square inch of pressure that failed to boil would make the generalization false.

Probability Statements   Perhaps the most troublesome class of statements to analyze is the range that falls in the area between particular statements of fact and laws of nature. At least since Aristotle's time, logicians and rhetoricians have struggled with the knotty problems posed by an analysis of probability statements. Is the statement "If this water is heated sufficiently, it will probably boil" a statement of fact? On what grounds can you decide the truth or falsity of such a statement?

Operational Definitions and Probability Statements   Certainly, if a statement of this sort is to be a statement of fact, not only must operational definitions be given to 'heated' and 'boiled' but also to the term 'probably.' Mathematical statistics are useful to give this term an operational definition. For example, the statement "Heating is correlated with boiling by a correlation coefficient of .90" is a probability statement that includes an operational definition of the term *probably*. In this case, *probably* refers to the set of operations involved in computing a correlation between observations of water that was heated and water that boiled. Such a statistical probability statement can be evaluated by checking the observations and the statiscal computations.

Laws of Nature and Probability Statements   When clarified in this way, the probability statement can be analyzed in the same fashion as a law of nature. If the investigator making such a statement says that for his two thousand samples of water the correlation coefficient was .50 and that this should not be generalized to another researcher's report that a study of one thousand samples of water revealed a correlation coefficient of .90, then the first is generalizing by complete enumeration. Such a probability statement is essentially a statement of fact that can be judged true or false on the basis of the observations of the water and the mathematical computation of correlation coefficients. However, the probability generalization can also be treated like a law of nature. Observation, plus mathematical computation can lead to rejection of such a probability statement. For example, if for two thousand samples of water the result was a correlation coefficient of + 1.0, the prior correlation coefficients of + .50, + .90, as well as the + 1.0 would all be false if they were treated as laws of nature. Like a law of nature, however, correlation coefficients cannot be run on all samples of water, so this probability generalization represents an inductive leap of the same sort a law of nature requires.

Probability Statements, Prediction, and Control   Statistical generalizations that hold for all events enable some prediction and control. For example, assume that success in debating correlates .70 with scores on a verbal proficiency test, .68 with scores on an IQ test, and .82 with college grade point. When student A , who has a high score on the verbal proficiency test and the IQ test and also a high grade point, wins a national debate tournament, the explanation might be: debater A won for the probability is high that the winner of this tournament will be someone who scores high on the verbal proficiency test and the IQ test and has a good grade point. In addition, if the three measures were computed for all entrants to the tournament and the prediction made that the winners would be in the top 10 percent rather than the bottom 10 percent on these scores, this would be a sound prediction. However, statistical generalizations could not have been used to invariably pick A as the winner prior to the tournament, as laws of nature would have.

Probability Statements and Generalization by Complete Enumeration   There are occasions when the social scientific researcher in communication wants to generalize about a class by complete enumeration. For example, a team of investigators may wish to study the television viewing habits of farmers in the United States, and they would like to find out about every farmer. The United States Census Bureau attempts to make some generalizations by complete enumeration of the class of United States residents every ten years, and the task is staggering. Probability statements can be used in such instances to save resources.

The Uses of Probability Statements   Because statements relating to the probability that the sample results provide a good inference as to the actual conditions in the parent population are the results of essentially taking a shortcut to the complete enumeration of the class of events, they are logically much different from probability statements which generalize about an open class, as do laws of nature. On occasion, careless investigators will confuse the two uses of probability statements by beginning a research report by justifying the importance of the study on the basis that discovering probability generalizations covering all similar communication episodes is a worthwhile research task, but ending their report with the assertion that the statistical descriptions made in the study are by complete enumeration and refer only to the subjects in the study.

If a research team makes a statistical estimate of the results of the complete enumeration of a large population such as the television-viewing audience in North America on the basis of a carefully drawn sample, the research may well be useful. However, to set out to discover a statistical probability statement analogous to the covering law of nature by complete enumeration of the sample of subjects is seldom useful. The knowledge that a sample of two hundred students at Y University reacted in a certain way to women using pornographic and profane words in 1950 or 1980 is not very important, unless the investigators are arguing that they can generalize from their sample. Usually what investigators who sample students for the study of communication tacitly assume is that they can generalize their results to all similar communication episodes, as the scientist can generalize the results of the study of the boiling point of water.

The general shape of the probability argument is that of indirect proof. The investigators assume lawfulness, set up the hypothesis of chance, reject the hypothesis that the results can be accounted for by chance alone, and argue that there is an underlying lawfulness. Having discovered lawfulness, the next logical step in the research program would be to refine quantification techniques, design research projects which isolate and control relevant variables, and develop precise quantification of the lawfulness so that it can be expressed in mathematics of functions such as algebra or calculus.

Recently a number of scholars discussing communication and rhetorical theory have argued that laws of nature analogous to those of the natural sciences are an impossible dream. They reject such "covering law" theories and suggest that investigators search instead for theories which account for the rule-governed regularities of communication episodes.

In this chapter I have stressed the differences between conventional and arbitrary rules and the stubbornness which characterizes the objects of our experience. Recall the conventional nature of much of the special theories of communication. Yet a rhetorical community of people who practice a communication style and share common language usages will exhibit strong patterns of regularity in their communication. These patterns resemble the invariable relations that characterize physics and chemistry. The rule-governed regularities, however, are not invariable. Water always boils when heated sufficiently, but a liar may assert in the message communication style that we are eating fried chicken when we are eating fried crow.

Probability statements may be used descriptively to indicate the relative strength of rule-governed communicative behavior. Investigators could examine the generalization "As a rule television newscasters do not use a singular verb with a plural noun or pronoun." They might study an extensive sample of television newscasts and conclude that the probability of a newscaster breaking the rule that the noun and the verb should agree as to number is one in five hundred.

Of course we might make rule-type statements about other elements of a communication episode than the constitutive and regulative rules which govern the playing of the language game. We might discover such regularities as these: as a rule political figures do not admit criminal actions in televised speeches; as a rule candidates do not publicly predict their own defeat before the election; as a rule people do not expect to be buttonholed and given a fifteen-minute honest answer when they pass an acquaintance on the street and ask, "How are you?"[14]

Statements of Value

Not all statements that are well formed are statements of fact. Statements like "Debate team A had a great case," "Prime-time dramatic shows on network XYZ are uniformly the most disgusting trash on television," and "The end does not justify the means" are not statements of fact. The community of social scientific investigators cannot agree upon the facts and deeds so that they can resolve their differences on these matters. Not that these statements are unimportant. Indeed, such statements are very important. Moral precepts are guidelines for behavior. Value systems and taste prescriptions form the basis for criticism and appreciation of the arts. However, researchers in communication must be careful not to confuse such statements with statements of fact. Observation is the court of last resort for statements of fact. Scientists do not argue about how many teeth there are in the mouth of a horse. They go and look and count. The clerics of the Middle Ages might well have argued about how many angels can dance on the head of a pin, for statements about angels dancing on pin heads are not statements of fact. Observations cannot yield evidence for the truthfulness of such statements. Statements about the good life or the great television program are open for argument, and they should be argued because they need to be accepted or rejected and there is no "true" or "false" answer. Each generation and each individual must decide which statements of this sort he or she will assert and believe, and argument and disagreement are thus to be expected and welcomed about these matters. About statements of fact, people should not, in principle, disagree, or again in Oppenheimer's words, "we may differ as to facts but we can resolve the differences."

Deduction

The final subclass of well-formed sentences are logical statements that assert something about the syntactical dimension of the language being used and not anything about "facts." This brings me to the third part of the scientific method, *deduction*. Induction and observation are related to semantical dimensions and analysis of the relationships that hold between statements of facts and observables. Deduction relates only to the syntactical dimension, and for the scientist this often involves a good deal of mathematics.

Empirical and Logical Statements   The statement $2 + 2 = 4$ is a tautology, and a decision can be made about the correctness or incorrectness of arithmetic statements simply by examining and checking the form of the statement. That is, if you understand the rules and the assumptions of arithmetic, $2 + 2$ implies 4. Such statements are the province of the syntactical dimension of language. The study and development of such deductive systems is the province of the discipline of logic. Therefore, the tools of logic are important in analyzing the theoretical structure of communication because the distinction between empirical statements and formal statements must be made in order to clarify the philosophical bases of communication theory. Much of the confusion in the philosophy and theorizing of the past has stemmed from failing to distinguish empirical statements from tautologies. Plato's philosophy of absolutes has this confusion in it; Kant's search for what he called "a priori" synthetic statements was essentially a search for empirical statements that could be known or intuited without relying on observation, much as tautologies are intuited. Nevertheless, one of the major contributions of Kant's impressive critique of pure reason (deductive logic) and practical reason (empirical knowledge) was the distinction he made between synthetic statements and analytic statements. By *synthetic statement* Kant meant roughly what I call a *statement of fact*, and by *analytic statement* he meant roughly what I have referred to as *tautology* or *formal statement*.

The Uses of Deduction   Investigators use deduction to arrange the symbols of statements of fact and generalizations into formal patterns permitted by the rules of logic or of mathematics to deduce or compute other statements of fact or generalizations that were implied but were not obvious in the original data. Mathematics adds nothing to the description of the world contained in the statements and generalizations provided by observation and induction. Mathematical statements are empty of content unless they are plugged into the world through observation and induction. When properly plugged in, they yield results that are just as reliable as the original inductions. What mathematical or logical deduction does in such a situation is make clear the additional implications of data. An infinite intelligence would not need mathematics because it would grasp all the implications of an induction or a theory immediately. Human beings, falling short of this infinite intelligence, must use mathematics as a tool to unravel the implications of their data which are not obvious upon inspection.

This emptiness should not be confused with triviality, for mathematics is an indispensable aid to seeing the implications of a theory and the relationships among laws of nature. Neither Newton nor Einstein could have formulated theories without the aid of mathematics; indeed, Newton was forced to develop sections of calculus to work out his theory. Psychologically the relationship between the invention of theories and mathematics may be even closer than this. Perhaps Newton could not even think his theory until he had the mathematics for it.

On the other hand, the impressive role of mathematics in science should not blind the researcher in communication to the analytic nature of deduction. Statistics are helpful, often necessary; but they cannot tell the researcher anything that is not firmly bedded in his data and in the theoretical rationale that shaped his gathering of data. If one's observations are inaccurate and the inductions unjustified, then the most elegant statistical analysis will not save the study.

Summary

Semiotic is the general theory of signs and languages and consists of three major areas of emphasis: (1) the syntactical dimension, (2) the semantical dimension, and (3) the pragmatical dimension. The syntactical dimension involves the relationships among the symbols in a formal sense. The semantical dimension concerns the relationships and the objects under study. The pragmatical dimension deals with language in use.

Much of science and social science is empirical in that observations are the basis for knowledge. I define statements of fact as syntactically sound formulations with clearly specified semantical rules such that observations furnish a basis for decisions as to their truth or falsity. These statements may be either directly or indirectly verifiable. Generalizations with empirical content may be laws of nature, in which case they express observable invariable relationships. When such generalizations are formed on the basis of observations, the process is called induction. Generalizations which describe a lawfulness in nature can never be demonstrated as true in an absolute sense. They apply to an open class and cannot, in principle, ever be verified. The observation of negative instances, however, is evidence that a generalization is false. Probability statements may be statements of fact or generalizations analogous to laws of nature in that they apply to open classes of events. In either case, observation plays a similar role in evaluating the quality of the data.

Operational definitions provide one technique for specifying semantical rules for statements of fact. To define a concept operationally requires a description of the procedures which trace the language back to the immediately observable.

Distinguishing between levels of language usage helps to clarify the difference between linguistic events and the objects of our experience. An object-language relates directly to things and can only be used to talk about objects. The object-language is the most basic level of language usage. An object-language is complete and has syntactical, semantical, and pragmatical dimensions. Natural scientists tend to phrase most of their observational statements in an object-language. Object-language discussions of natural scientists take place at the second level of investigation as discussed in previous chapters.

Metalanguage relates to both people talking in an object-language and to the things that they are talking about. The metalanguage is richer than the object-language in that it has symbols for the symbols of the object-language, for the linguistic rules of that language, for discussing characteristics of all three language dimensions, and for the action and behavior of the participants. Practitioners, teachers, and critics of communication at the second level require a metalanguage for their work. At the third level of social scientific analysis of communication, investigators require a meta-metalanguage rich enough to discuss communication styles, rhetorical communities, and special communication theories.

Not all statements are statements of fact. An important subclass of statements asserts propositions in regard to matters of value, taste, morals, and aesthetics. Such statements are not true or false according to the stipulated definitions used here. Observations cannot yield truth decisions about these matters. Another important subclass of statements that are not statements of facts are logical expressions and express linguistic relationships.

Logical statements are the province of deductive logic and for the scientists are most often expressed in mathematical expressions. They are, in one sense, without empirical content, and observations are not the grounds for their validation. Confusing linguistic statements with statements of fact has been the source of much trouble in various disciplines. Confusing statements of fact with statements of value and taste causes additional problems. Confusing metalanguage with object-language statements is a third source of difficulty. The framework of analysis that allows for the drawing of important distinctions among various linguistic elements will be applied in the remaining chapters to clarify the nature of communication theorizing.

A careful analysis of the nature of knowledge is prerequisite to sensible research programs and projects. Applying the techniques of philosophical analysis to general communication theories can yield direct applications to the problems faced by research workers by clarifying questions suitable for the development of general theories and indicating which questions can be answered on observational grounds and which cannot.

Notes

1. My own thinking has been influenced by the teaching and writing of Professor Gustav Bergmann.
2. See, for example, Stanley S. Stevens, "Psychology and the Science of Science," *Psychological Bulletin* 36 (1939): 221–263; and "Mathematics, Measurement and Psychophysics," in Stanley S. Stevens, ed., *Handbook of Experimental Psychology* (New York: Wiley, 1951), pp. 1–50.
3. Charles W. Morris, *Foundations of the Theory of Signs* (Chicago: University of Chicago Press, 1938), p. 3.
4. Paul Watzlawick, Janet Beavin, and Don D. Jackson, *Pragmatics of Human Communication: A Study of Interactional Patterns, Pathologies, and Paradoxes* (New York: W. W. Norton, 1967).
5. Ibid., p. 22.
6. Robert Oppenheimer, "Analogy in Science," *American Psychologist* 11 (1956): 128.
7. Ibid.
8. Gustav Bergmann and Kenneth Spence, "Operationism and Theory Construction," in Melvin H. Marx, ed., *Psychological Theory* (New York: Macmillan, 1951), pp. 56–57.
9. For a critique of operationism from the perspective of pragmatism, see Abraham Kaplan, *The Conduct of Inquiry: Methodology for Behavioral Science* (San Francisco: Chandler, 1964), pp. 39–42.
10. This is a paraphrase of the definition of anxiety found in a dictionary such as the unabridged *Random House Dictionary of the English Language* (New York: Random House, 1967), p. 68.
11. For a more complete analysis of the relationship between operational definitions and theoretical terms, with an emphasis on the concept of validity, see Daniel J. O'Keefe, "Logical Empiricism and the Study of Human Communication," *Speech Monographs* 42 (1975): 169–183.
12. For a discussion of the Personal Report of Communication Anxiety Test, see James McCroskey, "Oral Communication Apprehension: A Summary of Recent Theory and Research," *Human Communication Research* 4 (1977): 78–96; for a discussion of the use of heartbeat for indexing speech anxiety, see Ralph R. Behnke and Larry W. Carlile, "Special Reports: Heart Rate as an Index of Speech Anxiety," *Speech Monographs* 38 (1971): 65–69.
13. For a more comprehensive treatment of these developments, see Hans Reichenbach, *The Rise of Scientific Philosophy* (Berkeley: University of California Press, 1951), pp. 78–94; for another analysis see Romano Harré, "Concepts and Criteria," *Mind* 73 (1964): 353–363.
14. Toulmin has developed an elaborate taxonomy of the way the term *rule* has been used in ordinary usage. See Stephen Toulmin, "Rules and Their Relevance for Understanding Human Behavior," in Theodore Mischel, ed., *Understanding Other Persons* (Oxford: Basil Blackwell, 1974), pp. 185–216.

6

Science and the Nature of Knowledge About Communication

The Knowledge of Science

Universality of Scientific Laws   Science searches for universal agreement about invariable relations. Replication of experiments must result in agreement among the various researchers as to the nature and extent of these relations. The discussion of laws of nature in Chapter 5 outlined the basic features of scientific laws. The relations expressed, such as those between heating water and the boiling of water, must be invariable. In addition, all observers of all experiments must agree that water when heated boils. Bypassing all the philosophical niceties and problems raised by these broad requirements, the fact is that the natural sciences have achieved a community of agreement about a rather impressive number of such laws.

Concept Laws   Laws of two main types express the invariable relations in the natural sciences. The first is the concept law. Water is an example of a concept law. Iron, oxygen, and hydrogen are other examples of concept laws. The concept law *water* implies a host of invariable relationships. Once we determine that a given sample of fluid is water, we know that it will boil at one certain temperature and freeze at another. We know that it will combine with other compounds and elements in a certain fashion. These relationships are invariable. If ever a sample of pure H_2O were discovered that did not combine with iron to form rust under suitable conditions, the whole structure of chemistry would be affected.

Iron, too, is a law of nature. If we test a given sample of metal and discover it has the density of iron, we can predict that the metal will deflect a magnetic needle, will rust, and will have a certain melting point. These invariable relations are called properties. Thus, iron has the properties of rusting and melting.

Process Laws The second kind of law is known as the process law. It is expressed as a statement and is often represented in a mathematical formula. "Water, when heated, boils" is a process law. The law describing the invariable relations that hold between the distance traveled by a freely falling body on the surface of the earth and the time of the fall is also a process law. Expressed in a formula, the latter law is $S = \frac{1}{2}gt^2$. This same law can be stated in words as "the distance traveled is equal to half the acceleration of gravity multiplied by the time of the fall, squared." There is a close tie between process law and concept law. A concept law can be translated into process laws; and when all the process laws associated with the concept have been stated, the *meaning* of the concept law is exhausted. If a fluid is water, then a process law stating its specific gravity, another stating its boiling point, and another stating its freezing point can be specified. There is also reciprocal relation. Without the concept the process law could not be stated. The development of a concept such as "specific gravity" enables the statement of a process law involving both water and specific gravity.

Scientific Laws and Analogy Once laws of nature were discovered, people began to look for other laws of the same type. The discovery of the earliest laws is lost in prehistory, but once discovered these laws led the way to other discoveries by analogy. The interesting fact is that analogies have often worked. Once a new concept law has been discovered—a new element, for example— then by analogy a prediction can be made that the concept law will express a number of invariable relations of the order of a certain atomic weight, a certain melting point, and a certain specific gravity. Generally, these predictions have been accurate

In like manner, when process laws were discovered, many similar laws of the same form were discovered by analogy. Both process and concept laws are suitable for physics and chemistry, and their discovery opened the way for the development of theoretical structures in these sciences. We have no guarantee that laws suitable for communication will have these forms, and so far the attempts to find concept laws and process laws have been much less successful in the social sciences than in the natural sciences. If the behavioral sciences develop as the natural sciences did, however, once the appropriate forms for laws governing behavior are discovered, the way will be cleared for a rapid development of laws of a similar form.

The Knowledge of Rhetoric and Communication

Concept Formation in Rhetoric and Communication Historically, concept laws have been one of the archetypes for laws of nature in the natural sciences. Concept formation plays an equally important role in knowledge about communication and rhetoric. Few concepts in communication are laws of nature; they therefore serve different functions and constitute a body of knowledge that, while similar in some respects, differs in substantial ways from scientific knowledge.

Definition of Communication Concepts In Chapter 2 I indicated the important role played by definitions in communication and rhetorical theory. Theorists have been preoccupied with finding definitions for such terms as *rhetoric, communication, process, transaction,* and *persuasion.* Clarification of the definitional processes important to communication theorizing will aid in the understanding of the knowledge we have about rhetoric and communication and provide a basis for comparison with the concept laws of the natural sciences.

Operational definitions are often the basis for clarifying concepts in both the natural and social sciences, as indicated in Chapter 5. Quite often the definitions in communication theory are not operational definitions. The non-operational definitions include three important kinds: (1) conventional definitions, (2) descriptive definitions, and (3) prescriptive definitions.

Some definitions in communication are conventional. In a broad sense all language is specified by conventional rules. I could demonstrate the conventional nature of language by creating a mini-linguistic system.[1] To do so I must develop an arbitrary set of symbols, some rules as to how these symbols can be used syntactically to form sentences, and a set of semantical rules. The way contract bridge players have developed a mini-linguistic system in the form of bidding conventions provides a nice example of the procedure.

The way the players define the meaning of the terms such as "one club" or "four no trump" is conventional in that they indicate the semantical rules with statements like "Let us use 'one club' when we have the following kinds of cards." Another player might protest a given definition and point out the difficulties that the team would encounter if they used it. The players would be ill advised to conduct their discussion in terms of what "one club" really, in fact, means. They might profitably discuss what would happen to their effectiveness in the play if they used one definition rather than another. Interestingly enough, it is unfair for one team to use a convention without informing their opponents. When investigators in communication specify arbitrary semantical rules for the terms they use, they ought to recognize that they have not, therefore, discovered something about the phenomenon they wish to study. The terms will prove more or less useful as they conduct their investigation, but until they have done so the conventional definitions tell them no more about the observables than do the abstract formulations of the pure mathematician.

Natural languages such as English are not conventional in some important respects. A natural language-in-use has a history, and scholars can explain the structure of the way the language developed. Psychological learning is a factor in language development as well. In terms of human learning potential and the historical development of a natural language-in-use, it is not entirely conventional, and phoneticians, anthropologists, and psycholinguists may study empirical data to find explanations of how language-in-use is determined by the nature of human beings and the way they have interacted with their environment. But if we reconstruct language in order to understand its logical functioning, then my analysis of the conventional nature of language is useful as a tool for the critical analysis of communication theory and research.

One important kind of definition used in communication is the conventional definition. We may, within certain limits, make our terms mean what is most suitable for our purposes, as long as we agree about the meanings. Thus, the authors of a textbook quite often begin with a series of definitions of key terms. The authors might define *persuasion* arbitrarily. They might contrast their definition with those found in other books until they clearly establish the conventional meanings they will employ. When people make stipulated definitions, they ought not to argue about the definition unless they have a full realization of what is at stake. They should ask of the conventional definition, "Does this stipulation serve the purposes of the discussion or analysis?" They might legitimately contend over whether a definition of *persuasion* which stipulates that the term will henceforth be used to denote all communication is a useful one. Perhaps they might decide that a more restrictive definition of persuasion as that subclass of communication in which a person designs a message with an intent to influence a target audience is the best for their purposes. Certainly they ought not to argue about whether persuasion truly is one or the other. At this stage of the analysis the investigators do not know what is the case, for they are simply sharpening their linguistic tools before they go out and use them to study their material and social reality.

The conventional definition is a *metalanguage* statement about how a term in the *object-language* is to be used to denote observables. I can use the single quotation marks around the term as I define it to keep the distinction clear. For example, "'persuasion' denotes all communication" would be a conventional definition.

Some definitions in communication are descriptive statements about observable features of reality phrased in the same form as conventional definitions. Descriptive definitions are not specifications of the semantic rules to be used in the investigators' object-language but are statements of fact about objects and phenomena phrased in that object-language. If we take the inclusive definition of *persuasion* as a descriptive statement in the object-language, then it asserts that every event named "communication" exhibits the quality of being persuasive. Although, on occasion, the two are confused, both the conventional and the descriptive definition are widespread and important in communication theorizing.

When definitions are used in a descriptive way, the investigators will often find controversy useful. Just as scholars might challenge the reliability and validity of data, so also might they profitably challenge whether or not the things named in their object-language statements exhibit the qualities asserted in the descriptive definitions. A descriptive definition is often a complex set of statements of fact organized by some tacit assumptions, and insofar as the definition contains or implies factual descriptions those descriptions need to be tested empirically for their truth or falsity.

About conventional definitions we might say, "That is all very plausible and consistent in the abstract, but it has nothing to do with the world." About descriptive definitions we would be well advised to say, "Observations support those definitions," or "Observations indicate that the definition is false."

The scholars who use conventional definitions can construct an essay on that foundation alone. By means of stipulating definitions for ordinary language words or for invented terms, I can create persona, abstract entities, concepts which have no semantical ties to observables in any language. I can take the term *unicorn* and define it as "a mythical beast resembling a horse with a horn in the middle of its forehead." I could then go on to take up various parts of the unicorn for more detailed definition. I could define the horn and its properties. If I got carried away I could plausibly continue my definitions by analogy with observable beasts such as horses, which the stipulated definition says that the unicorn resembles. I could define the unicorn's mating habits, its eating preferences, and its herd instincts. What I have done is to abort the process of defining a term conventionally as done by the bridge players at the point where they connected their language to the card holdings within hands.

The complete process of applying geometry to a problem such as measuring the distance across a river requires stipulating a definition and then acting out that definition with surveying instruments by sighting, measuring, and so forth. However, if I begin by stipulating a definition and then do not provide any connections among the language and observable facts, my fancy is left as free as the creative artist's to create massive thought structures by defining and further defining my invented terms.

With my mythical beast I am not likely to shift my language in the middle of my story to begin to treat the unicorn as though we could observe individual unicorns. Many authors of articles theorizing about rhetoric and communication, however, begin by stipulating conventional definitions for key terms and by the middle of the essay their language has shifted from a "let us stipulate or assume" tone to an assertive mode which suggests that they are no longer using conventional definitions but are instead describing material or social realities. Thus, they can spin out plausible, consistent, and detailed theories of communication without any semantical connection to observables (without data).

I think it would be gratuitous to single out any of the number of sometimes brilliant essays in the literature which have fallen into the mode of constructing theory on stipulated definitions. Instead, I will indulge in a fanciful example of how conventional definitions can provide the substance for communication and rhetorical theory.

My fanciful essay is entitled "Toward a Theory of Psychic Communication." I start with a stipulated definition of *psychic communication*: the transmission of meanings between or among spiritual entities alive or deceased without the use of the ordinary senses such as taste, hearing, seeing, etc. *Spiritual entities* are disembodied essences that may either emit or receive vibrations which carry meanings. A *psychic communication center* is a spiritual entity that emits meaningful vibrations. A *psychic communication clairaudient* is a spiritual entity that intuits the meanings in the vibrations. *Vibrations* are psychic phenomena that convey meanings in psychic communication. The *ether* is the medium that transmits vibrations and is not impeded by time, space, or physical objects. Thus, vibrations may travel from a center to a clairaudient through hundreds of years, light-years of distance, and any amount of matter.

I am now prepared to develop a model of psychic communication complete with a psychic communication center with certain celestial needs and purposes, determining to communicate a message and envibrating the meanings into ether that radiates outward through time, space, and all obstacles to be devibrated by a clairaudient.

All of my definitions are stipulated, and what is more the stipulations do not specify semantical rules for connecting to observables.

My point is not that scholars developing theories of rhetoric and communication should eschew conventional definitions. Indeed, good conventional definitions are extremely useful. They are the heart of mathematics, and the power of mathematics to aid in the creation of knowledge and its application is well demonstrated. They are important to the method of philosophical analysis as well. Scholars might well begin with stipulated definitions and then provide clear semantical rules for the definitions so that investigators can use them in observing communication phenomena. Modified by discoveries of what is the case, the stipulated definitions could yield to descriptive definitions which provide knowledge about material and social reality. Authors of essays in the philosophy of rhetoric and communication might begin with conventional definitions, keep the tone of their linguistic style clearly in the assumptive mode, and conclude with recommendations for the empirical testing of the theoretical account. Alternatively they might not only develop the theoretical rationale but report some preliminary or extensive testing of their notions.

Some definitions in communication and rhetoric are prescriptive statements. Although their linguistic form is similar to that of the other definitions, they function as guides to action and to ethical choice. A definition such as "an orator is a good man speaking well" is a value judgment of the order "Good speakers ought to be good men." Some years ago, textbooks in public speaking often defined the purpose of speechmaking as communicating with the audience. The definition was not a factually accurate description of the purposes of actual speakers, but may well have been an ethical imperative to students that they ought not to be motivated by other purposes. Many of the value judgments which are an important part of the theorizing about the arts of rhetoric and communication are couched in definitional form. Controversy over ethical imperatives is important and to be encouraged. Indeed, ethical controversies go on continually and are not resolved in the same fashion that factual differences may be resolved. I might argue, for example, that the definition of *orator* should be modified to "an orator is a good human being speaking well" because I believe that a woman ought to be allowed to be an orator as well as a man. In the history of the United States the ethical question of whether or not women ought to be orators has been the basis for long and acrimonious debates.

We need to distinguish which of the three kinds of definitions a theorist is using in order to sort out the nature and to evaluate the quality of an explanatory account of communication. If two scholars are arguing about the nature of persuasion and one of them is starting from a conventional definition for the purposes of their interchange and the other interprets the definition as a description of the observational data, they will fall into a serious misunderstanding. Similarly, if one describes the world on the basis of social scientific data with a definition of persuasion while the other uses a definitional form to describe the world as it *ought* to be according to some ethical imperatives, they will be talking at cross-purposes.

The three ways of interpreting definitions are illustrated by examining Aristotle's famous definitions of rhetoric. When Aristotle's book on the subject is translated into English, the term *rhetoric* is sometimes defined as "finding all the available means of persuasion." This definition may be interpreted as conventional, descriptive, or prescriptive. (At this point, arguments that the translation is a poor rendering of the original or that Aristotle intended the definition to be of a certain kind, while interesting scholarly questions, are irrelevant to my analysis.)

If this definition is interpreted as a conventional one, then Aristotle would be suggesting that throughout the discussion whenever he uses the term *rhetoric* he means in a given situation "finding all the available means of persuasion." Certainly, this is a legitimate way to begin a book, and the only quibble a scholar might have with Aristotle in this regard would be over whether or not some other definition might have been more helpful for the kind of analysis he was about to make.

The definition might also be interpreted as a *description* of the practice of rhetoric. In this interpretation Aristotle would be asserting that whenever the events called rhetoric are *observed* in the world they have the quality of "finding all the available means of persuasion." Some scholars have asserted that the Aristotelian approach to knowledge is based on descriptive definitions. G. Burniston Brown, for example, has interpreted Aristotle's definitional approach to knowlege as an attempt to apply the methods of geometry to *demonstrate* knowledge about the world. Geometry proceeds by starting with definitions and axioms and then deducing a number of unforeseen implications from the definitions. A triangle can be defined as a plane figure bounded by three straight lines and, given the axioms of geometry, a number of essential properties of triangles can be deduced. When all of these essential properties of triangles have been demonstrated, we know all there is to know about a triangle. Aristotle, according to G. Burniston Brown, attempted to demonstrate knowledge about observables in a similar way. He began by defining concepts in terms of similarities and differences.

Such definitions were designed to reveal the essence of a subject. Thus, the definition of *man* must reveal the essence of man just as the definition of *triangle* must reveal the essence of triangles. When the definition that contains the essence of man has been discovered, Aristotle would use axioms suitable to the study of man to deduce, by means of syllogisms, the further essential properties of man. The definition of 'rhetoric' could proceed in the same way. 'Rhetoric' could be classified in the same genus as 'dialectic', and the definition could then proceed to establish the differences between rhetoric and dialectic. This process should lead to a definition that catches the essence of rhetoric, and by using suitable axioms and syllogistic reasoning, we should then be able to deduce all the essential properties of rhetoric. When we have done this we know all about rhetoric and the task of science is finished.[2]

Stripped of all its elaborate Platonic and Aristotelian metaphysics, this sort of definition turns out to be a descriptive definition. That is, under this interpretation Aristotle's definition of 'rhetoric' is an attempt to describe the practice of rhetoric as he observed it in Greece. The scholar who interprets Aristotle's definition as a descriptive definition might well take issue with its adequacy and conduct his inquiry at some length. His argument should be based upon observation and judgment about the adquacy or inadequacy of the description as a reflection of the practice of speaking that the scholar observes. The scholar might assert that Aristotle's definition describing the facts of rhetorical practice is false because the scholar has observed speakers who did not find all the available means of persuasion.

Finally, Aristotle's definition could be interpreted as a prescriptive statement. That is, Aristotle is asserting a value statement that whenever speakers practice the arts of rhetoric they ought to find all the available means of persuasion. The scholar who interprets Aristotle's definition as prescriptive may disagree with the definition, but since it is a value statement and not a statement of fact about observables the scholar's argument will come down to some counterstatement such as that rhetoric ought to have a broader (or narrower) function than finding all the available means of persuasion.

Concepts and Taxonomies   To clarify the concepts used in theorizing in communication that are established by conventional definitions, by observation of phenomena, and as value judgments, I will compare them to the concepts in laws of nature. The definitions used for concept laws and process laws in the sciences are not conventional definitions in the narrower sense. The discovery of the concept of specific gravity was an important discovery based on empirical data. Scientists cannot say, "Let us agree that specific gravity means thus and so." Their experiments in the laboratory would force them to match their concepts with their observations. Yet, conventional definitions are helpful and important in theorizing about rhetoric and communication. I might define the concept of ethical proof as the rhetorical devices used during the delivery of a speech or I might broaden the definition to include the reputation of the speaker and the actions that the speaker takes before he or she gives the speech.

There is no laboratory to consult in a case like this, and whatever definition is most helpful in the analysis at hand can be agreed upon by the people involved in using the concept. If the statment is rephrased to say that traditionally *ethos* has meant what the speaker does before the speech and *ethical proof* has meant what the speaker does during the speech, then it becomes a statement of fact and is either true or false. Indeed, one of the important ways in which conventional definitions can be sanctioned is by tracing the way the term has been used in the past. Part of a scholar's task in a given research project might be to trace the way key terms have been used historically. These terms, however, may be defined conventionally despite their traditional usage. Words can be used as tools; and if we understand the difficulty in washing past connotations from a term, we can make the word denote whatever concept is most helpful in our analysis. If the traditional usage is likely to add confusion to the discussion, a new term may be coined for the concept. Introducing a new term ensures that old language habits do not cause misunderstanding; however, inventing new terms exacts a price, too. The new terms must be learned and used, and too many novel terms can contribute to an abstruse style and make for heavy going until they become second nature. In addition, theoreticians can become addicted to making up new words. The result is often a pretentious jargon that they then use for the restatement of common sense. The problem is illustrated by the development of fantasy theme analysis. Traditional usage for the term *fantasy* adds some confusion to the stipulated definition, which includes both fictitious and nonfictitious dramatizations. However, the traditional usage does connote creativity, interpretation, and an important process for providing meaning. On balance the term seems to me to have more strengths than weaknesses. Others who have studied shared fantasies in groups and organizations as well as in society in general have used such terms as *sagas* and *myths* to denote the same phenomenon.[3]

In any event, scholars making conventional definitions in rhetoric and communication have employed both strategies, sometimes redefining the traditional terms in new ways and sometimes using a new term for the purpose of study and teaching.

When the definition is an object-language statement describing the properties of the phenomena, the approach is similar to that of the scientist explaining a concept law. In both instances, observation is the court of last resort in resolving differences. Descriptive definitions provide empirical content for investigators in communication. They function much as concept laws do in the natural sciences, and for some investigators the search for descriptive definitions is, indeed, a search for the equivalent of concept laws.

The differences among conventional definitions, descriptive definitions, and concept laws are reflected in one of the major theoretical frameworks for all disciplines—that of classifications. The setting up of classes in such a way that knowledge can be ordered, related, and explained is dependent upon concept formation. Systems of classification can be found in the natural sciences such as chemistry (table of elements), botany (classification of plants), zoology (classification of insects), communication (classification of contexts), rhetoric (classification of rhetorical devices), and radio and television (classification of program types).

The classification of knowledge in the sciences is the result of concept laws or of descriptive definitions of considerable precision. The classification of knowlege in rhetoric and communication is often the result of conventional definitions. The difference is important in both the development and use of classifications as knowledge. For example, if the concept *swan* includes qualities A, B, C, D, let us say, swimming, long-necked, two-legged, white, we may build a classification system that has one category for swans. What happens to the classification system that has only one class for swans when an individual is discovered that is long-necked, swims, and is swanlike in all respects, except he is *black*? If the classification system is constructed on the basis of conventionally defined concepts, there is no problem. The system is expanded; and the definition of the concept *swan* is cut so it includes only swimming, long-necked, and two-legged. There are now black and white swans. The class *swan* has been divided into two parts; and the classificatory system is a bit larger and, perhaps, more unwieldy but it still accounts for our experience. However, if the concept *swan* was a concept law like *iron*, then the discovery of a black swan would be a serious matter. One of the bases of classification would then be color, which is asserted by the concept law to be invariably associated with membership in a given class. When this is disproved by the discovery of a representative with an unpredicted color, doubt is thrown on all the rest of the invariably associated qualities upon which the system rests. The black swan is the equivalent of a piece of iron that has the wrong atomic weight. Such a piece of iron would cause a serious reevaluation of the table of elements.

The classificatory systems in rhetoric and communication range from almost purely arbitrary ones to those based upon descriptive definitions as precise as those of the zoologist or botanist. If we classify speeches according to a set of concepts such as *forensic*, *deliberative*, or *epideictic*, the concepts are usually defined in arbitrary fashion. Thus, when an individual speech appears that has qualities A, B, C, which are the qualities included in the arbitrary definition of *deliberative*, but does not have quality D, and has several additional features, E and F, which were not included in the concept of *deliberative* but are part of the *epideictic*, it is not at all unusual or disturbing. A new concept can be developed or the old concept can be divided into several subcategories. The classification system can be expanded to include a new category of epi-deliberative speeches. The growing interest in generic rhetorical criticism brings the nature of concept laws and classificatory systems to the fore for contemporary students of rhetoric.[4]

The voice scientist's classification of phonemes in terms of the position of the articulatory mechanism during their production is an example of a classificatory system based upon precise descriptive definitions. To say that (b) is a bilabial plosive is to say something about its relationship to certain positions of the articulatory mechanism during its production. When a (b) is found that is not produced by making a small explosion by blowing apart the compressed lips, it is not as damaging as the discovery of an element that does not have the qualities predicted; but it is a surprise and may be considered as much of an anomaly as an albino pheasant. If too many such individuals are found, the whole classificatory system may need to be evaluated.

Concepts and Process Laws   Concepts play a crucial role in the development of process laws, as well as in classificatory frameworks of knowledge. Imaginative people can dream up operationally defined concepts by the gross, but the concepts ought not to be random flights of fancy; they must be worth doing. Specific gravity is an example of a concept that was worth the trouble to develop. The reason it was worth developing is that it became part of a series of process laws. I could dream up an analogous concept such as specific levity that would not be useful in the same way. Specific levity might be found by taking the weight of the speaker, times the number of hairs on his head, divided by the number of words spoken per each audience laugh. I could determine specific levity operationally (although it is a bit tedious to do the necessary counting), but there would be little point in doing it unless we could find a process law or a probability generalization using the concept.

The importance of concepts like specific gravity in the physical sciences has led researchers in the social sciences to try to develop similar concepts. Intelligence quotient is an example of an operationally defined concept in the behavioral sciences. The point of developing a concept such as intelligence quotient is to find a process law such as "If a student has an IQ of 140 or more, then he can successfully complete four years of college." This statement, however, does not hold true in every instance. Thus, the notion of IQ has not led to any process laws; but it is a more useful concept than would be the concept of specific levity because it has been the basis of a number of probability statements such as "IQ test scores correlate with the Brown Carlson Listening test with a correlation coefficient of .55."[5] Such probability generalizations are useful and constitute part of our knowledge about psychological phenomena. They enable prediction, not about individuals, but about general trends when large numbers of individuals are involved; and they furnish a kind of explanation of events.

Some concepts in experimental phonetics are very close to concept laws. The concept of vowel *formants* is such a notion. Certain patterns of energy distribution in vowel sounds (formants) are closely related to the perception of the vowels. The development of concepts such as *bel* in the area of psychophysical measurement is very close to a process law that states an invariable relationship between certain measurable qualities of the sound wave and certain other qualities related to sound percepts.

Communication Concepts and Generalizations   A number of generalizations in communication take the form of process laws and incorporate concepts in the same fashion as a law of nature. In small group communication I might combine such concepts as *group productivity* and *group cohesiveness* into a generalization such as "Group productivity is proportional to group cohesiveness." I have phrased a generalization in the same form and employed concepts in the same way that the natural scientists do when they formulate a law of nature such as "The velocity of a uniformly accelerating object is proportional to the time of acceleration." However, I may have started with a conventional definition for each of the key concepts. I may define *group productivity* as the ability of the group to do the job that it is set up to do. I may define *cohesiveness* as the willingness of the individual group members to work for the group, the ability of the group to stick together, its *esprit de corps*. Now, more than likely I come to these conventional definitions with some background experience and commonsense knowledge about groups and how they communicate and work. My definitions are framed on the basis of conventional wisdom. Nonetheless, the definitions are conventional in that I hope to study my hypothesis about the relationship between productivity and cohesiveness empirically.

In order to proceed in a way analogous to the natural scientists I define my concepts about small group communication in operational terms. That is, I provide clear semantical rules which connect my conventional definitions to observables. I develop a procedure whereby I can count units of product to provide a numerical description of quantity and use that as my operational definition of productivity. I develop a paper-and-pencil index of members' reported feelings of group attraction and quantify cohesiveness in this manner. I then set up groups and count production outcomes, test for cohesiveness, and do a statistical analysis of the data to see whether productivity is proportional to cohesiveness. Investigators have followed essentially the same procedure to try to support generalizations about relationships among such concepts as *leadership, cohesiveness, productivity, communication flow*, and so forth. Their results have not been as clear-cut as the results of experiments in the natural sciences which have provided a rationale for laws of nature.

Instructors in small group communication may also develop knowledge on the basis of concepts formed from experience in a more general descriptive way. That is, I might define a general tendency that asserts, "All other things being equal, the more cohesive a group the greater its productivity." My claim now is not that I have discovered a law of nature but that a good many people who have a professional interest in studying, teaching, and working with task-oriented groups have observed their dynamics and come to the conclusion that the generalization does describe an important tendency in group dynamics. What do such generalizations tell us? The scholar with a strong scientific bias might not even consider a statement asserted on the basis of general experience as knowledge at all.

Certainly my generalization about small group communication based upon practical experience tells us a good deal less than it would if it functioned as a law of nature. But if it does prove to help us anticipate group productivity and if we can then often increase productivity by increasing cohesiveness, it does tell us something.

Such statements are like scientific laws in several important respects. First, they are based upon empirical data. People working with groups have observed them and noticed an important feature that they name with a specific term so that they can discuss the feature with greater ease and precision. The way people observe, notice, and name a striking aspect of the phenomenon they are curious about can be thought of as the process of concept formation. They form concepts in such instances because they can discriminate and separate out certain features of the group activity which seemed analogous to one another. Once they have formed the concept on the basis of a searching procedure in which they observed $group_1$, $group_2$ . . . $group_n$, they will tend to have a mental set with concepts to aid in their study of other groups. Having formed the hunch that two concepts are related in proportional fashion on the basis of working with a number of groups, they can now observe other groups and check out the hypothesis.

Second, the generalizations are like scientific laws in that they are supported, modified, or rejected on the basis of experience. Should further observations fail to verify the generalization, the practitioners may try to account for the failure in terms of other factors which were unusual and which submerged the tendency of productivity and cohesiveness to be linked. People are often reluctant to discard a hard-earned generalization, because tentative as it may be it does provide some security and some base point for the study and practice of small group communication. If the generalization fails repeatedly, it will often be discarded.

Teachers and practitioners in all areas of communication have discovered a large group of generalizations such as "Group productivity is proportional to group cohesiveness" on the basis of practical experience. Many of the generalizations aid them in anticipating the way communication episodes will unfold. The skillful practitioner can use such knowledge and combine it with talent in the art of communication to explain, anticipate, and partially control communication events.

Probability Laws Investigators often take the generalizations developed by practitioners as the basis for more systematic empirical investigation. When they do so they give the concepts operational definitions and may search for statistical interpretations that provide evidence for *correlations* among the concepts. To take my example of the operational definitions for productivity and cohesiveness, social scientific investigators might set up studies in such a way that they discover that the two sets of scores are correlated or covary in a statistically significant fashion. When investigators develop and support a generalization asserting that a positive correlation exists between two operationally defined concepts in all similar contexts, they are providing an explanation that is somewhere between the generalizations expressing the hunches of practitioners and the laws of nature characterizing some of the natural sciences.

All three kinds of generalizations are based upon direct observation. The hunches of practitioners usually are more ambiguous than either the statistical correlations or the laws of nature. The ambiguity makes for more differences of opinion over the meaning of descriptive definitions and the reliability of the generalization. The probability statement's meaning is specified by the operational definitions of the concepts and the statistical inferences of correlation. The result is that probability assertions tend to be more precise than the hunches of practitioners. The scientific laws of nature are the most precise of all three formulations. Not only that, laws of nature assert invariable relationships, whereas the probability statements provide an estimate of the degree of correlation.

Are probability statements then *statistical laws*? Can the statistical correlations supported by the research literature in communication plus those to be discovered furnish the basis for a science of communication? Like so may questions of this nature, the answer depends upon what one means by science. Contemporary physicists and chemists have reduced many of the late-nineteenth-century laws of nature to statistical laws. Since the hardest of the hard sciences have shifted emphasis to statistical laws, is that evidence that statistical correlations in communication research can provide analogous explanations? A more precise question can lead to greater understanding of the issue. Can statistical laws like those in physics become the basis for knowledge in communication? To answer this question I must draw a distinction between the probability generalizations that express correlations and the statistical laws in the natural sciences.

Analogies are the core of theorizing. When we discover analogous events in our experience, we are at the foundation of concept formation, and yet poorly drawn analogies often cause intellectual mischief. The analogy between statistical correlations in communication and the use of probability mathematics in physics, for example, is a poor one. Recent developments at the subatomic level of analysis indicate that some physical phenomena seem to follow no regular laws of nature but rather operate according to the assumptions of randomness. For probability mathematics to be useful, several assumptions must be made. The first is that the phenomenon under study is lawless, operating in random fashion, purely by chance. When investigators make the assumption of chance, they can apply probability mathematics to their problem; and if they are dealing with a large enough number of cases, they can predict fairly accurately what will happen at a *grosser* level of analysis.

The typical probability example of flipping an unbiased coin indicates how this is done. Assume an investigator wants to discover the laws governing the flipping of the coin. If she wants to know if a given instance of flipping the coin will turn up heads, she will try to find the laws of nature governing the movement of this particular flip. She must measure the force given the coin, the air resistance, the position of the coin before it was flipped, the distance of the fall, and other relevant information. By careful application of the laws of dynamics she could predict the toss. However, if the discovery of all relevant information proved too tedious and burdensome or proved to be impossible to determine, the researcher could begin to study the pattern of coin flips at a *grosser* level of analysis. She could ask herself if there are some laws governing the number of heads and the number of tails and the order in which they appear. She might, for example, compute the correlation between three heads in a row being followed by a tail. When this proves a dead end, she could decide to make the assumption that she should not look for laws at this level of analysis but rather that she should assume these events take place according to pure randomness and chance. Once she makes the assumption of chance governing the number of heads and tails she can apply the *laws* of statistics to her problem. Speaking of statistical laws in this way is much different from using the term to refer to probability statements indicating correlation between two variables. By statistical computation the researcher can now predict the number of runs of six heads in a row as larger and larger samples of coin tosses are collected. Such computation will also predict the equal distribution of heads and tails.

The important probability rule in such instances is the law of large numbers. There is always a margin of error in making predictions on the basis of probability mathematics. The larger the number of events under consideration, the smaller the margin of error. If, for example, we want to be 99 percent sure of our predictions, the margin of error will depend on the number of tosses under consideration. For 100 tosses, if we wish to be 99 percent sure, we must say that there will be between 35 and 65 heads in 100 tosses. Obviously this is a crude sort of prediction when dealing with only a small number of events. Increasing the number of tosses and keeping our level of accuracy at 99 percent, probability laws predict between 450 and 550 heads in 1,000 tosses, and between 4,850 and 5,150 in 10,000 tosses. The margin of error increases from 15 for 100 to 50 for 1,000 to 150 for 10,000, but the *percentage* of the margin in relation to the total number of tosses decreases from 15 percent to 1.5 percent.[6] With increasingly large numbers the percentage of error becomes so small that at a gross level of observation for extremely large numbers of events, probability mathematics predicts with almost the accuracy of a law of nature.

Statistical laws of this sort are important where other methods of investigation seem inappropriate, where we can make the assumption of randomness, and where large numbers of events are involved. In such cases, statistical computations can make predictions with considerable accuracy; and if *observations* verify these predictions, we can accept them as substantiated. The statistical rules governing the flip of a coin tell us nothing about the likelihood of the next flip turning up heads. Only when we observe a large number of events can predictions be made. Statistical laws can make no predictions about the next play of a slot machine, but over thousands of plays they enable more and more accurate predictions about how much money the machine will pay out. In terms of such statistical predictions the natural sciences have some advantages compared to the behavioral sciences. On occasion, the scientist investigates random activity in large numbers of atomic particles. This means that the statistical predictions can be made at the commonsense level of perception with such accuracy that the margin of error is not very noticeable. For example, radium, as found in nature, disintegrates slowly. If we have one gram of radium, we can compute the number of atoms it contains. Scientists have discovered that a portion of these atoms will split away each year. They have no notion as to which atom will split at any given moment. Any individual atom may split away in the next second or remain for years. If there are laws governing the splitting of an individual atom, the scientists do not know them. They take the alternate position of assuming that the process is a random one and use probability statistics to compute the rate of decay of radium with great accuracy. For a pound of uranium, for example, the rate of decay is about five million atoms a second, which indicates the feasibility of applying the law of large numbers to such phenomena.

Statistical laws of this kind are not applicable to small numbers of events. Therefore, they have limited practicality for the communication researcher unless he is dealing with mass media and can assume randomness in a million or so speech events.

The analogy between such statistical laws in the natural sciences and statistical laws in communication does not hold. What about the probability statement that asserts that the null hypothesis was rejected at the 5 percent level of confidence or that there is a positive correlation of .87 between two test scores? Let us examine first the statement rejecting the null hypothesis with a certain amount of confidence. A researcher asserting such a statement is doing just the opposite of the researcher who first searched for lawfulness in the flipping of a coin and, finding none, decided to assume there was no lawfulness and used statistical laws to predict the distribution of heads and tails according to chance. Instead, this researcher *begins* by assuming that the events under study can be explained as happening by chance; this is the meaning of the notion of the *null hypothesis*. When the researcher tests the null hypothesis, he checks the notion that the results of his study can be explained on the basis of chance. When he finds that the odds are against such results as he found happening by chance, he can reject the null hypothesis. When he does this, he may bet that there are laws operating in the data he is studying. If he asserts that he rejects the null hypothesis at the 5 percent level of confidence, he means that according to statistical assumptions of chance the odds are 95 out of 100 that he would *not* get such results. Thus, probability mathematics cannot be applied to these data as the scientist applies statistics to the decay of uranium. He has discovered that the variations in his data are not likely to be due to chance. What has he accomplished? He has established a strong case for assuming that there are regularities operating in his data, and he must now try to find them.

Such probability statements can be thought of as the basis for a science of communication, but they remain different in important respects from laws of nature or from the use of statistical computations and the assumption of randomness to predict such things as the rate of decay of radium. They are a way station between the more crude formulations of commonsense probabilities and the laws of the natural sciences.

Explanatory Systems in Science and Communication

One of the most important functions of theories of all kinds is their power to explain events. Since this function is an important part of any systematic body of knowledge I will analyze some of the typical techinques used to provide explanations for events in both material and social reality.

When I examine an explanatory account of a class of communication phenomena from a metalanguage perspective, I can emphasize one or more of the three basic linguistic dimensions. Thus, I can concentrate on the explanation as a clarification in the syntactical dimension. If I explain the theorem in geometry that asserts that the sum of the square of the two legs of a right triangle are equal to the square of the hypotenuse by tracing back the steps of my computation to several axioms, I have provided a syntactical explanation. If I explain the rust on an object by asserting that the object is iron and iron in the presence of water will oxidize, I have provided a description in the object-language and I have provided a semantical explanation. If I explain an individual's behavior in terms of a superstitious belief in magic, I have provided a metalanguage analysis in the pragmatical dimension.

Two features of the explanations of science and communication are worth noting. The first is the notion that emphasizes the pragmatical dimension and suggests that an explanation is a communication transaction and must be understood and believed by the other parties involved in the communication. Thus, when I explain an unhappy event in terms of a bad omen like the sighting of a black cat at midnight, it does not become an explanation until the other person understands the functioning of black magic and believes it. The second is the notion that emphasizes the semantical dimension and suggests that an explanation is not an explanation unless iron does rust in the presence of water and the bad omen did cause the unhappy event. From the second perspective I would see the account of the rusty iron based upon chemical laws as an explanation even though a community of people did not believe it, and the account of the sighting of the black cat as causing the rust not explanatory even though a community did believe it.

Natural scientists may couch many of their explanations in the object-language. Scholars studying communication *must* couch their explanations in a metalanguage. Thus, I might study the communication associated with the word *magic* but to do so I would have to study both the material reality and the social reality of a given community of people. In my explanation of communication I might include an account of my interpretation of what certain physical movements mean to the actors. Thus, I might not only describe the throwing of a pinch of salt over the shoulder but go on to account for the throwing on the basis of what the act meant to the persons involved in the action.

Explaining by Giving Causes   One of the most widespread ways that natural scientists provide an explanation for material reality is by linking results to causes. The notion of explanation in general is thus often closely entangled with the concept of *causality*. Frequently when we talk in commonsense ways about "cause" and "effect," we refer to a somewhat ambiguous notion of an invariable relation in time. Thus, if event B is always preceded by event A and if event A is always followed by event B, we may conclude that B is caused by A or that B is the effect of A. If someone is hit in the eye and the eye turns black, we say that the blow caused the black eye. If someone takes strychnine and dies, we say the poison caused the death, or that the death was the effect of the poison.

This viewpoint of cause and effect as an invariable relation in time is not enough to explain the logic behind these commonsense notions. For example, there are pairs of events that are invariably associated in time and yet we do not think of them as causally related. Birth invariably precedes death, but we do not think of birth as causing death. There are still other sequences in which event A invariably precedes B and then invariably follows B. Sunrise precedes sunset and then follows sunset, yet we do not talk of the sunrise causing the sunset. Actually the idea of causation as an invariable relation in time is rather sophisticated common sense. It transcends the cruder notion that the cause somehow is doing something to bring about the effect.

Both of these notions overlook the relationship between causality and laws of nature. Behind every statement of cause and effect a law of nature is implied. To say that heat causes water to boil does not necessarily mean that heat must precede boiling, for the heating and the boiling may take place simultaneously; nor does it mean that the heat is somehow in the water blowing bubbles. What it does mean is that *if* water is heated, *then* it will *always* boil. Asumed in every statement of cause is an if-then-always statement of this sort. The laws that state the relationship between pressure, volume, and temperature of gases do not imply a time dimension, but they can be used as the basis of cause-and-effect statements.

An important meaning of explanation, therefore, is to give the causes of an event. In the natural sciences this kind of explanation is furnished by laws of nature and theories such as Newton's. For example, if a curious child observes a book fall off the table and asks "Why?" an explanation can be given by furnishing a generalization that covers the specific event. Perhaps you answer, "Because whenever an object is unsupported it falls." To the next "Why?" you may answer with a still broader generalization such as "Because the earth attracts all objects and causes them to fall." To the next "Why?" you may answer that in the universe all masses attract each other in a straight line with a force proportional to the product of the mass and inversely proportional to the square of the distance between their centers. To the next "Why?" you can give no further answer within the framework of Newton' theory because you have reached its broadest generalization.

For this meaning of explanation, therefore, the question "Why did that happen?" means "According to what prior conditions and what laws of nature and theories did that occur?"[7] Scientific explanation of this sort has predictive power. You might say, "Be careful or you will knock the lamp on the floor." If someone asks "Why?" you may proceed as above to give an explanation of your prediction. Should the lamp be unsupported it will fall as you predicted.

Many explanations in rhetoric and communication take the same form as scientific explanation related to a covering law and use the terminology of *cause* and *effect* or *factors* or *variables* to explain communiction processes. The difference between communicatin theories based on probabilities and scientific explanation is that communication theories lack predictive power. The effect of a mass-media persuasive campaign might be explained after the event in terms of the mood of large segments of the public, the skill of the publicists in developing themes, purchasing media time, and so forth, but it could not have been invariably predicted prior to its implementation.

Probabilities as Explanation   In my earlier discussion of probability generalizations I noted that one possible interpretation of a series of empirical studies which reject the null hypothesis in regard to a generalization governing communication processes is that the processes are not random chance events but lawful in the same way that chemical processes are lawful. On such an interpretation, I would argue that the investigators have uncovered an area where laws of nature are in operation and what is now needed is further investigation and clarification, and the result will eventually be the discovery of covering laws.

In my discussion of process laws as invariable relationships and in the notion that one negative instance is sufficient in principle to falsify a law of nature, I have emphasized the logic of scientific laws, explanations, and causality in principle. In practice, most scientific laws have exceptions. Scientists have formulated and used laws of nature even though contrary instances were possible and sometimes when contrary instances were known to have occurred.

Kaplan noted that the term *quasi law* has sometimes been used to indicate widely accepted generalizations with known exceptions. They are accepted as explanatory on the argument that the exceptions are the result of special and as yet unknown conditions, and when these are discovered, the generalizations will function as laws of nature. He went on to judge, "In behavioral science our knowledge is virtually all in the form of quasi laws, at best. But if we cannot, in the present state of our knowledge, explain the exceptions, it surely does not follow that we know nothing at all."[8] One interpretation of probability generalizations is that they are steps toward quasi laws which in turn are steps toward laws of nature.

I might, however, make a second interpretation, which is that the generalizations expressing correlations and covariances are accurate numerical descriptions of the communication processes and the generalizations cannot in principle ever become covering laws. On such an interpretation I would argue that communication events are not governed by laws of nature, nor are they random and chance events; they are characterized by regularities and patterns, but these regularities are not the invariant iron laws of nature.

My interpretation could account for the regularities on the basis of *inherent tendencies, or social norms*, or *conventional rules*.

One answer to the question of why a certain process unfolded is to say that there is a tendency in the system for things to work out in that way. The tendency does not always materialize, but it is often present. Thus, if someone asks why a person emerged as leader of a group even though no formal leader was appointed, I might respond that there is a tendency in leaderless small groups for one person to emerge a leader. The first person might then note that in another group similar to the first, no leader emerged. I might answer that even though there was a tendency in the group, other things happened and created forces sufficiently powerful that the tendency was not realized. We might speak of the tendency of water to seek its own level but recognize that wind tends to raise waves and that the gravitational force of the moon tends to raise tides. I might note a tendency for the firstborn child in a family of three children to be talkative and task-oriented in small-group discussion meetings. However, a given individual might be anxious and withdrawn, and I account for the unanticipated communicatin behavior on the grounds that the person suffers from trait anxiety. When asked to explain the trait anxiety, I might respond that the person was a battered child and battered children have a tendency to develop trait anxiety.

Another answer to the question of why a certain communication episode developed as it did is to say that it was governed by social norms or mores. The rhetorical community has developed normative behavior in regard to its communication style which newcomers and children born into the community come to learn through a general acculturation process. Most people follow the norms most of the time and thus facilitate the communication in the community. Norms, of course, can be broken either by error or by conscious nonconformity.

What is the difference between a tendency and a normative regularity? The tendency explanation assumes a general pattern similar to that described by a law of nature. The normative explanation assumes patterns specific to given groups and communities. Thus, I might account for a community's observed greeting behavior which consists of saying, "How are you?" and answering, "Pretty good. How are you?" or some equivalent as the general custom. When I observe someone responding to the greeting by buttonholing the other person and delivering a fifteen-minute oration on his spiritual condition, his physical condition, his mental condition, and his financial condition, I might account for the deviant behavior in terms of the individual seeking attention. The individual failed to conform to the norms. I ought not to say that there is a tendency to use the normative greeting pattern in the community as I might in ordinary usage. What I might do in line with my stipulated definition is to answer the second-order question "Why do these people have the norm of using this ritual greeting?" by saying that there is a tendency in all rhetorical communities to develop ritualistic norms for greetings and goodbyes.

In ordinary language usage, I might also say that as a rule people in the community will use the ritualistic pattern of greeting. In the general sense the term *rule* might include my stipulated definition of *tendency* and of *norm*. In addition, *rule* could include habitual behavior of individuals which did not conform to the group's norms. I might say, "As a rule she is late for our conferences." There is, however, another more specialized meaning for *rule* which indicates another way in which we can explain communication phenomenon. Communication events have many of the same earmarks as gaming behavior in general. Athletic contests, card games, and board games such as chess are like communication events in that they take place within a designated place, and they are governed by conventional agreement among the players as to what behavior constitutes playing the game and what can and cannot be done within the play.

Communication events take place within physical space and time. Thus, two people may have a conversation defined in time by the boundaries of greeting and goodbye communication and fenced off in space by the orientation of their bodies and their verbal and nonverbal communication. A small group meets at a certain place, the members arrange themselves into a pattern which defines the group's boundaries, and the boundaries of the meeting are defined in time by some ritualistic opening and closing comments.

The constitutive rules which govern gaming behavior are conventional and like social norms may be broken. However, participants must learn and follow the rules in order to play the game. The result is that an anthropologist might observe the athletic events of a culture and discover repetitive patterns of behavor. In like fashion, the observer of a card game might see regularities in turn-taking and play. I once participated in a bridge game observed by a younger brother of one of the players. The younger brother had never seen the game played before. As we began to play, the unusual distribution of cards resulted in our being unable to bid the first hand. All of the players said "Pass" and we threw in the cards. A second hand was dealt. Again we were unable to bid. In all we dealt the cards four times without being able to play a hand. At this point the younger brother as amateur anthropologist remarked, "There's not much to that game, is there?"

One way to explain the behavior of football players, bridge players, or people involved in a communication transaction is to explicate the rules which provide the goals, the basis for winning or losing, and the allowable and disallowed actions. Thus, I might explain the communication behavior of a group of young men in a ghetto of a north American city in the 1960s by describing the rules of the game of "dozens" which they were playing. Or I might explain the communication of another group of people in a North American university in the 1980s by describing the rules of the game of "graduate oral examination" which they are playing.

To sum up, the investigators who make systematic studies of communication behavior and reject the null hypothesis or establish correlations among behavior may be supporting the presence of a pattern which is tied to tendencies, to norms, or to rules rather than laws of nature "seen through a glass darkly."

Motives, Meanings, Purposes, and Plans as Explanation   A growing number of communication theorists are drawing a distinction between human motion and human action. The theorists argue that a description such as that provided by a radical behaviorist gives an inadequate explanation of human behavior. They suggest that a better road to understanding is to account for human behavior on the basis of the conscious motives, meanings, purposes, and plans of the people involved in the action.

Weber is said to have insisted that "the fundamental subject-matter of the social sciences is the self-conscious actions of individual persons."[9] In this view the scientific explanation of the social world often should refer to the meanings of the actions of the human beings who are living in and continually recreating their social realities by their communication.

Explanations of communication behavior can be based upon attributed motives. I might explain the nature of a persuasive campaign by arguing that the candidate's publicists designed it to appeal to clearly specified segments of the American voting populace because they were motivated by a desire to win the election. I could go on to note the results of in-depth interviews and private polls that indicated the social reality of the various segments of the audience and how the publicists adapted to audience motives and purposes. I could outline the way the campaigners formulated plans for campaign events, media specials, and other details of the persuasive effort.

Some scholars argue that an adequate explanation requires more than a descriptive account of the self-conscious purposes and plans of the individuals involved in the events. They would require that the scholar go on to indicate *why* the individuals came to develop the motivations, meanings, and purposes and to draft the plans which explain their action.

Plausible Narrative as Explanation   On occasion, scholars who are providing an explanation for human action on the basis of attributing motives end up by presenting a causal narrative that suggests that the unfolding action can be accounted for on the basis of motives, plans, and purposes. A plausible narrative in which a cast of characters—human beings or other entities endowed with human characteristics—enact a believable scenario accounting for the unfolding of events is a powerful and attractive way for human beings to gain understanding of their environment.

The way a skillful lawyer develops a narrative to account for the circumstantial evidence that is established beyond reasonable doubt illustrates the explanatory power of the technique. The prosecuting attorney's narrative may explain the facts in a case as follows. The defendant was trying to obtain a divorce from his wife. She would not give it to him. The defendant and his mistress plotted to have the wife killed and hired a hoodlum to murder her. When the gunman failed to follow through as promised, the defendant and his mistress accosted the wife and asked again for a divorce. When the wife refused, he shot and killed her. Therefore, the defendant is guilty of murder in the first degree. The defense lawyer may explain the same set of facts in some different fashion. His client did not try to hire the hoodlum to kill his wife. The hoodlum, who so testified, is a liar and a convict who stands to gain by helping the prosecuting attorney in this case. His client loved another woman and wanted a divorce, but he is intelligent enough to know he would destroy his life by committing murder, particularly such a crude and inept killing as this one. What happened was that his wife caught the defendant and his lover in the garage of their home and threatened both their lives with her revolver. He grappled with her and in trying to take the gun away from her it accidentally discharged and killed her. Therefore, his client is not guilty of first-degree murder.[10]

Religious narratives such as the account of God creating heaven and earth and placing Adam and Eve in the garden of Eden serve a similar explanatory function, as do the mythic stories of Greece and Rome.

Historical explanations are often cast in the form of plausible narratives in which important personages such as heads of states, military officers, and social and cultural leaders make decisions and enact plans which explain the way events unfolded.

Empathy as Explanation   Scholars may try to create understanding by writing their accounts in such a way that the readers empathize with the human actors. The explanations furnished by works of art are often of this kind. We may attend a play, empathize with a leading character, and come away feeling that we now have a greater understanding of the human conditions revealed in the play. In the sense of empathy as explanation, Shakespeare's characterizations of King Claudius and of Macbeth explain ambition and murder.

Some humanistic scholars strive to create empathic understanding by writing history in such a way that they recreate the experience of the people involved. If I could write the history of Revolutionary rhetoric in America in such a way that the reader could empathize with Patrick Henry or his listeners when he spoke on the encroachments of the British crown on the liberty of Virginians, or if I could write a rhetorical criticism of the televised speeches of Richard Nixon in such a way that the reader who had not seen them could empathize with those who did, I would provide understanding in the empathetic sense.

Summary

Science searches for universal agreement about invariable relations. These regularities are expressed in low-level laws of two general types: (1) concept laws which express a number of invariable relationships such as *water* or *iron*, and (2) process laws such as "Water, when heated, boils."

Concept formation plays an equally important part in the knowledge about communication and rhetoric. Few concepts in communication are laws of nature. Operational definitions are often the basis for clarifying concepts in both the natural and the social sciences. Quite often, however, theorists have been preoccupied with finding other than operational definitions for terms such as *rhetoric* and *communication*.

Some definitions in communication are conventional. We can, within limits, make our terms mean what is most suitable for our purposes as long as we agree about the meanings. Some definitions in communication are descriptive statements about observable features of reality phrased in definitional form. Some definitions in communication and rhetoric are prescriptive statements. Although they take the form of definitions, they function as guides to action and ethical choice.

Concepts are the basis for one important type of theoretical structure in both communication and science. Taxonomies (systems of classification) that order elements, species, genres, communication contexts, rhetorical figures, or television-program formats are based on concepts. If the concepts of a taxonomy are conventional, the classification system resembles the theory erected by scientific taxonomies based on concept laws, but it does not provide the same sort of knowledge. If experience does not square with a conventional taxonomy it is a simple matter to set up new conventional definitions. However, should experience falsify the taxonomy thought to be invariably related to a concept law, it would throw doubt on the lawfulness of the other concepts in the taxonomy.

Concepts in the natural sciences not only are laws in themselves but frequently are invariably related to other concepts in the form of process laws. There are generalizations in communication that take the form of process laws and use concepts in much the same way; such concepts, however, are often the result of conventional or descriptive definitions and provide, at best, a quasi law.

Probability can be phrased in terms of operationally defined concepts and statistical inferences. Probability statements tend to be more precise than the hunches of practitioners. They should not, however, be confused with the statistical laws of physics, which are based on the assumption that the random activity of subatomic particles will result in predictable general patterns of such things as the decay rate of radioactive materials.

One important function of theories of all kinds is to explain the events covered by their scope or domain. One form of explanation involves clarification in syntactical terms. Another explanatory form emphasizes the semantical dimension.

One of the ways that theories in the natural sciences may provide explanations is by providing a process law which links results to causes. Some communication theories provide explanations in the form of causal accounts, but since they are based on probability statements, they provide explanations of likely contingencies rather than invariable connections.

Explanations in communication may take the form of attributing results to inherent tendencies or of accounting for patterns of communicative behavior in terms of social norms or conventional rules.

Other explanations of communication events may take the form of attributing motives, meanings, and purposes to the human actors involved in the episodes.

Plausible narratives provide a meaningful interpretation of events, and empathic participations in such narratives provide a qualitative explanation of what the events were like.

Notes

1. An interesting experiment which created an arbitrary mini-linguistic system is reported in W. Barnett Pearce, Vernon E. Cronen, and Ken Johnson, "The Structure of Communication Rules and the Form of Conversation: An Experimental Simulation," paper delivered at the annual meeting of the Speech Communication Association, Minneapolis, Minn., 1978.

152

Science and the Nature
of Knowledge about
Communication

2. Guy Burniston Brown, *Science, Its Method and Its Philosophy* (London: Allen and Unwin, 1950).

3. My definitions of fantasy themes, fantasy chains, and rhetorical visions can be found in Ernest G. Bormann, "Fantasy and Rhetorical Vision: The Rhetorical Criticism of Social Reality," *Quarterly Journal of Speech* 58 (1972): 396–407. Sykes uses the term *myth* for much the same phenomenon; see A.J.M. Sykes, "Myth in Communication," *Journal of Communication* 20 (1970): 17–31.

4. See, for example, Karlyn Kohrs Campbell and Kathleen Hall Jamieson, eds., *Form and Genre: Shaping Rhetorical Action* (Falls Church, Virginia: Speech Communication Association, 1978).

5. Ralph G. Nichols and Thomas R. Lewis, *Listening and Speaking* (Dubuque, Iowa: Wm. C. Brown, 1954), p. 8.

6. This discussion of statistical laws is drawn from John G. Kemeny, *A Philosopher Looks at Science* (Princeton: Princeton University Press, 1959), pp. 65–81.

7. This explanation follows the general analysis of Carl Hempel and Paul Oppenheim, "The Logic of Explanation," in Herbert Feigl and May Brodbeck, eds., *Readings in the Philosophy of Science* (New York: Appleton-Century-Crofts, 1953), pp. 319–352. For a review of literature on theory construction, explanation, necessity, and causality see Virginia McDermott, "The Literature on Classical Theory Construction," *Human Communication Research* 2 (1975): 83–013.

8. Abraham Kaplan, *The Conduct of Inquiry: Methodology for Behavioral Science* (San Francisco: Chandler, 1964) p. 97.

9. W. G. Runciman, *A Critique of Max Weber's Philosophy of Social Science* (Cambridge: Cambridge University Press, 1972), p. 72.

10. For an article on storytelling as legal explanation, see W. Lance Bennett, "Storytelling in Criminal Trials: A Model of Social Judgment," *Quarterly Journal of Speech* 64 (1978): 1–22; fantasy themes are essentially narratives or stories. For an account of how they provide explanations of events, see Bormann.

7

Critiques of Communication Theory

Having laid the groundwork for a critique of general communication theory in Chapters 5 and 6, I turn now to the examination of knowledge about communication. I begin with a summary of the various expressions of unrest that characterized the 1970s and then turn to a focused critique on the quasi-paradigm of variable analytic studies.

The Controversy over Covering Law, Rules, and Systems

In the 1970s the scholars making humanistic and social scientific studies of communication began to examine alternative approaches to the development of communication theory. The lack of progress in developing adequate theories, as documented in earlier chapters, resulted in an impulse to make a systematic study of the research enterprise.

The first strong expression of that impulse came in the mid-1970s with a number of convention programs and journal articles concerned with alternative approaches to theory and research. The impulse took the form of a three-part frame of analysis. Various partisans compared and contrasted the covering law, systems, and rules viewpoints as feasible and useful perspectives from which to develop theoretical explanations of communication.

The impulse toward philosophical analysis first came to general attention in convention papers and programs. For example, in 1975, Berger, Cushman, and Monge presented papers dealing with the covering law, the rules, and the systems perspectives.[1] The title of a symposium that subsequently appeared as the entire issue of *Communication Quarterly* in which the three papers were published was "Alternative Theoretical Bases for the Study of Human Communication." The issue also contained essays by Pearce, Delia, Hawes, and Rossiter.[2]

The debate began by attacks on the assumption that theories of a hypothetico-deductive type such as Newton's were either possible or appropriate for human communication. Monge in suggesting a systems viewpoint and Cushman and his associates in arguing for a rules viewpoint either directly or by implication suggested that covering laws were unlikely to provide satisfactory explanations of human behavior. Berger and Miller were leaders among those who stepped forward to argue the usefulness of searching for covering laws.[3] Those advocating a rules or systems viewpoint suggested that covering laws might be found for biophysical motion and behavioristic stimulus-response patterns, but that laws were unlikely to cover human action that involved the conscious choice of actors who had intentions, made plans, followed conventional rules, or applied practical arguments to their planning and decision-making.

The attacks on the lawfulness of human behavior also included the notion that the unified, dynamic, process nature of reality was unlikely to be adequately explained by mechanistic laws. The process nature of communication implied some organismic metaphor characterized by dynamic and reciprocal interrelationships.

Implied, but seldom specifically articulated, was the age-old philosophical (and theological) question of freedom of the will versus determinism. If human actors can choose to establish norms, rules, and conventions and can further choose to conform or not conform to those arbitrary constraints, then freedom of will is implied. If systems can be closed, then investigators may be able to discover enough concept and process laws so that by defining the state of the system at a given time, they can, by the application of the suitable laws, predict the state of the system at any subsequent time. If, however, human communication systems can never be closed because of human symbolic action, then such predictions cannot be made.

In Chapters 5 and 6 I examined essentially the same issues discussed in the controversy over covering laws, systems, and rules, with the exception of the question of whether or not concept and process laws convering human communication are logically impossible. As I will indicate in greater detail later in this chapter, I believe that laws in the form of generalizations such as "Water, when heated, boils" are unlikely. However, the question of whether or not investigators can develop scientific laws governing human communication is a question of fact. They will or will not be developed, and conjecture about future facts, while interesting and sometimes entertaining, seldom contributes to the scholarly enterprise in the long run. My hunch is that some scholars will continue to search for covering laws and theories no matter what discussions we have about the possibility of discovering such laws. Historically the reductionists have been remarkably successful. There were early arguments that although investigators could find scientific laws for inanimate matter, they would fail when they came to study the living organism. Subsequent scientific investigations of cell biology began to reduce cellular activity to chemical electromagnetic laws. The next barrier was said to be the point where living matter merges with consciousness. Again, some argued that while physical laws might be useful in accounting for life processes, the higher mental processes and consciousness itself could never be reduced to physiological bases. Subsequent scientific investigations of such things as the brain and brain waves have made substantial progress in explaining conscious states in physiological terms. My point is that those interested in a science of communication ought to be encouraged to continue. Past failures can be accounted for without recourse to the assumption that covering laws can never, in principle, apply to human communication.

A Critique of the Tripartite Analysis

The excitement and enthusiasm the immediate postwar years for scientific study of human communication was fading by the 1970s. Studies became mechanical and research summaries pedestrian; theorizing seemed, in the words of Delia and Grossberg, "so distanced from the meaningfulness of the social world as to yield abstractions without grounding." These abstractions seemed "either trivial or nonsensical to everyday social actors."[4] The tripartite analysis served a useful function in bringing to the attention of scholars the problems plaguing their research and theory. Those who were practicing the quasi-paradigm of variable analytic studies began to join one or another position or to reexamine their research and theory and come to its defense.

Dividing the world of communication theory and research into three parts, however, brought with it certain confusions and served to muddy some important distinctions. One major confusion related to the indiscriminate use of the term *theory* in the early discussions. Some scholars referred to the viewpoints reflected in the discussions as covering law *theories*, systems *theories*, and rules *theories*. Using the same name for each implied that all were of the same kind. Closer examination revealed that the three differed in substantial ways.

There are difficulties inherent in including covering law theory in the same class for comparative purposes with rules and systems perspectives. Every investigator has a viewpoint. The term *rules theory* often turned out to be another label for the assumption that important human action, particularly communication action, is based upon regularities which can be accounted for in terms of human intentions, agreed-upon norms, conventions, and rule-conforming behavior and that the best that covering laws can do is to to describe human motion. *Systems theory* often turned out to be another name for the assumption that all things and all human actions are organically interrelated, that while investigators can define boundaries for systems and subsystems, these boundaries are seldom closed, and that systems, however defined, are all interrelated and in totality come to more than the sum of their parts. Investigators seeking to discover covering laws have a viewpoint also. They assume the phenomena under study exhibit some invariable relationships, that these invariable relationships will hold in the future as they have in the past, and that they can discover and describe these relationships.

A covering law theory, however, is not a viewpoint. A hypothetico-deductive system such as Newton's is an actual thought structure with certain properties and potentials for prediction and control and with the power to give a scientific explanation for phenomena. By confusing a viewpoint with a theory, investigators often made unreasonable demands on viewpoints; they tried to get them to yield research topics, which such perspectives cannot do. In other words, we should not draw an analogy between a covering law theory (which can serve as a mathematical system from which we can derive hypotheses for research) and a viewpoint like a rules perspective.

Cronkhite and Liska made somewhat the same point that I am making by drawing a distinction between two kinds of scientific metaphors. They suggested that a distinction be drawn between *epistemological* and *explanatory* metaphors. They would reserve the term *explanatory metaphor* for hypothetico-deductive and similar theories and the term *epistemological metaphor* for what I have been calling viewpoints.[5]

Another problem with the tripartite analysis relates to the more fundamental issue of whether or not scientific laws can be discovered to account for human communication. In a critique of the "laws-rules-systems trichotomy," Cronen and Davis argued that "the analytical implications of this typology are serious because it confounds distinctive levels of theoretical decision making."[6] Cronen and Davis pointed out that the discussion often equates laws with the invariable relations associated with hypothetico-deductive theories or with deterministic causality, equates system with logical necessity, and equates rules with indeterminancy and contingencies. Approaching the question of freedom of the will from the tripartite framework beclouds the issue, since, according to Cronen and Davis, a good theory of human communication might involve a mixture of invariable relations, logical necessity, and practical force. They suggested that a rules perspective might result in a theory that included laws of nature as well as accounts of conventional regularities. They also argued that an open system perspective would involve practical necessity as well as logical force.

Berger made a similar point when he argued that the rules perspective need not rule out causal laws. Berger suggested that knowing the rules operative in a given communication episode enables one to explain only those episodes that unfold in conformity to the rules. Knowledge of the rules does not enable one to explain those incidences when participants decide not to follow the rules. A hypothetico-deductive theory that provided laws describing the decision-making processes of the participants would provide a better explanation than the description of the conventional rules relating to the episode. To step even further back, Berger argued that laws would be possible and useful to answer such questions as what social forces produced what kinds of conventions and rules, how rules and conventions are transmitted to neophytes, and how they evolve and change through time.[7]

I am in essential agreement with Cronen and Davis when they charged the tripartite analysis with confounding "distinctive levels of theoretical decision making."[8] In earlier chapters I have explicated the same issues and discussed the problems involved in the development of laws, probability generalizations, tendencies, norms, and rules. Conceptualizing the problems of theory building in terms of the levels of analysis depicted in Figure 3, Chapter 3, provides another framework that spells out the problems of theoretical scope as well as the issue of scientific determinism versus human freedom and choice.

The Controversy over Epistemological Positions

The impulse to critique the state of research and theory in communication expressed itself in discussion of philosophical assumptions as well as controversy over theory types. The argument began with a challenge to behaviorism, which the critics equated with logical positivism; moved to a summary of the arguments presented by professional philosophers who had attacked logical positivism some years earlier; and concluded with the presentation of an alternative philosophical position.

Typical of the attack was that of O'Keefe, who argued that logical positivism was now largely abandoned by philosophers of science.[9] He summarized the typical charges that philosophers had made against logical positivism. He reiterated the arguments against such tenets of positivism as that observational statements are straightforward and to be sharply distinguished from theoretical statements, that operational definitions provide an adequate account of the meaning of scientific concepts and laws, and that good data are comparable no matter what theoretical framework governed those who gathered them.

O'Keefe applied the analysis to communication theory and research and found that "as long as one holds the positivistic view that observations are theory-free, one can afford to go about randomly doing whatever experimental study comes to mind and strikes one's fancy."[10] The investigators governed by such an assumption produce research findings which "all too often end up as a string of unconnected results, devoid of significance."[11] O'Keefe suggested that communication theorists and researchers should take the assumption that there is no possibility of a theory-free observational language as a basis for their work and submit their assumptive systems to public analysis and controversy. "What must be encouraged is public discussion of the conceptual foundations of theoretical approaches to communication."[12] He concluded that in addition to the renunciation of the positivistic philosophy of science, what was required was "a reconceptualization of the study of human communication . . . that stresses conceptual analysis and programmatic research."[13]

Delia subsequently elaborated on the O'Keefe attack on logical positivism by suggesting an alternative philosophical base for communication research.[14] Delia labeled the assumptive system *constructivism* and characterized it as one based on the "underlying root metaphor . . . of the 'organism.'"[15] The whole is that which is organic and "the multiple forms created in the course of development are dependent upon the nature and organization of the whole."[16]

In contrast to the logical positivistic position that knowledge is based upon relatively theory-free observations, the constructivist position assumes that "observations are theory-laden."[17] Relying heavily upon Kuhn's analysis of paradigms, Delia argued that operational definitions, quantification techniques such as the semantic differential, and other methodological concerns are inherently tied in with the assumptive system of the investigators. Too often researchers in communication worked from tacit assumptions that were crude and unexamined tenets of logical empiricism, and the result was that fuzzy concepts led to fuzzy results. He urged programmatic research based upon consciously articulated assumptive systems in which the role of the intellectual community as the arbiter of ideas would be emphasized.

Where O'Keefe had summarized philosophical arguments against logical positivism, Delia presented a detailed and thorough critique of the variable analytic research tradition in communication. Specifically, he examined the source credibility studies and, building upon previous critiques by Applbaum and Anatol, Baudhuin and Davis, Tucker, and Cronkhite and Liska, submitted them to a slashing attack from their conceptualizations and theoretical groundings to their research designs and implementations.[18]

Delia suggested that a constructivist world view which sought to examine credibility in such a way that it squared with the commonsense experiences of people in everyday affairs would provide a better assumptive system for the study of ethos. Delia described constructivism as a view that saw human beings striving after meaning and that defined perception in terms of the selective attention to particular aspects of the environment. For Delia the proper study of credibility involved the study of the impression processes by which people actively interpreted their environment and evaluated others within specific communicative contexts. He submitted as good examples of the constructivist approach a series of studies that he and his associates had made in examining the processes of impression formation, the persuasive strategies of children, and the processes of social construal and behavioral control of communication.[19]

Delia's approach to constructivism had a phenomenological flavor.[20] Hawes, however, presented another critique of logical positivism and contrasted it with a more thoroughgoing phenomonology. He recommended that communication researchers adopt a "hermeneutic phenomenology of communication."[21] Hawes characterized logical positivism as preoccupied with epistemological questions—a concern with the causal patterns to be found in a taken-for-granted world. Phenomonology, on the other hand, deals with ontological questions—a concern with how the world is continually being constituted. The question for phenomenologists of communication relates to "what is real" and "how realness is accomplished."[22]

Hawes viewed communication as central to the ontological questions, since "the primary stuff of which social worlds are constituted is communication." People construct their social realities by and through communication. Critical analyses of communication which put out of play the familiar commonsense world and make the everyday communication unfamiliar open the way for interpretative criticism. The phenomenological investigator would ask what "communicative work members" do to "accomplish perpetually their being" and how they do it. By contrast, positivists assume the social world and interpret it for the participants in social scientific terms.[23]

Hawes would have phenomonological communication scholars formulate research questions "from the perspective of the members and in the terms they use to account for their actions."[24] They should be concerned with what a communication event is and how it is produced. Where the positivist is concerned with the nature of the product, the phenomenologist is concerned with how things came into being. Hawes submitted the work that he and his associates had done in the analysis of natural talk as examples of the way research could relate to a phenomenological perspective.

Pragmatism, particularly through the influence of the progressive education movement under the leadership of such philosophers as John Dewey, was influential during the years of rapid growth in the study of communication. The tenets of pragmatism served as important elements in the assumptive system governing early investigators in public discussion, which was the forerunner of small group communication. Dewey's formulation of the process of reflective thinking served as the basis for the steps in the discussion process.[25] Thonssen and Baird wrote much of their methodological advice on how to criticize speeches from a pragmatist perspective.[26] Kaplan's influential research manual was based largely on pragmatism.[27]

Pragmatism, like logical positivism, is an empirical position which relies upon experience as the ultimate justification for knowledge and truth. However, the two positions differ on the nature of proof for linguistic statements. Logical positivism divides statements into sense and non-sense; into those which are meaningful and those which are not. Logical positivism sees all meaningful statements as analytic or as statements which say something about the world. Positivists would then verify the truth or falsity of empirical statements by observing whether or not what they assert is the case. Pragmatism examines all statements in terms of what William James called their "cash value." Pragmatism sees all statements whether of value, of mathematics, or of fact as potentially useful. Pragmatists would establish meaning not by operational definitions but by exploring all the practical implications of believing the concept or statement to be true. For pragmatists a difference to be a difference must make a difference. A leading pragmatist, Peirce, suggested that a statement is meaningful if "it can enter into the making of a decision, and its meaning is analyzable in terms of the difference it makes to the decision taken."[28]

For pragmatists, statements and logical forms used in the process of inquiry are not true or false; rather, they are warranted by virtue of having facilitated successful inquiry. The more frequently ideas and logical forms are used in successful inquiry, the more warranted assertibility they have.[29]

Bloom also submitted logical positivism to a critique, but he recommended pragmatism as the preferred perspective for research in communication. He argued that positivism relegates "statements which express values to the limbo-like domain of emotive or affective meaning . . . the scientifically meaningless."[30] Bloom noted that declaring value statements to be of no scientific use severely limited communication inquiry. He turned next to operationism and made an argument similar to O'Keefe's against the usefulness of a narrowly operational approach to definitions.

Bloom's major argument in behalf of a pragmatic perspective was that it opened up the possibility of investigating values and moral decisions. The pragmatists would argue that when moral decisions are made in a reflective way, they follow the pattern common to the process of inquiry.

> After recognizing a problem, we formulate possible solutions to the problem. After considering the consequences of these hypotheses and judging which are most relevant, the chosen hypothesis is put to the test. If the results of that test—whether vicarious trial-and-error or experimental demonstration—provide a solution, i.e., produce a belief or warranted assertion, inquiry ceases. If not, the process begins anew. For the pragmatist, the difference between scientific and moral questions is a contextual rather than a substantive matter.[31]

The controversy with respect to research and theory in the 1970s expressed itself in several directions. These various attacks represented an impulse rather than a movement, and the impulse tended to land tangential blows on what I believe should be the main target, i.e., a clearly identifiable concrete research tradition which is characterized by exemplar research designs, which has a common assumptive system and world view, and which is devoted to solving puzzles within that quasi-research paradigm. Elsewhere in this book I describe the research tradition that I have in mind and label it the *quasi-paradigm of variable analytic studies*.

An attack on behaviorism is an attack on the historical roots of the variable analytic studies in communication, but it is unfocused in that the evolution of the research approach has removed such studies from a radical behaviorist position. Attacks on logical positivism are too diffuse and broad in that an investigator could be a logical positivist and undertake a wide range of scholarly studies in addition to the variable analytic investigations. Indeed, as Miller and Berger have cogently argued, it is very difficult to have a scientific perspective without some form of empiricism as a foundation.[32] Attacks on operationism are likewise applicable to a much broader range of investigative method than that characteristic of the variable analytic quasi-paradigm. While philosophically a strictly operational position may be difficult to defend, in practice most of the natural and social sciences do depend upon very carefully specified observational procedures as the bedrock for their studies.

The logical positivist tradition, while it may have had excesses and while philosophers have found weaknesses in original formulations of the positions, has made some strong contributions to research in the social sciences. Such concepts as validity and reliability of quantification and the importance of integrating mathematical systems with the data so that they fulfill the assumptions of the mathematics are essentially due to logical positivism. Even such a thoroughgoing pragmatist as Kaplan admits the usefulness of such analysis.[33] My point is that we can focus our critique on the quasi-paradigm of the variable analytic studies without denying the usefulness of the social scientific study of communication, the potential power of behaviorism, or the fruitfulness of an essentially logical empirical perspective for research.[34]

Focusing the Criticism

Generally we ought to be open to alternative modes of study of communication, since we have not as yet developed any widely successful approaches in accounting for communication. However, when scholars have spent three decades on a certain line of investigation and have developed clear recipes for conducting studies and when the program has failed on its own terms to develop theory, I believe we ought not justify continuing the approach with the general argument that we ought to encourage all approaches to the study of communication. Further, I believe that some potentially fruitful alternatives will incorporate social scientific investigations and humanistic studies in complementary and supportive ways. But we must first clear the ground of the biases against such complementary work which are part of the variable analytic tradition.

I believe that the uneasiness with research and theory in communication in the 1970s was largely due to the shortcomings of the influential quasi-paradigm of variable analytic studies, but because the attack was diffused into wider and more abstract philosophical issues, it was less useful than it might have been.

The quasi-paradigm is solidly based upon discovering and isolating the variables which invariably interact in dynamic communication processes. Bowers, in a handbook on doing research within the variable analytic tradition, used a series of studies by Miller and Hewgill as models of communication research. He noted that the Speech Association of America awarded them a prize for excellence in 1967.[35] The Miller and Hewgill studies will serve me as a way to define by example what I mean by the quasi-paradigm of variable analytic studies.

Miller and Hewgill studied the interactions among the variables of fear appeals, source credibility, and attitude change. They based their research hypotheses on consistency "theories" such as cognitive dissonance and congruity. Their research problems were based on previous research in that earlier investigation had indicated that mild fear appeals were more effective than strong ones. They developed a hypothesis that strong fear appeals might be more effective than weak ones if all the relevant variables were taken into account.

Miller and Hewgill manipulated the variables of source credibility and fear appeals. Their research hypotheses included statements like "If a source has high credibility with a listener, appeals that elicit strong fear for persons highly valued by the listener will effect greater attitude change than appeals that elicit mild fear."[36] They then developed two messages in the form of interviews discussing such civil-defense measures as building fallout shelters. They selected subjects from Michigan elementary school PTA groups. They manipulated the source credibility variable by introducing the interviewee as a national authority on the effects of radiation for some statements and as a high school sophomore for others. After the subjects heard the message they were given a test booklet with semantic differential type scales to index the credibility of the sources and with other semantic differential type scales to check attitudes.

They interpreted the results using sophisticated statistical treatments such as the Kruskal-Wallis one-way analysis of variance. They discovered that the interaction effects among the two manipulated variables (level of fear appeal and source credibility) and the dependent variable (attitude change) were in the direction anticipated and so unusual that they were unlikely to have happened by chance.

The general earmarks of variable analytic studies are illustrated by the Miller and Hewgill investigations. Generally, investigators clearly delineate relevant variables, develop brief written or oral messages or short group meetings, manipulate variables by changing the directions they give the subjects in experimental and control groups, and "measure" the variables by scaling techniques often of the semantic differential type. Investigators usually seek some "theoretical" basis, since the quasi-paradigm stresses the importance of deriving research hypotheses from theory. Usually the theoretical implications of the results are discussed at the conclusion of a research report in the interest of the theory-building function of research.

Investigators doing research within the quasi-paradigm tried to develop experiments that would test and establish hypotheses in order to discover functional laws that would predict outcomes in the same way the laws of physics and chemistry do. They sought to find a theory of the Newtonian type to cover human communication behavior.

The shortcomings of the quasi-paradigm have become obvious, and the first-rate practitioners within its assumptions are admitting that it turned out to be a dead end. Berlo, who was an important figure in the postwar development of the quasi-paradigm, wrote in 1977:

> The fact of the matter is that, like many of my colleagues, I simply did not understand the underlying assumptions and theoretical consequences of what I believed and had not grasped the limited fertility of the research tradition in which I had been trained.[37]

Berlo went on to judge, "If we are trying to implement the view that the only *substance* is *flux*, that *the what of being is the how of becoming*, that *organization is change in relationship*, we need a new game, new rules, new guidelines for inquiry [Berlo's italics]."[38]

Miller and Burgoon, two leading practitioners of the quasi-paradigm, noted that the research tradition was waning in popularity and had failed to make much of a contribution to theory. They equated research in persuasion with variable analytic studies, discredited the attitude change investigations, and went on to suggest better ways to investigate persuasion. They suggested that investigators concentrate on such complex phenomena as *strategy* and *style* which might well move the studies out of the assumptive system of the variable analytic quasi-paradigm.[39]

Simons, in 1978, launched a slashing attack on the "persuasion/attitude change area within social psychology." As I interpret his analysis he is attacking what I call the quasi-paradigm of variable analytic studies. Simons was concerned with what he regarded as "the dominant social-psychological approach to the study of persuasion—the attempt to infuse high-level theorizing about so-called basic psychological processes with practical applications." He argued, "Drawn from the physical sciences, this 'covering law' approach has had considerable appeal for three decades now, but the record does not bear out its promise." More directly to my point, he claimed "that the approach not only has not fulfilled the exaggerated claims that have been made for it, but also that it *cannot* fulfill these claims. [Simons' italics.]."[40] In order to explain why the variable analytic tradition cannot in principle fulfill the claims of its proponents to develop theory, I must examine in considerable detail the nature of theorizing in physics. Many of those who have criticized the covering law approach to communication theory have done so in abstract terms and in the style of philosophical analysis of general issues. In order to focus my analysis on the quasi-paradigm I must examine it in light of scientific theory and practice in sufficient detail to make the crucial points. I will take as my exemplar of a covering law theory that of Newton.

Newton's Theory as Covering Law

The puzzle-solving nature of scientific activity, once the basic paradigm is established, can be illustrated by the study of the behavior of a body moving under the impetus of a steady rate of acceleration. If a body starts from a position of rest and has a constant acceleration of 10 feet per second, then its velocity at the end of the first second will be 10 feet per second or a (the same as the rate of acceleration itself). After two seconds the velocity will be 20 feet per second or $2a$. To find the average velocity of a trip in which a body starts from rest and travels for a time at a constant rate of acceleration, one needs to know how long the trip took and the velocity of the object at the end of the trip. Thus, in the example above when the body started from rest the velocity at the beginning of the journey was zero, and if the trip took two seconds, the velocity at the end of the trip was $2a$ or 2×10 feet per second or 20 feet per second. The average speed was then half of 20 feet per second or 10 feet per second.

Because all of these laws or relationships are expressed as mathematical functions, an investigator can use algebraic manipulations to reason from premises to conclusions.

The three features of the scientific method of the physicist and chemist at the turn of the twentieth century kept playing back and forth. Original observations resulted in the induction that velocity equals the distance traveled divided by the time of the journey as well as the inductions about velocity as a function of acceleration and time. Deductive manipulations using the assumptions and rules of algebra result in the derivation of a further relationship. The new relationship could then be checked by investigators who created the proper conditions in the laboratory. Once laboratory investigations supported the derived functional relationships, engineers could approximate the laboratory manipulations in much larger environments and predict the outcomes accurately enough to change them. A vital part of the entire procedure was the ability of the scientists to count accurately and assign numbers to their observations in such a way that the rules of arithmetic applied. They were able to assign a precise numerical value to the distance a body traveled, to a proportion derived by the dividing of one number by another, and to the time involved in a journey. While such counting always had a margin of error, the errors were small enough and the techniques to resolve them well enough agreed upon so that scientists in different laboratories at different times could agree that their observations supported the conclusion, say, that $v^2 = 2as$.

The theory which covers the specific functions outlined above was that originally formulated by Newton. Newton did not formulate his theory until the natural sciences had developed to the point where a number of explanations of phenomena were available to him. The low-level functions integrating the motion of bodies on the surface of the earth which I illustrated with the formulas about velocity and accelerations above were well developed by Newton's time. Galileo had done extensive work with the swing of the pendulum and with falling objects on the surface of the earth, which established the law that the distance an object fell was equal to one-half a constant force of acceleration times the time of the fall squared ($S = \frac{1}{2}Kt^2$).

Copernicus and others had developed an account of the motion of the planets that assumed that the sun was the center of the system rather than the earth. Ptolemy had provided an explanation of the motion of the planets that assumed that the earth was the center and that had worked to predict the position of the planets with considerable accuracy. Copernicus' account worked as well as (but no better than) Ptolemy's explanation. Interestingly enough, a number of scientists were drawn to Copernicus' explanation not because it was better able to predict but because it was simpler and more elegant. That is, they came to accept the new formulation on aesthetic grounds. Kuhn in his historical account of such major changes in scientific theorizing as the one represented by Copernican revolution and by Newtonian theory argues that the participants in the new research paradigms saw the world so differently than did those in the older perspectives that there was no rational basis for argument across perspectives. According to Kuhn's interpretation, a scientist came to Copernicus' account only by translating the old language into the new until the individual was able to "go native" and begin to think in terms of the new paradigm.[41] The aesthetic dimension of scientific and mathematical theories is an important part of their appeal. Poincaré was of the opinion that the right solution to mathematical problems was always aesthetically of the right form. On those few occasions when he had a flash of creative insight into the solution of a mathematical problem and upon checking out the answer discovered that he was wrong, the erroneous solution was *of the same form* as the right solution when he discovered it. Indeed, Poincaré maintained that his creativity contained a "delicate sieve" which only allowed solutions of the proper form to surface from his foreconsciousness to his consciousness.[42]

Newton was working at a time when the field of terrestrial mechanics was developed to a point where mathematics and quantification in terms of measurements of distance, time, and mass were possible. Meantime the field of celestial mechanics was developed to the point where the sun was posited to be the center of the solar system and the astronomers had telescopes and other instruments which allowed them to make precise measurements of the angles and positions of heavenly bodies.

Newton's theory was based upon an unifying analogy. Indeed, a fruitful analogy is often the basis of scientific theories and provides another clue to the aesthetic dimension of such thinking.[43] Newton's insight was to see that the fall of the earth toward the sun was analogous to the fall of the apple toward the earth. Newton constructed a number of precisely defined concepts that fit into one overarching functional relationship and that, when accompanied by a dictionary or a set of directions as to how to apply the function to a given concrete situation by mathematical deduction, would yield mathematical formulas, which further experimentation could confirm or disconfirm. Newton's theory was similar in form to the law relating distance to the time of fall for a freely falling body ($S = \frac{1}{2}Kt^2$). Mathematicians could derive applications of Newton's theory in the same way they could derive $v^2 = 2as$ from the basic laws relating to time, distance traveled, and acceleration. The major difference was that Newton's general formula covered Galileo's laws of motion and Copernicus' laws of astronomy. Thus, the argumentative structure of the theory had three rather than two levels, as indicated in Figure 5.

The power of Newton's theory and its great impact on intellectual life in the years following its discovery resulted partially from the way experiment after experiment and practical application after practical application turned out as the derived mathematical computations predicted they would.

Newton's theory consists essentially of the general law that the force pulling two bodies together is proportional to the product of their masses and inversely proportional to the square of the distance between their centers. Again the law can be expressed as a mathematical function in terms of concepts which can be assigned precise numerical descriptions.

$$F = K\frac{M_1 M_2}{R^2}$$

In the formula, F is the force of attraction, M_1 and M_2 are the masses of

Figure 5 Argumentative structure of Newton's theory as related to laws of terrestrial and celestial mechanics.

Third Level:	Newton's Theory	
Second Level:	Galileo's laws derived from Newton	Copernicus's laws derived from Newton
First Level:	$v^2 = 2as$ as derived from Galileo's laws	Computation of a given planet's position at a certain time in the future
	Observations of objects set in motion in laboratory	Observation of planet's position through telescope

the bodies, R is the distance between their centers, and K is a constant force known as the constant of gravitation. By applying the general formula to the motion of the planets an astronomer can compute their orbits around the sun. The essential technique is that of discovering the vector forces upon the earth, for instance, when the direct fall into the sun is modified by the gravitational pull of other planets and the speed of the earth around the sun. Objects on the surface of the earth fall with a uniform acceleration because the distance from the surface to the center of the earth is so much larger than the distance above the earth from which the objects fall that the acceleration of gravity in the formula $S = \frac{1}{2}at^2$ turns out to be a constant. On the surface of the earth the constant of gravity is a bit more than 32 feet per second per second.

Newton's general law could thus predict the course of the planets as well as the fall of the apple. However, Newton's theory was so abstract and covered so many instances that before technicians could make practical applications to such matters as ballistics or predicting eclipses of the sun they had to do a great deal of mathematical computation.

Newton's theory was based upon the assumption that the force of gravity was unvarying and ubiquitous throughout the universe and for all time. The theory anticipated that the earth's orbit would continue in the future according to the dictates of gravity and that the earth's orbit in the past was a function of the same force. One could postdict eclipses as well as predict them. All objects in all climes and geographical places would drop toward the earth with the same acceleration, according to the Newtonian theory.

In the practice of normal science, the community members participating in a disciplinary matrix focus their attention on certain puzzles that require solving. Their tacit assumptions and the rules of the research paradigm bring them to examine a uniquely defined set of concepts and the related observations of factual material. One of the important areas of factual study is those materials which the paradigm singles out as particularly useful in accounting for the nature of things. Thus, scientists practicing normal science in the Newtonian paradigm investigated such facts as velocity, the constant of gravitation, mass, and time. As a science matures, investigators tend to develop more and more precise ways of determining the nature of such facts. In the natural sciences the tendency has been to build more and more complex and special apparatus for the observations relating to the basic concepts.

While not a paradigm in the sense in which Kuhn defines scientific paradigms, the exemplar of the variable analytic studies functioned in many ways analogously to the way paradigms function in the practice of normal science. Participants in the attitude change school of research, for example, focused their attention on such concepts and related factual observations as *source credibility, message variables,* and *receiver attitudes.* They developed more and more precise ways to elaborate and observe receiver personality traits such as dogmatism, tolerance for ambiguity, and complexity of cognitive style. The majority of the methods for observing the features of a communication event that the exemplar focused upon as being particularly important for explaining communicating were paper-and-pencil rating, evaluating, and testing procedures.

Variable Analytic Quasi-Paradigm Compared to Newtonian Paradigm

The analogy between Newtonian mechanics and behaviorist psychology proved to be more figurative than literal. The experimentalists in communication research caught up in the exemplar of variable analytic studies stretched the analogy even more, since they were, almost of necessity, interested in symbolic matters for which the behavior of subjects was often a poor index. A follower of Hull or Skinner could observe the rat running a maze for its food or performing in a Skinner box, but the investigator studying a subject's change in attitude could not see the motion within the central nervous system which accompanied the change. Their general procedure was a testing technique called the *semantic differential.*[44] In using the semantic differential the investigator asks the subject to introspectively assess the change within his or her symbolic interpretation of the world and supply an estimate as to how many units along some two- or three-dimensional space the meanings had been rearranged as a result of the manipulation of the communication variables involved in the experiment. Usually the investigator provides a pictorial representation of the space in the form of some scale and asks for pencil marks to indicate distance on the scale.

The physicists were dealing with invariable relationships. The law of gravity seemed to work everwhere in the universe and seemed to have operated through history. The law of gravity yielded computations which postdicted events in the past as well as predicting the future. The operations of the whole magnificent system were exemplified by the fall of one apple. (No need for the investigator in the Newtonian paradigm to take a careful random sample of falling apples to assure that some were large and some small, some green and some ripe, some crab and some winesap.)

The investigators employing their analogy of Newtonian mechanics to the study of communication events were unable to quantify their variables as did the natural scientists. Communication scholars knew that quantification was the key to the success of the method. Historically the breakthrough in the development of functional laws came when investigators found ways to measure such variables as time. The researchers in communication used scaling devices and other psychological testing procedures to quantify variables. But the resulting numbers did not fulfill assumptions of such mathematics as arithmetic, algebra, geometry, and calculus. Communication theorists could not use the numbers to express functional relationships in mathematical terms and have their observations confirm or negate the functional connections.

Since they could not use the mathematics of functions, particularly algebra and calculus, investigators turned to statistical mathematics for the bulk of their deductive systems. Statistical mathematical systems were able to provide estimates of the odds that a given variance between two factors was due to chance or due to some lawful relationship or probable regularity. The statistical treatments could not provide a functional relationship between two factors so that knowing the value of one at a given time a person could compute precisely the quantitative value of the other at that time. Thus two of the most important features of the scientific paradigm of Newton were lacking from the quasi-paradigm of early investigators in communication who saw as one of their central variables the concept of "attitude change."

Since the Newtonian theory was based upon a number of prior mathematically expressed functional relationships, the efforts of theoreticians in the new "science" of communication to develop communication theory along the model of Newton were bound to fail. They never had the equivalent of $S = \frac{1}{2}Kt^2$ to work with. Newton would not have been able to formulate the law of gravity without the prior work of Galileo, Copernicus, and others. Given the state of laws relating to mechanics in Newton's day, someone else might well have formulated the theory had Newton never been born. Without low-level laws expressing functional relationships, without measurements to fulfill the assumptions of mathematical systems that express functions, the search for a consistently integrated body of laws bound together by a unifying analogy was logically impossible.

Many communication scholars also wished to derive their hypotheses from theory so that they would not dissipate their efforts in isolated, meaningless, and random studies unrelated to one another. But where would they find the theory to guide their investigations? One answer was that handbooks, textbooks, and other instructional materials embodied a crude kind of theory of communication. As we have seen in Chapter 3, in one sense of the term *theory* they were quite right. The communication practices of the mid-twentieth century were intimately related with style-specific special theories that guided practice and supplied the basis for criticism. However, the style-specific theories were artistic rather than scientific. Investigators nonetheless drew from the theories such questions as: Is the anticlimactic order of arguments more persuasive than the climactic order? Is the citation of the source of evidence more convincing than reference to the evidence without mentioning the source? Is it better to mention arguments against your position as well as those in favor of it, or is it better to mention only your side? They raised questions that grew out of style-variant principles (special theories) and that could not in the very nature of the case turn out to guide the investigator to the discovery of invariant laws (general theories).

Many communication scholars also sought deductive completeness and consistency according to the ideal type of hypothetico-deductive theories. Their desire for logical completeness led them to formulate their conclusions and hypotheses into the form of algebraic equations and to manipulate the equations in a deductive way. Unfortunately the equations did not fulfill the assumptions of arithmetic, much less algebra, and so practical applications of the conclusions were not possible.

Historical perspective indicates that even in sciences such as physics and chemistry, ideal types of scientific theories drawn from a given period of scientific development in one disciplinary matrix are so different from theories drawn from a different period that the notion of a universal ideal type for all times and all disciplines is a mistake. Certainly the search for a communication theory based upon the touchstone of the hypothetico-deductive systems of late-nineteenth-century physics and chemistry turned out to be a mistake. Thus, communication scholars striving to learn from the best experience in scientific methodology, practice, and theorizing started down some promising paths in emulating the behavioral psychologists and in studying the philosophers of science. With the hindsight of historical analysis we can now see that the promising paths proved to be dead ends. We also can have an appreciation of their dilemma and their search for appropriate ways to study and account for human communication. They came to the task when science was prestigious. Research, particularly scientific research, was an avenue to personal and professional status. With the sciences at their height of power and prestige, the intellectual communities tended to denigrate communication. The lure of science was thus double strong.

My point is not that they were inept, untalented, or opportunistic. Many psychologists and social psychologists followed the same path. The were, instead, part of the vanguard of scholars studying human behavior and social phenomena who wished to apply the scientific method to their concerns and who found themselves in an intellectual milieu that encouraged the developments that I have described. My foray into a brief historical analysis is primarily to indicate to today's scholar the drift of the past so that future scholarship can be productive. Their effort was not wasted in one sense, because promising paths must be followed even if many come to nothing so that future generations do not keep on going down the same dead ends.

As investigators continued to search for theoretical explanations, deductively integrated and consistent, that would yield further hypotheses for investigation and would serve to provide the basis for practical applications to predict and control communication events, they developed general communication theories designed to provide broad explanatory accounts analogous to Newton's theory. Among the most popular of such formulations which grew out of and supported the quasi-paradigm were the balance theories.

Balance Theories of Communication

One whole family of communication "theories" consisted of *balance* explanations of attitude change. Theorists formulated these explanations after a body of research in the quasi-paradigm of variable analytic studies had accumulated. They expressed the formulations in general terms and then derived hypotheses for future research efforts from the theories. The general shape of the balance theories thus resembled that of the hypothetico-deductive theories.

Balance theories provide an account of why people change their attitudes that suggests that people strive to keep their internal symbolizations consistent. People whose cognitions are in balance maintain their old attitudes. However, when something happens to upset the equilibrium, to unbalance the cognitive consistency, then people strive to achieve equilibrium again, and in doing so they change some of their attitudes. A general law that derives from the balance theories is that to change attitudes a persuader must first upset the equilibrium of the listener and create a strain.

A number of investigators derived research hypotheses from the consistency or balance theories. From among the various balance accounts presented in Chapter 2 and formulated by such scholars as Heider, Newcomb, Osgood, and Tannenbaum I will take Festinger's cognitive dissonance theory as an example.

One team of investigators derived the following conclusions from the dissonance notion: People who make difficult decisions must feel dissonance; therefore, after making the decisions these people will be motivated to reduce the dissonance. One way people might reduce dissonance would be to seek out information and argument in support of their decision and avoid information and argument contrary to it. These investigators then set up a study in which they could observe what advertisements people read after the purchase of a car. Their hypothesis was that people would read more positive advertising about the car they bought than about other cars. They discovered that more people than one would expect by chance did so.[45] Another investigator tested essentially the same hunch by offering subjects eight different appliances in a simulated marketing-research survey and asking them to rate each appliance's attractiveness. The investigator told each subject that she would be given one of the appliances in return for participating in the survey, but since the items were in short supply it would be necessary to choose one of the two attractive appliances. After making the choice the subjects were asked to rate all of the appliances again. The subjects tended to rate the chosen appliances slightly higher than the rejected ones in the post-decision situation.[46]

Investigators derived a number of other hypotheses from the notion of cognitive dissonance, such as that a person who publicly advocates an attitude that goes counter to his or her real attitude will experience dissonance and thus be motivated to shift attitudes, or that a person who is forced to do something that is inconsistent with his or her attitudes or who is handsomely rewarded for doing so will feel less dissonance than someone who acts under less compelling circumstances.

A whole host of investigators launched studies of such derived hypotheses and with each successful rejection of the null hypothesis claimed further support for the theory of cognitive dissonance.[47] Aronson concluded his 1972 review of the theory and research related to cognitive dissonance with this appraisal:

> It is evident that the theory of cognitive dissonance has been a very useful theory. Indeed, in the fifteen years since its inception, it has generated far more research and uncovered more knowledge about human social behavior than any other theory in psychology. At the same time, it should be pointed out that, in formal terms, it lacks the elegance that one usually associates with rigorous scientific statements.[48]

Although the theory of cognitive dissonance, did indeed lack elegance, it did roughly conform to the pattern of the ideal model of hypothetico-deductive theories of the Newtonian type. The basic law that cognitions that are inconsistent cause psychic discomfort and arouse a drive similar to the physiological drives of hunger and thirst and, thus, motivate human beings to seek consistency has wide scope. The assumption is that the cognitive dissonance phenomenon is an unvarying human drive that can account for Julius Caesar's crossing of the Rubicon as well as predict the behavior of a cigarette smoker in the future who reads of new evidence of the danger of smoking. The theorists derive hypotheses from the basic law, which they then submit to experimental test. If subjects behave as the theory predicts in a greater proportion than chance would anticipate, the theory is supported.

The differences between the theory of cognitive dissonance and Newton's theory, however, are more than just a matter of elegance, important as elegance is in the construction of a theory of this sort. Statistical inferences are different from the solutions of the equations of the differential and integral calculus. The mathematics that provides a precise numerical description of variables in a functional relationship is of a different order from the mathematics that provides a numerical estimate of the probability that experimental outcomes can or cannot be accounted for on the basis of chance happenings.

Newton's theory contained three laws of motion, which were often expressed in natural language sentences (as opposed to mathematical sentences). For instance, Newton's first law of motion can be expressed by the sentence "Every body continues in a state of rest or uniform motion in a straight line, unless it is compelled to change that state by the application of some external force." Newton's third law can be expressed by the sentence "To every force or action there is always an equal and opposite reaction."

On the surface the cognitive dissonance notion bears a resemblance to Newton's first law of motion when expressed in ordinary language. With a bit of rephrasing I might say, "Every individual's cognitive system continues in a state of rest unless it is compelled to change that state by the intrusion of some conflicting cognition by an outside message source." However, the analogy is superficial and the similarities are such that I choose to call the cognitive dissonance formulations a *quasi-hypothetico-deductive theory*. Newton's second law can be expressed by the sentence "The net or effective force acting on a body is proportional jointly to the mass and acceleration produced by the force." The second law can also be expressed by the functional relationship $F = ma$. With the translation of the sentence from a natural language assertion to a mathematical function the Newtonian theorists began the development of a mathematically consistent set of laws. Cognitive dissonance theory contains no sentences that can be translated successfully into mathematical functions.[49] The translation difference between the two theories is of such a magnitude that it justifies thinking of cognitive dissonance as a quasi-hypothetico-deductive theory.

A quasi-hypothetico-deductive theory is one that has the form of a theory of the Newtonian type without the substance. The quasi-theory may beguile and mislead us in ways that theories that make no claim at resembling those of nineteenth-century physics and chemistry seldom do.

What difference does it make that cognitive dissonance (and other balance formulations) are in the form of Newton but lack the substance? Might I not argue that the analogy is still a powerful heuristic form, and that consistency and balance theories, by seeing similarities in attitude changes to the changes in position and velocity of bodies at rest and at motion and by drawing the analogy between inertia in mechanical systems and balance among cognitive systems, provide an important explanatory service for communication scholars? In addition, experimental evidence indicates that if the theorists cannot derive hypotheses deductively in the form of mathematics for laboratory testing, they can at least argue plausibly from the assumptions to hypotheses for laboratory investigation, and such studies do indicate a better-than-chance ability to anticipate changes in attitude and behavior. Not only that, but does not the accumulated evidence in support of the derived hypotheses gradually give communication scholars the practical ability to design persuasive messages and campaigns in such a way that they can *engineer* public opinion in much the same way that scientists could apply Newtonian mechanics to engineer a bridge?

Aronson suggests such practical applications when he discusses a hypothetical new owner of a television station setting out to change the audience's opinions on an important issue.

> How do you set about doing it?. . . you present a two-sided argument (because two-sided arguments work best on intelligent people). You arrange your arguments in such a manner that the argument in favor of free medical care is stronger and appears first (in order to take advantage of the primacy effect). You describe the plight of the poor . . . in a manner that inspires a great deal of fear; at the same time you offer a specific plan of action. . . . You present some of the arguments against your position and offer strong refutation of these arguments. You arrange things so that the speaker is an expert, is trustworthy, and is extremely likeable. You make your argument as strongly positive as you are able in order to maximize the discrepancy between the arguments presented and the initial attitude of the audience.[50]

However, Aronson goes on to argue that the world is much more complicated than the summary of research results indicates, and he then provides a series of hypothetical examples in which the above advice would fail to change attitudes.

Despite these similarities, the differences in reasoning between the quasi- and the hypothetico-deductive theory are of such consequences that they essentially negate most of the claims of explanation, prediction, and control for the quasi-hypothetico-deductive theory. Since claims of explanation, prediction, and control are the major justification for theories of the Newtonian type, the failure of consistency theories in these regards is most damaging.

My charge against theories of the cognitive dissonance type is a strong one, and I turn now to my argument in its support. I have been at some pains earlier in the chapter to show how arithmetical and algebraic computations allow one to deduce laws relating to Newtonian mechanics from other laws. The payoff of that discussion comes now as we examine the subtle differences in reasoning between deriving a hypothesis for study from the assumptions of cognitive dissonance and deductively computing a conclusion from the laws of motion.

The process of deduction in the hypothetico-deductive theory proceeds according to the rules of mathematics, while the process of reasoning in deriving a hypothesis from the assumptions of cognitive dissonance theory proceeds linguistically. The procedure by which a theorist draws out plausible meanings from ambiguous terms in the basic formulation of cognitive dissonance is more analogous to the exegetical reasoning of a theologian than to the deductive logic of a physicist. Figure 6 presents a layout of the reasoning process by which a person might compute a conclusion from several laws of motion, by which a person might derive a research hypothesis from assumptions relating to cognitive dissonance, and by which Jonathan Edwards reasoned to a conclusion in a famous sermon. Notice that in the mathematical computation the form of the argument is crucial. We can check the validity of the argument simply by making sure that all of the steps in the proof follow the rules of algebra and arithmetic. In Edwards' exegetical argument, on the other hand, the meanings he attributes to words and combinations of words becomes crucial. Notice, too, how a person moving from the premise that a state of "tension" occurs to the next premise that the tension is "unpleasant" is essentially drawing out one of the possible interpretations of "tension" and making it explicit. The next step in the proof that asserts that people try to avoid the unpleasant is but another way of defining *unpleasant*. That is, the third step is brought in when the concept of unpleasant is brought in in step two.

The important difference between deductive logic and exegetical reasoning is that two theologians may argue vociferously about the validity of a move which goes from the text "Their foot shall slide in due time" to the conclusion "There is nothing that keeps wicked men at any one moment out of hell, but the mere pleasure of God." Two mathematicians would not argue about whether or not one can reduce the formula $s = \frac{1}{2} \frac{av^2}{a^2}$ to $v^2 = 2as$. Two social scientists can, like the theologians, argue over whether or not the tension associated with cognitive dissonance is unpleasant even if they agree that holding two cognitions that are psychologically inconsistent causes tension. One could, for example, argue that the tension resulting from holding two inconsistent cognitions is

FIGURE 6 Layout of reasoning from premise to conclusion in hypothetico-deductive systems, in quasi-hypothetico-deductive systems, and in theological arguments.

Newton	Cognitive Dissonance	Johnathan Edwards
Given: $v = at$ $t = \dfrac{v}{a}$ $t^2 = \dfrac{v^2}{a^2}$ Given: $s = \frac{1}{2}at^2$ Then: $s = \frac{1}{2}\dfrac{av^2}{a^2}$ $2s = \dfrac{v^2}{a}$ $2as = v^2$ Conclusion: $v^2 = 2as$	Given: A state of tension occurs whenever an individual holds two cognitions that are psychologically inconsistent. Therefore: The tension associated with cognitive dissonance is unpleasant. Given: People always try to avoid the unpleasant. Given: What reduces the unpleasant increases the pleasant. Therefore: Cognitive dissonance is reduced, tension is reduced, pleasure increased by changing one or both cognitions. Given: Advocating a position which goes counter to one's attitude creates cognitive dissonance. Conclusion: Counter-attitudinal advocacy will change attitudes in the direction of the advocated attitude.	Given: "Their foot shall slide in due time." Deuteronomy, 32, 35. Therefore: "They are always exposed to destruction." Therefore: They are exposed: "to sudden unexpected destruction." Therefore: They are liable to fall of themselves. Therefore: The only reason they have not yet fallen is because "God's appointed time has not come." Conclusion: "There is nothing that keeps wicked men at any one moment out of hell, but the mere pleasure of God."

pleasurable in that the individual feels on the verge of a creative breakthrough into a newer consciousness and that the tension of creativity is pleasurable.[51] At any rate, the difference in the way the scientist derives a hypothesis for a critical experiment is so different in kind from the way a social scientist derives a hypothesis for an experiment from cognitive dissonance assumptions that they are not the same sort of thing.

Another basic problem with the quasi-hypothetico-deductive theories in communication is that the form is inappropriate to the context. The Newtonian paradigm grew out of investigations into natural phenomena and included a mechanical world view, a way of studying and organizing factual observations, and a way of doing normal science appropriate to the study of material objects. By trying to impose that paradigm on a new set of research problems into human symbolizing and communication phenomena, the communication researchers created an explanatory system divorced from the social realities with which they hoped to deal.[52] Their quasi-paradigm directed their attention to research issues and questions unrelated to the important underlying issues that changing historical circumstances were creating for people everywhere. Although Aronson quickly modified his list of things to do to apply communication research to practical problems by asserting that things are not so simple as the checklist made them seem, his list is not atypical of serious attempts by theorists to synthesize research results and develop practical applications from them.

Newton's theory can be supported or disconfirmed by observations that check predictions deduced mathematically by application of the laws. Festinger's dissonance theory cannot be supported or disconfirmed by observations in the same way. Thus, an experimental subject whose marking of an attitude change scale fails to change significantly after he or she has listened to a message does not disconfirm the dissonance notion, because we can assert that the message failed to create dissonance and thus no change resulted. A body at rest to which an external force was applied and which did not react with an equal and opposite force would disconfirm Newton and throw the whole theory into disarray.

Aronson notes the difficulty but finds it a feature which makes the theory "exciting." He writes "Conceptually, the major weakness in the theory stems from the fact that its application is not limited to situations that are inconsistent on *logical* grounds alone. Rather, the inconsistencies that produce dissonance are *psychological* inconsistencies [emphasis Aronson's]." Psychological inconsistencies, unfortunately, are hard to discover or anticipate. "It is sometimes difficult to be certain what will be psychologically inconsistent for any one person."[53]

Similarly, we can provide alternative explanations for attitude change of the same form as the balance notions, which are plausible and of considerable scope, and there is not a way to choose between them on logical or empirical grounds. As I pointed out in my discussion of Newton earlier, somewhat the same situation was the case with the astronomy of Ptolemy and Copernicus before the development of Newton's theory. However, after Newton, the fact that Galileo's terrestrial mechanics fit into the same conceptual framework as Copernicus's celestial mechanics provided an argument which strengthened the Copernician notions. Alternative explanations for attitude change cannot in principle be distinguished in the same fashion as the Copernician was distinguished from the Ptolemiac astronomy.

We might posit a family of spontaneous combustion "theories" of attitude change which would provide an alternative explanation for the phenomena explained by balance theories. The spontaneous combustion theory asserts that people are always churning out new fantasies, new symbols, new attitudes, and new beliefs. Unless the individual continually receives outside messages supporting and maintaining the status quo or the equilibrium, the individual will experience spontaneous internal upheavals as the forces of the unconscious mind keep boiling up new symbolic fantasies. Because the holding down of the spontaneous eruption is unpleasant and leads to tedium and boredom, people are moved to break out of it or avoid efforts to hold it back; this is roughly analogous to the process involved in trying to keep such drives as hunger and thirst from expression—except that here, the driving force is cognitive discomfort rather than psychological discomfort. How does the individual reduce discomfort? By freeing himself or herself from the forces which restrict free and authentic expression of creativity.

An interesting thing about the spontaneous combustion theories is that they assume that the system cannot, even in principle, be closed. The cognitive dissonance assumption implies the closed system of the nineteenth-century physicist and chemist. That is, the balance theories are a natural outgrowth of the research paradigm that the communication scholars borrowed from physics. The behaviorists of the early twentieth century did not want to posit any internal mediating states between stimulus and response, for to do so would be to clutter up their theories with unnecessary constructs. Thus, the balance theory was based upon a view of human nature that saw an inert human being pushed and pulled by external stimuli and responding to messages rather than creating them. The spontaneous combustion theory is based upon a view of human nature which sees a human being creating attitudes spontaneously and continuously. In the balance view, one has to account for change; in the spontaneous combustion view, one has to account for stability and the continuance of attitudes.

We could think up a number of theories of the same form as the balance theories, each with its own implied view of human nature, each plausible, and each capable of suggesting possible hypotheses for empirical investigation. I will suggest only one more and invite the reader to "dream up" several others. We might posit a family of entropy theories of attitude change which would provide an alternative explanation for the phenomena explained by balance theories and by spontaneous combustion theories. The entropy theory asserts that continual decay and disorganization is the normal condition of internal symbolic states, attitudes, beliefs, and cognitions. If an individual's internal organization of mental images, meanings, and so forth is left to itself, it will erode away into chaos. Unless the individual receives continuous communication that reorganizes and builds it up again—i.e., continuous inputs of negative entropy—he or she will gradually cease to function as an integrated personality. Negative entropy always requires energy to fight the forces of entropy. Both the source and the receiver of the message must expend energy to build up the organization of the receiver's attitudes.

Theories which posit some idealized nature of human beings and account for human behavior on that basis are common in the social sciences. Thus, some economic theory is based upon an idealized economic person who acts for economic gain or in economic self-interest. The three theories I elaborated above are all versions of an idealized human being responding to communication in a certain way. One idealization asserts that human beings strive for cognitive consistency, another asserts that human beings are continually creating messages and changing attitudes, a third asserts that human beings participate in the general decay of information discovered in machines by the scholars investigating communication systems and cybernetic processes.[54]

One way to interpret the theoretical accounts that provide a plausible explanation of human behavior based upon an idealization of human beings is as an abstract fantasy type in which an everyman character plays out a series of scenarios, always motivated by the one salient feature highlighted by the theory—economic self-interest, cognitive consistency, or whatever. While such theories are oversimplifications of human nature, they are useful in providing understanding of human action insofar as an appreciable number of people do exhibit the appropriate behavior. That is, if a large number of people often act as though they are out for their economic self-interest, some of the principles of economics based upon such scenarios will be played out in economic activity, and if a large number of people often act as though they are straining for cognitive consistency, then some of the conclusions based upon such scenarios will be played out in communication activity.

The theorist who starts by positing a plausible motivation as the one motive in human communication behavior and who has some skill at developing scenarios—that is, at fantasizing—can evolve a plausible theory of the same form as the theory of cognitive dissonance. The usefulness of such theorizing is only partially based upon the plausibility of the formulation which justifies it, however. Eventually the scenario must account for the way people act in a somewhat comprehensive fashion in order to lead to useful understanding.

As I indicated in Chapter 2, the variable analytic quasi-paradigm and the consistency theories are not the only formulations that relate to the development of a general theory of communication. I have singled out the variable analytic studies and consistency theories for detailed critique because, to my mind, they have made their maximum contribution and we ought to turn to other ways of research and theorizing.

The influence of the variable analytic tradition served to inhibit new directions until recently, but by 1980, a number of alternative ways of studying communication were well under way. Most of the new approaches, such as conversational analysis, ethnographic studies of rhetorical communities, and investigations of communication strategy and style, individual rules for interpersonal communication, patterns of networks and interactions in communication systems, and fantasy theme analysis are still in their developmental stages. They have not yet emerged clearly enough to allow for a focused critique such as the one I have provided for the variable analytic quasi-paradigm. I shall examine some of their apparent strengths and weaknesses as well as their potential for the future in Chapter 8.

Summary

In the 1970s the scholars making humanistic and social scientific studies of communication began to examine alternative viewpoints relating to the development of general communication theory. The first strong expression of that impulse took the form of a three-part frame of analysis that compared and contrasted the covering law, the systems, and the rules viewpoints as feasible and useful perspectives from which to develop theoretical explanations of communication.

The debate began with attacks on the assumption that theories of a hypothetico-deductive type such as Newton's were either possible or appropriate for human communication. Those advocating a rules or systems viewpoint suggested that covering laws might be found for biophysical motion, or for behavioristic stimulus-response patterns, but that laws were unlikely to cover the conscious choice of actors who had intentions, made plans, followed conventional rules, or applied practical arguments to their planning and decision-making. The attack on covering law theories also included the notion that they were mechanical and unlikely to explain the unified, dynamic, process nature of reality. Implied was the basic question of freedom of the will versus determinism.

The tripartite analysis served to bring to the fore the problems plaguing communication research and efforts to develop general theories of communication. Dividing the world of theory into three parts, however, brought with it some confusions. Critics who made comparative analyses of covering law, rules, and systems perspectives often reached faulty conclusions. Distinguishing between actual theories on the one hand and perspectives for study on the other provides a basis for clarifying some of the confusions. Another problem with the tripartite analysis was that some who used it drew inaccurate distinctions among causality, logical necessity, and practical necessity.

The impulse to critique the state of research in theory and communication also expressed itself in a discussion of the basic assumptive system of investigators and theoreticians. The argument began with a challenge to behaviorism (which the critics tended to equate with logical positivism), moved to a summary of arguments against logical positivism, and concluded with the case for an alternative philosophical position. The pattern was followed by Delia, who urged constructivism; by Hawes, who argued for phenomenology; and by Bloom, who recommended pragmatism.

The uneasiness with research and general theories of communication in the 1970s may well have been largely due to the shortcomings of the influential quasi-paradigm of variable analytic studies and its associated quasi-hypothetico-deductive theories of balance and consistency. The influential research tradition resembles the disciplinary matrix and exemplars of Newtonian mechanics in form, but key features of the Newtonian paradigm are missing. The quasi-paradigm does not have low-level laws of nature, such as those of Galileo which formed the bases for Newton's general theory. The quasi-paradigm was not composed of mathematical functions that could be translated into measurable properties and that could form a syntactical system from which new generalizations and specific applications could be derived mathematically as was the Newtonian system.

Since the exemplar of good investigations for the quasi-paradigm included the requirement that research hypotheses be derived from theory, investigators tended to draw research notions from special style-specific theories. Questions about such matters as whether or not high or low fear appeals would be more or less persuasive are related to stylistic features and not to general characteristics of human communication.

The consistency theories, once they evolved to account for research results, had the form of Newtonian mechanics without the substance. Investigators tried to derive research hypotheses from the consistency theories but could not do so by means of mathematical deduction as the physicists could with nineteenth-century mechanics. They thus had to use exegetical forms of reasoning to develop their research questions. Exegetical arguments resemble the process of conventional definition and may be changed arbitrarily. As a result, one could not test consistency theories by research results in the way that one could apply Newtonian mechanics.

A final problem with those who developed the quasi-paradigm was that they tried to transfer in too literal a fashion a research paradigm from another century and another field of inquiry to contemporary social scientific study of communication. The result was that their explanatory system became more and more divorced from the social realities with which it was supposed to deal.

Cognitive dissonance and other balance theories provide explanations by positing an image of human beings which sees people motivated to action only when their psychological consistencies are brought into a state of imbalance. Similar research results could be explained by positing different images of human communication. In the final analysis, the usefulness of such images of human beings is based upon the extent to which people act in accordance with the central image.

Notes

1. *Communication Quarterly* 25 (1977), Charles R. Berger, "The Covering Law Perspective as a Theoretical Basis for the Study of Human Communication," 7–18; Peter R. Monge, "The Systems Perspective as a Theoretical Basis for the Study of Human Communication," 19–29; Donald P. Cushman, "The Rules Perspective as a Theoretical Basis for the Study of Human Communication," 30–45.
2. *Communication Quarterly*, 25 (1977), W. Barnett Pearce, "Metatheoretical Concerns in Communication," 3–6; Jesse G. Delia, "Alternative Perspectives for the Study of Human Communication: Critique and Response," 46–52; Leonard C. Hawes, "Alternative Theoretical Bases: Toward a Presuppositional Critique," 63–68; Charles M. Rossiter, "Models of Paradigmatic Change," 69–73.
3. See Berger; also, Gerald R. Miller, "The Current Status of Theory and Research in Interpersonal Communication," *Human Communication Research* 4 (1978): 165–178; Gerald R. Miller and Charles R. Berger, "On Keeping the Faith in Matters Scientific," *Western Journal of Speech Communication* 42 (1978): 33–57.
4. Jesse G. Delia and Lawrence Grossberg, "Interpretation and Evidence," *Western Journal of Speech Communication* 41 (1977): 37–38.
5. Gary Cronkhite and Jo Liska, "Introduction to a Symposium: On What Criteria Should be Used to Judge the Admissibility of Evidence to Support

Theoretical Propositions in Communication Research?" *Western Journal of Speech Communication* 41 (1977): 3–8.

6. Vernon E. Cronen and Leslie K. David, "Alternative Approaches for the Communication Theorist: Problems in the Laws-Rules-Systems Trichotomy," *Human Communication Research* 4 (1978): 120.

7. Berger, pp. 12–13.

8. Cronen and Davis, p. 120.

9. Daniel J. O'Keefe, "Logical Empiricism and the Study of Human Communication," *Speech Monographs* 42 (1975): 169–183.

10. Ibid, p. 177.

11. Ibid.

12. Ibid., p. 181.

13. Ibid., p. 183.

14. Jesse G. Delia, "Constructivism and the Study of Human Communication," *Quarterly Journal of Speech* 63 (1977): 66–83.

15. Ibid., p. 68.

16. Ibid., p. 69.

17. Ibid., p. 68.

18. Jesse G. Delia, "A Constructivist Analysis of the Concept of Credibility, "*Quarterly Journal of Speech* 62 (1976): 361–375.

19. Delia, "Constructivism and the Study of Human Communication," p. 78, fn. 40.

20. "The most direct avenue to the study of communication processes not doing violence to the phenomenological perspectives of study participants and to the preinterpreted quality of the social world lies in the use of data collection techniques which generate data unstructured by the collection procedures themselves." Ibid., p. 78.

21. Leonard C. Hawes, "Toward a Hermeneutic Phenomenology of Communication," *Communication Quarterly* 25 (1977): 30–41.

22. Ibid., p. 35.

23. Ibid., p. 36.

24. Ibid., p. 37.

25. The basic pattern of reflective thinking as outlined by Dewey was adapted to provide a discussion agenda. See, particularly, John Dewey, *How We Think* (New York: Heath, 1910).

26. Lester Thonssen and A. Craig Baird, *Speech Criticism* 1st ed. (New York: Ronald Press, 1948).

27. Abraham Kaplan, *The Conduct of Inquiry: Methodology for Behavioral Science* (San Francisco: Chandler, 1964).

28. Paraphrased in Ibid., p. 43.

29. See, for example, John Dewey, *Logic, the Theory of Inquiry* (New York: Holt, 1939).

30. Vincent L. Bloom, "Pragmatism: The Choice of a Critical Perspective for Communication Inquiry," *Western Speech* 39 (1975): p. 5.

31. Ibid., p. 11.

32. Miller and Berger. For a perspective which denies empiricism, however, see Frederic A. Gruber, "Why Empirical Methods Cannot Apply in Communication Research: The Case Against Behaviorism," in Fred L. Casmir, ed., *Intercultural and International Communication* (Washington, D.C.: University Press of America, 1978), pp. 7–41.

33. Kaplan analyzes interval, nominal, ordered metric, and ratio scales, pp. 189–198. He also discusses reliability, p. 200, and validity, pp. 198–206.

34. When in the past I have critiqued the quasi-paradigm I have often been accused of being biased against science, against social science, against the social scientific study of communication, and so forth. I should like to be very clear that I am committed to careful and rigorous empirical investigations of communication episodes. What I am critiquing is a clearly specified type of investigation and theorizing. Discarding the quasi-paradigm would in no way jeopardize social scientific studies of communication.

35. John Waite Bowers, *Designing the Communication Experiment* (New York: Random House, 1970), pp. 119–124.

36. Two articles are relevant here. The first was Murray A. Hewgill and Gerald R. Miller, "Source Credibility and Response to Fear-Arousing Communication," *Speech Monographs* 32 (1965): 95–101; and the second was Gerald R. Miller and Murray A. Hewgill, "Some Recent Research on Fear-Arousing Message Appeals," *Speech Monographs* 33 (1966): 377–391. The second article is the one referred to by Bowers, but it surveys several studies, including the one reported in the first article. For my purposes I will use the study reported in the first article as my exemplar. The quotation is from Hewgill and Miller, p. 95.

37. David K. Berlo, "Communication as Process: Review and Commentary," in Brent D. Ruben, ed., *Communication Yearbook I* (New Brunswick, New Jersey: Transaction Books, 1977), p. 12.

38. Ibid., p. 17.

39. Gerald R. Miller and Michael Burgoon, "Persuasion Research: Review and Commentary," in Brent D. Ruben, ed., *Communication Yearbook 2* (New Brunswick, N.J.: Transaction Books, 1978), pp. 27–45.

40. Herbert W. Simons, "The Rhetoric of Science and the Science of Rhetoric," *Western Journal of Speech Communication* 42 (1978): 38–39.

41. Thomas S. Kuhn, *The Structure of Scientific Revolutions*, 2nd ed. (Chicago: University of Chicago Press, 1970), pp. 144–59. Kuhn argues, "The early versions of most new paradigms are crude. By the time their full aesthetic appeal can be developed, most of the community has been persuaded by other means. Nevertheless, the importance of aesthetic considerations can sometimes be decisive" (p. 156).

42. Henri Poincaré, "Mathematical Creation," in Brewster Ghiselin, ed., *The Creative Process* (New York: New American Library, 1955), pp. 40–41.

43. For an insightful discussion of the role of analogies in scientific theories see Norman Campbell, *What is Science?* (New York: Dover Publications, 1952).

44. The procedure is described in detail in Charles E. Osgood, G. J. Suci, and Percy H. Tannenbaum, *The Measurement of Meaning* (Urbana: University of Illinois Press, 1957). For a review which examines objections to and the strengths of the procedure, see Donald K. Darnell, "Semantic Differential," in Philip Emmert and William D. Brooks, eds., *Methods in Communication Research* (Boston: Houghton-Mifflin, 1970), pp. 181–196.

45. Danuta Ehrlich, Isaiah Guttman, Peter Schönbach and Judson Mills, "Post-decision Exposure to Relevant Information," *Journal of Abnormal and Social Psychology* 54 (1957): 98–102.

46. Jack Brehm, "Postdecision Changes in the Desirability of Alternatives," *Journal of Abnormal and Social Psychology* 52 (1956): 384–389.

47. For a survey of some of the studies relating to cognitive dissonance, see Chester A. Insko and John Schopler, *Experimental Social Psychology* (New York: Academic Press, 1972), ch. 4, "Dissonance in Free-Choice Situations," pp. 107–127; ch. 5, "Dissonance in Forced-Compliance Situations," pp. 128–162; for a general summary and critique see Chester A. Insko, *Theories of Attitude Change* (New York: Appleton-Century-Crofts, 1967).

48. Elliot Aronson, *The Social Animal*, 1st ed. (San Francisco: Freeman, 1972), p. 137.

Aronson's second edition, published in 1976, still evaluated dissonance theory in positive terms: "As we have seen, dissonance theory has proved to be a useful way of looking at human interaction. In two decades since its inception, it has inspired more research and generated more discoveries about social behavior than any other theory in psychology." By 1976, however, Aronson had reservations. He noted that "there are some serious conceptual problems with the theory as originally stated" (p. 132). He argued that in recent years much of the vagueness of the original formulation had been reduced. He had modified the formulation to situations in which the individual's behavior violates his or her self-concept. Aronson reacted most strongly to criticism by Daryl Bem, who argued that dissonance effects are nothing more than the result of people's making reasonable inferences about their attitudes. Bem did several studies in the variable analytic mode and found the same results based on his explanation as had been obtained by studies based upon cognitive dissonance (pp. 135–137). Aronson's response is not unusual. Bem's challenge to cognitive dissonance has received a good deal of attention from the proponents of the theory. My interpretation of this is that people solving puzzles within the quasi-paradigm are much more likely to take seriously a different solution to the puzzle developed from within the assumptive system than they are a critique of the entire system from outside that perspective.

Cognitive dissonance theory has been attacked extensively, but often from within the quasi-paradigm. See, for example, in Shel Feldman, ed., *Cognitive Consistency: Motivational Antecedents and Behavioral Consequents* (New York: Academic Press, 1966), William J. McGuire, "The Current Status of Consistency Theory," pp. 1–38; Milton J. Rosenberg, "Some Limits of Dissonance: Toward a Differentiated View of Counter-Attitudinal Performance," pp. 135–170; and Albert Pepitone, "Some Conceptual and Empirical Problems of Consistency Models," pp. 257–297.

49. Krause made an ambitious attempt to translate cognitive dissonance concepts into mathematical formulas but he failed to find ways to measure the concepts so the numbers could be used in mathematical functions like $F = ma$. See Merton S. Krause, "An Analysis of Festinger's Cognitive Dissonance Theory," *Philosophy of Science* 39 (1972): 32–50.

50. Aronson, 2nd. ed., p. 80.

51. Anthony Storr, *The Dynamics of Creation* (New York: Atheneum, 1972), discusses cognitive dissonance and suggests that "there is another way of dealing with incompatibles and opposites within the mind. . . . One characteristic of creative people, as we have seen, is just this ability to tolerate

dissonance. They see problems which others do not see. . . . it is the creative person's tolerance of the discomfort of dissonance which makes the new solution possible" (pp. 226–227).

52. For a fuller discussion of these issues see Walter B. Weimer, "Communication, Speech, and Psychological Models of Man: Review and Commentary," in Ruben, ed., *Communication Yearbook 2*, pp. 57–77.

53. Aronson, 1st ed., pp. 137–138.

54. See Weimer for an analysis of explanations posited on psychological models of human beings.

Humanistic Studies of Communication

Chapter 1 concluded with the intriguing notion from the editors of *Drama in Use* that the most promising way in which humanistic scholarship might be brought into fruitful collaboration with the rigor of social scientific investigations might be through "new and fertile communications theories (or hypotheses) that recognize the complexity of human behavior as manifest in symbols."[1]

This chapter examines humanistic scholarship in general and the work in rhetoric and communication in particular to explore more fully its nature and to examine its potential relationship with communication theories.

Simons, who has been in the forefront of those with a social scientific perspective who are trying to integrate rhetorical and communication theory, characterized certain humanistic scholars as "muddleheaded anecdotalists." He argued that he had learned more about communication from them than from the bulk of the hardheaded empiricists. Simons provided a partial list of the thinkers that he found insightful. This list was headed by Gregory Bateson and Kenneth Burke but also included "such creative spirits as Erving Goffman, Jules Henry, R. D. Laing, Thomas Schelling, and Paul Watzlawick."[2]

Scholars interested in communication have often found philosophers, psychiatrists, literary critics, sociologists of the symbolic interactionist school, cognitive and humanistic psychologists, and critics of social theory stimulating and useful to their theorizing. Simons' list is illustrative. A perusal of the citations in important and representative journals and books on communication theory would reveal a growing interest in works by scholars such as McLuhan on mass media; Cassirer and Langer on symbolism; Edelman on symbolic uses of politics; Buber, Kierkegaard, and Sartre on human relationships and the human condition; Jung and Levi-Strauss on myth; Maslow, Gibb, Schutz, and Rogers on interpersonal relations, I.A. Richards, Weaver, Perelman, and McKeon on rhetoric; and Mead, Cooley, and Simmel on social relations. Recently there has been a reawakening of interest in the Frankfort School with communication scholars finding the works of such social critics as Marcuse, and especially Habermas, enlightening.[3]

Towers has provided an interesting comparison between two émigrés to America from Europe, Paul Lazarsfeld and Theodor Adorno.[4] Both had an association with the Frankfort Institute for social relations. Lazarsfeld did some work on contract for the Frankfort Institute's study of authority and the family while a member of the Psychological Institute at the University of Vienna, and Adorno was affiliated with the Institute for a time. Lazarsfeld came to America in the 1930s and incorporated the American preoccupation with quantitative methodologies into the social institute concept. For many years he worked with the Bureau of Applied Social Research at Columbia University. Adorno emigrated some years later, but continued his work from an essentially humanistic, philosophical-critical perspective.

Lazarsfeld represented an orientation which was popular in America in the decades from 1935 to 1965. The growing contemporary interest in the work of the Frankfort Institute and social criticism as represented by Adorno is suggestive of what may become a future shift of interest among at least a substantial group of communication scholars.

How does someone trained in the "hypothetico-deductive-statistical" approach such as Simons, who maintains that he "too [can] appreciate its logic,"[5] find humanistic studies of use for the understanding of communication? How can the "muddleheaded anecdotalists" make a contribution to research and theorizing in communication?

To answer such questions this chapter begins with a survey of one important stream of humanistic studies, dramatism. Dramatism is not the only major humanistic perspective of current interest to scholars in communication, but it is one of the more influential and will serve as illustrative of humanism in general. The chapter goes on to examine the work of rhetorical critics and historians in terms of the several levels of analysis and special and general nature of communication theories that I earlier applied to social scientific studies. The chapter surveys the historical development of the study of the history and criticism of public address and examines critiques of that tradition. The final section of the chapter deals with the similarities and differences between historical and critical studies.

Dramatism and the Study of Human Communication

In Chapter 6 I noted the growing tendency of communication theorists to draw a distinction between motion and human action. One possible explanatory scheme, as we saw, was to attribute intentions and motives to human actors. Weber provided an influential analysis of such explanations with his concept of *verstehen*. Weber suggested that *understanding* in his sense of *verstehen* requires that behavior be examined in its social and institutional context. That is, the investigator must understand the social customs, rules, norms, and meanings surrounding behavior. The investigator must, further, account for the actor's intent in performing behavior and must provide a motive to account for the intent. Thus, if all we know is that we have observed a man adding up a column of figures, we have little understanding of what is going on. If, however, we know the context in which the behavior of adding up a column of figures is embedded, we have greater understanding. Assume that the adding up is part of the balancing of an account book and that such balancing is part of a complex web of financial practices. If we come to know the nature of the surrounding customs, norms, and meanings, we have taken a further step toward an explanation. If we go on to discover the intent of the person adding up the figures and find that it is to balance the books rather than to check to see whether someone has doctored the books for the purpose of hiding an embezzlement, we have still greater understanding. In addition, however, *verstehen* in a more complete sense requires an account of why the individual is moved to achieve the intent. Why did this particular person at this time decide to actually do the balancing of accounts? In Runciman's words:

> . . . in the example of the priest celebrating mass to say "he is celebrating mass" is to account for his (intentional) words and gestures but not to explain either what has motivated him to celebrate mass or how it comes about that such a thing goes on in the culture in question in the first place. For Weber, sociological explanation begins when the observer attributes a motive to the agent, and ends when an empirical demonstration is afforded both that this *was* the motive and how (in terms of the particular hypotheses which the sociologist selects out of the limitless range of possible causes and effects) it came to be so.[6]

Cognitive psychologists also draw a distinction between action and bio-physical behavior. Harré, for example suggested that in cognitive studies "a human being is treated as a person, that is as a plan-making, self-monitoring agent, aware of goals and deliberately considering the best way of achieving them."[7]

Kenneth Burke makes a somewhat similar point from a dramatistic perspective by drawing a distinction between action and sheer motion. "'Action' is a term for the kind of behavior possible to a typically symbol-using animal (such as man) in contrast with the extrasymbolic or nonsymbolic operations of nature."[8]

Among the humanists studying communication episodes, the dramatistic perspective has been influential and heuristic. The contributors to the anthology *Drama in Life; The Uses of Communication in Society* include Kenneth Burke, Hugh Duncan, Peter Berger, Maurice Natanson, Georg Simmel, Eric Berne, Erving Goffman, William Stephenson, Daniel Boorstin, and Murray Edelman. These scholars are but representative of a host of writers who have provided insights for communication theorists and researchers.

Burke is a cosmic thinker, philosopher, and literary and social critic; Goffman is an anthropologist and sociologist. Although, as we have seen in earlier chapters, communication theorists and researchers have borrowed most heavily from psychology and social psychology, they have always had an interest in sociology, anthropology, and psychiatry, and since the mid-1960s they have turned increasingly toward those disciplines for assumptive systems and research methodologies. Some of the schools of sociologists have been little influenced by behaviorism. For example, scholars interested in the sociology of knowledge and committed to a symbolic interactionist position have often been humanists who relied upon philosophical and critical perspectives for much of their conceptualizations.

Burke's dramatistic analysis focused on an act that requires an agent within a scene employing an agency to achieve some purpose. The dramatistic pentad of act, agent, agency, scene, and purpose has been widely used by symbolic interactionists in sociology and by contemporary rhetorical critics and theorists. However, the entire corpus of Burke's writings, which encompass all symbolic action, has been influential.

Max Black reviewed one of Burke's important works, *The Grammar of Motives*, and characterized it as a "vast rambling edifice of quasi-sociological and quasi-psychoanalytical speculation" that rested upon "a set of unexamined and uncriticized metaphysical assumptions."[9] Burke's writings range over all human history and sociology and account for it in terms of symbolic action. His works are opaque and often provided the exegetically minded communication scholar with ample ambiguity to justify the practice of drawing out the meanings implied by the text along the lines of those charted in Figure 6, p. 174 and illustrated by Jonathan Edwards.

Burke also provided communication scholars with a number of insightful aphorisms and other seminal quotations. Few humanists have been as widely cited by students of communication and rhetorical theory as Kenneth Burke. That fact alone might provide evidence for the possible usefulness of dramatism as a unifying perspective for communication and rhetorical theory. The sociologist Duncan took Burke's work and provided a systematic approach to symbol usage in society which makes the perspective more available to communication theorists.[10]

Goffman provided a more concrete application of the dramatistic perspective to human interaction and communication. Unlike Burke, Goffman often based his conclusions on field work in such settings as mental hospitals.[11] Goffman explained ritual elements in social interaction in terms of the enactment of roles, the following of a line, and the importance of places and scenes.

Goffman's study of what he called "face-work" provides an example of his use of the dramatistic perspective. He explained *face* as follows:

A person may be said to *have*, or *be in*, or *maintain* face when the line he effectively takes presents an image of him that is internally consistent, that is supported by judgments and evidence conveyed through impersonal agencies in the situation. At such times the person's face clearly is something that is not lodged in or on his body, but rather something that is diffusely located in the flow of events in the encounter and becomes manifest only when these events are read and interpreted for the appraisals expressed in them.[12]

Goffman's analysis included a discussion of basic kinds of avoidance of loss of face, correcting dramas when face has been lost, and games in which face is challenged and points made by the antogonists. He emphasized the role of immediate spoken interaction in the challenges to, the loss of, and the maintenance of face in a way that has obvious applications to interpersonal communication, and concluded with an examination of ritual order.

"To study face-saving," according to Goffman, "is to study the traffic rules of social interaction; one learns about the code the person adheres to in his movements across the paths and designs of others, but not where he is going, or why he wants to get there. One does not even learn why he is ready to follow the code, for a large number of different motives can equally lead him to do so."[13] Ethnographic studies of the communication associated with face-work thus provide only part of what Weber suggested was required for adequate understanding. Goffman maintained, however, that "underneath their differences in culture, people everywhere are the same." He saw people as having a universal human nature which could not be explained by looking to them but rather, "One must look . . . to the fact that societies everywhere, if they are to be societies, must mobilize their members as self-regulating participants in social encounters."[14]

My analysis of rhetorical communities and their special theories of communication in Chapter 3 raised the question of how rhetorical criticism that revealed the communication theory of such communities might provide a more general explanation of communication and of how ethnographic studies of such communities might generate general theories of communication. Goffman clearly understood that the field studies themselves only provided an account of the "traffic rules" and the "code" and did not explain *why* people were motivated to follow or not to follow the rituals. He addressed the central issue as follows:

> The general capacity to be bound by moral rules may well belong to the individual, but the particular set of rules which transforms him into a human being derives from requirements established in the ritual organization of social encounters. And if a particular person or group or society seems to have a unique character all its own, it is because its standard set of human-nature elements is pitched and combined in a particular way. Instead of much pride, there may be little. Instead of abiding by the rules, there may be much effort to break them safely.[15]

Despite idiosyncrasies among communities, Goffman concluded, "It is as if face, by its very nature, can be saved only in a certain number of ways, and as if each social grouping must make its selections from this single matrix of possibilities."[16]

The symbolic convergence approach to research and theory in rhetoric and communication represents a third dramatistic viewpoint. Symbolic convergence differs from the other dramatistic approaches in that it grew directly from the study and criticism of communication. The central focus of the symbolic convergence persepective is upon the communicative processes by which human beings converge their individual fantasies, dreams, and meanings into shared symbol systems.

Chapter 7 discussed the way in which a general theory of communication may be based upon some central image of men and women taken in isolation. Such accounts then explain communication episodes in terms of how such idealized personae respond to and create messages. Thus an idealized image of the individual human being might posit an essentially logical person who strives for cognitive consistency. The convergence viewpoint, by contrast, is based upon a model of how groupings of people come to share common symbol systems. It focuses on communicative interaction rather than on the individual characteristics of people.

The convergence viewpoint provides an assumptive system for the analysis of messages in order to discover the manifest content of fantasy themes and evidence that groups of people have shared the symbolic interpretations implied by them. The shared fantasies may begin to cluster around common scripts or types, and when members of the community allude to such shared scripts they provide further evidence that the symbol systems are shared. Once a community has shared a number of fantasies, they often integrate them by means of some organizing principle such as a master analogy into a coherent rhetorical vision.[17]

The central explanatory hypothesis of symbolic convergence is the dynamic process of the sharing of group fantasies. Investigators observing small group discussions and small group conferences first discovered and isolated the process. They found that they could reliably identify the verbal and nonverbal communication associated with the convergence or chaining process.[18] Subsequent investigators discovered that such symbolic convergence processes also take place on the occasion of public speeches when audience members begin to participate in the dramatizations, narratives, anecdotes, stories, and hypothetical examples of the speaker and indicate in their verbal and nonverbal communication that they share in the tone and connotation of the dramas.[19] Evidence is accumulating that audiences for the mass media also share fantasies.

Symbolic convergence integrates humanistic scholarship with social scientific methods. A number of scholars have utilized fantasy theme analysis of rhetorical visions to document the presence of shared fantasies and rhetorical visions and then provided a rhetorical criticism of the consciousness of those publics who share the visions.[20] Other scholars have started with rhetorical criticism to discover the common fantasy themes within a body of discourse, constructed rhetorical visions from those common message elements, and then developed Q-sorts to test the constructs.[21] A logical extension of such efforts is to develop survey research instruments to use with suitable large-sample techniques to estimate the distribution of shared fantasies and rhetorical visions among various mass publics.[22]

The symbolic convergence hypotheses represent a framework for the development of a general theory of communication, since they transcend rhetorical communities and apply to the process by which human beings in a variety of communication contexts come to share a common symbol system and vision.

The hypotheses provide the basis for anticipation of human behavior such as voting and for practical applications in preparation of messages which are consonant with the shared fantasies, fantasy types, and rhetorical visions of various groups. [23]

Both Burke and Goffman encompass the unfolding of events. They are, therefore, more inclusive in their scope than the symbolic convergence account that deals only with the rhetorical interpretation of realities as located in the give and take of verbal messages. Symbolic convergence differs from Burke's dramatism in that it relates only to the content of messages, whereas Burke emphasizes the totality of unfolding human action. Burkean rhetorical critics have often portrayed a speaking occasion in terms of the dramatistic pentad where the speaker is the agent, the speech the agency, the occasion the scene, and so forth. Goffman's dramatism also viewed everyday behavior in dramatistic terms. He analyzed ordinary conversation as part of the presentation of self or of face-saving.

Fantasy theme analysis studies the way communicators discuss fictitious and nonfictitious events in the past or in the future or at some other place than the here-and-now of the immediate communication episode. The ongoing flow of experience may seem chaotic or confusing; immediate behavior may seem impulsive; occurrences may seem accidental. The speaker who recounts such experiences (after the fact) places the events into narrative form and provides an explanatory structure for them. The narrative form implies or attributes motivations to the personae and may provide an explanation based on lawfulness or the will of a supreme being rather than on chance or accident. The same is true of an account set in the future. The group may come to share a dream of what they want to achieve in the future by means of dramatic portrayals of characters in that future scene. Such dreams of the future are also structured interpretations of events.

Clearly dramatism provides a viewpoint that enables humanistic scholars and social scientists to bring their perspectives and research methodologies to bear in a collaborative fashion on communication. Some useful cooperative efforts between the muddleheaded anecdotalists and the hardheaded empiricists have already taken place in such explanatory approaches as those provided by Goffman's field studies of the presentation of self and of saving and maintaining of face, and by the application of Burkean notions to sociological questions, and by rhetorical criticism and empirical tests to the symbolic convergence hypotheses.

Somewhat the same line of analysis would indicate that the application of classical mythology to psychoanalytic matters, the use of psychodrama, role-playing, and the analysis of contemporary drama for the study and illustration of pragmatic communication by psychiatrists provide further evidence of the interplay between humanistic and social scientific scholarship. [24]

Given the potential of humanistic studies to contribute to the development of communication theories, I turn next to the humanistic studies that have historically been central to the study of communication, namely, the study of rhetorical history and criticism.

Both social scientists and humanists find the practice of criticism related to the communicative activity of rhetorical communities an important feature for study. Social scientists may employ ethnographic field-study techniques, survey methods, or naturalistic studies of ordinary talk, whereas the humanists will tend to study documents and other human artifacts. The line of demarcation is not clear, though, and social scientists may use data from historical sources and historians often use statistical information collected by field study and survey methods. Scholarly criticism may also aim at more general understanding of human symbol-using.

Scholarly historical studies may function in terms of providing identity, cohesion, and purpose for a community. Histories may take their place alongside rhetorical messages that use the past for the same purposes.[25] Scholarly history may also provide comparative studies across communities and search for more general patterns of communication. In the instances where critics or historians provide explanatory structures relating to communication across styles, their function is analogous to social scientists' search for general theories and hypotheses.

There has been a tie between historical and critical scholarship in the study of what is often termed *public address*. *Public address* refers to speeches and public affairs programs, typically of persuasive intent aimed at public audiences. In practice, the study of public address has concentrated on oratory, public speeches, debates, and public discussions of political, military, social, educational, and economic issues. Because of the historical importance of this particular field of study, the practice of history and criticism of public address needs to be examined in greater detail and the opposing viewpoints need to be contrasted and discussed.

History and Criticism of Public Address

The Effect of the Speech   Herbert A. Wichelns of Cornell University wrote a seminal essay on speech criticism in 1925. He entitled his essay "The Literary Criticism of Oratory." After examining in considerable detail the literary criticism of a number of speakers, Wichelns decided that "the common ground of literary criticism is its preoccupation with the thought and the eloquence which is permanent." Literary criticism tends to view all literature as written literature and to ignore the difference between spoken and written works. Rhetorical criticism, however, "is not concerned with permanence, nor yet with beauty. It is concerned with effect. It regards a speech as a communication to a specific audience, and holds its business to be the analysis and appreciation of the orator's method of imparting his ideas to his hearers."[26]

In 1929, Harshbarger completed his doctoral dissertation at Cornell, "Burke's Chief American Works." This study was one of the first to be developed along the lines suggested by Wichelns in his essay "The Literary Criticism of Oratory." The "guiding principle" in Harshbarger's study was that Burke's "works are to be regarded as resulting from the interplay of three forces—

speaker, occasion, and audience."[27] In addition, "The effect of the speeches on the debates in which they occurred is analyzed, and the effect of all the work on Burke's fortunes and those of his cause is recapitulated."[28]

Graduate students at other institutions were also beginning to write studies that examined speeches as resulting from the interaction of speaker, occasion, and audience and that evaluated the effect of those speeches. At the State University of Iowa, for example, A. Craig Baird was beginning a long and distinguished career of guiding graduate students in studies in public address. In 1930, one of the first of Baird's students to complete a doctoral study in public address, William Norwood Brigance, completed his study of Jeremiah S. Black. Baird directed more than one hundred master's theses and some fifty doctoral dissertations, largely in the history and criticism of public address. Basically Aristotelian in his approach to rhetoric, Baird used classical canons in criticism, but followed Wichelns' doctrine of the importance of the audience and of effect.[29]

Brigance edited two volumes of critical studies entitled *A History and Criticism of American Public Address* in 1943. In the preface to this collection, Brigance stated of the studies that "final judgment is here based on effect instead of beauty, on influence instead of appeal to the imagination."[30] Indeed, the majority of the twenty-nine critical essays in these two volumes reflected the Wichelns-Baird approach to criticism. Wichelns contributed an essay on Emerson. A number of the contributors were trained at Iowa or Cornell, and many of the essays were based on doctoral studies completed at those two institutions.

In 1947, Baird coauthored, with his former student Lester Thonssen, an article entitled "Methodology in the Criticism of Public Address." In this article the emphasis is still clearly on criticism. "What is the goal of the rhetorical investigator?" the authors ask, and they answer, "It is chiefly criticism." While researchers may study many aspects of speechmaking as well as biographical material relating to the speeches under consideration, "The chief business of the rhetorical scholar, nevertheless, is the evaluation of a speech or speeches. His questions are, 'Is this a good speech? If so, why?' The answers are the essence of his primary research task." Further reflecting the distinction between history and criticism, the authors say of the process of criticizing speeches that the "judgment here is essentially like that of other art forms. The critic of speeches is confronted with an art, just as is the evaluator of a novel or play."[31] Wilchelns' notion that rhetoric "is concerned with effect" had become the central touchstone for evaluating a speech, according to Baird and Thonssen. They wrote, "The judgment concerns the effect of the discourse, or response. To what degree does the audience react favorably to the purpose of the speaker? Such a question, whatever may be the difficulty of interpreting the terms *audience* and *responses*, is the heart of the problem."[32]

In 1948, Thonssen and Baird published a detailed treatment of the methodology of rhetorical criticism entitled *Speech Criticism.*[33] The book elaborates the basic position of the article "Methodology in the Criticism of Public Address" and makes an important addition. It presents standards of criticism, developed from rhetorical theory. These standards are to be applied to a given speech and the speech will be found to measure up or to fall short. If it were not for the audience, that all-important feature that distinguishes rhetorical criticism from literary criticism, this would be sufficient for the critic to make a judgment. However, since the audience is involved, and the major canon is effect upon an audience, the rhetorical critic makes a further investigation into the historical context of the speech to discover if the speaker accomplished his purposes. If the speaker did, then a judgment can be made not only about how well the speech reflected the rhetorical theory but also about the effectiveness of rhetorical rules themselves. If the speaker was ungrammatical and yet effective, and the rhetorical theory used as a criterion stated that ungrammatical language will hurt a speaker's ethos and thus his or her effectiveness, then the rhetorical theory itself must be modified.

Thus, criticism can serve a practical function in that it can test and modify theory. Effectiveness becomes the crucial consideration in judging the worth of the rhetorical theory as well as the speaker's ability.

With *Speech Criticism*, the line of development begun by Wilchelns came to fruition. The viewpoint included a classical, predominately Aristotelian, set of categories for the description and analysis of speeches. The emphasis in this criticism is upon the oral nature of speechmaking and the reciprocal interaction between speaker and audience. The nature of the audience and the occasion affects the quality of the discourse, according to this viewpoint, and the speech, in turn, influences the audience and, perhaps, the course of history. Finally, critics of this persuasion used rhetorical theory as an aid in evaluating speech practices but assumed also that the results of critical studies of effective speakers will serve to correct and modify rhetorical theory.

By the early 1960s the label *history and criticism of public address* served to indicate a clearly discernible and popular school of humanistic scholarship. Although there were controversies regarding the purpose and practice of the scholarship, they tended to relate to solving puzzles within the general assumptive system of the viewpoint.

One of the puzzles related to using the effect of the discourse as a touchstone for critical evaluations. In 1956, Nilsen published an article devoted to the wisdom of using the effect criterion.[34] He concluded his examination by supporting the importance and necessity of evaluating the social consequences of speeches, although he suggested that these consequences be viewed in the broader context of the ultimate effect for good or evil on society rather than in the narrower sense of effectiveness of the speaker in realizing his or her purposes. Other writers stressed the need to consider effect. Griffin, in discussing the rhetorical criticism of historical movements, took as "a first and obvious principle" that "the critic must judge the effectiveness of the discourse."[35] Croft, in his 1956 essay "The Functions of Rhetorical Criticism," accepted the effect criterion as a starting place for his analysis.[36]

Using the effect as the ultimate criterion for rhetorical criticism posed ethical problems. If the critics based their theory on critical standards tested by their effect, they often found themselves in danger of praising rhetorical practices which on other grounds might seem questionable. The effects tended to sanction any manipulative technique that worked. Thonssen and Baird devoted the last chapter of the first edition of *Speech Criticism* to a discussion of the importance of including ethical judgments in rhetorical criticism.

Awareness of the problem was not always sufficient to deal with it, however. Judging discourse by effect was amoral, and critics' attempts to make ethical judgments about it resulted in trying to apply criteria external to rhetorical standards. Baird's work was illustrative. He tended to use classical answers, such as Aristotle's doctrine that rhetoric should be used to defend the truth and Quintilian's notion of the orator as a good man.[37]

As more and more scholars produced works in the history and criticism of public address, other weaknesses surfaced. The approach proved barren in terms of the promised modification of theory. Despite the fact that hundreds of critical case studies of effective speakers indicated that the speakers broke certain established rhetorical rules, the rules continued to find their way into the textbooks.

Finally, the scholars practicing criticism according to the perspective of the history and criticism of public address discovered that they were having great difficulty establishing a convincing structure that would support a claim of either short-range or long-term effects for a given speech, for the entire speaking career of a famous speaker, or, indeed, for the rhetorical discourse associated with a campaign or movement.

The Effectiveness Criterion   Because of the problems with the effect of the discourse, other scholars began to suggest different solutions to the problem of what should be the ultimate criterion against which to evaluate discourse. One of these, also stemming from Wichelns' approach, is represented by Parrish. Parrish modified the notion of effect. In an introductory essay to a volume of *American Speeches,* of which he was coeditor with Hochmuth, Parrish started from an Aristotelian position and suggested that "the critic's concern is not with the literal results of the speech, but with the speaker's use of a correct method; not with the speech's effect, but with its effectiveness." For Parrish, effectiveness involved the concept of an ideal audience. The immediate audience certainly was not necessarily the best guide to evaluating effectiveness. "We admire Burke's great addresses, not because they were well adapted to the boozy country squires who sometimes sat in Parliament, but because they were designed for a better audience." Thus, the critic ought to "interpret and evaluate a speech in terms of its effect upon an audience of qualified listeners."[38]

The Artistic Viewpoint   McBurney and Wrage further extended the notion that correct method was a better key to excellence in discourse than effect. They rejected the effect criterion completely and advocated in its place an "artistic theory" of criticism. Since speech is an art reducible to principles, judgment of that art should be based upon those principles, and the persuasive discourse in any context for any purpose is good insofar as it demonstrates adherence to the principles of the art of rhetoric and bad insofar as it departs from them. On the basis of the "artistic theory," a critic should be able to judge the excellence of a speech in manuscript before it is delivered to an audience—if, indeed, it is delivered to an audience at all.[39]

The Critique of the History and Criticism of Public Address

In the 1950s the scholarly practice of writings in the tradition of the history and criticism of public address reached its height. In 1955 the third volume of *A History and Criticism of American Public Address* was published, under the editorship of Nichols.[40] The volume supplemented the two volumes edited by Brigance in 1943. In addition to published volumes of essays, the scholarly journals printed a large number of studies in the same tradition.

By the early 1960s the weaknesses in the humanistic study of public discourse were becoming more and more apparent. In Chapter 1 I traced the style as the dominant rationale for scholars in academic settings. The style incorporated an adaptation and modification of classical rhetorical notions as part of theory associated with it. When scholars engaged in the teaching of public speaking moved to the humanistic study of oratory, they essentially established criteria from the public speaking style and applied it to the analysis and evaluation of an important speech, a series of speeches, or the entire career of a given speaker. The second part of *Speech Criticism* could, with slight modification, be used as a textbook in public speaking.

The authors of essays in the history and criticism of public address were working within the confines of a rhetorical community practicing a communication style with its associated theory and criticism. They were well acquainted with how criticism and theory fed into and out of practice. They attempted to transfer that process to the third level of analysis and produce a grand universal rhetorical theory composed of principles which would be applicable across time and culture. By scholarly criticism they would modify the covering principles and gradually refine a universal rhetorical theory. In short, they made the mistake which the social scientific investigators were to repeat in the next decades of confusing special rhetorical theories with a universal general rhetorical theory.

When the scholars applied the style-specific theory of academic public speaking to historical materials, they tended to produce trivial studies. Historically important speakers were often practicing a different communication style than was popular among connoisseurs of public speaking, so critics using the public speaking theory provided little insight even about that style. But even when applied to contemporary discourse which grew out of the same style, the leisurely pace of scholarly publication and its limited audience assured that teachers criticizing and coaching students in the classroom while they were practicing the style would be more influential in changing theory and practice than would the writers of scholarly essays in rhetorical criticism.

Because the public speaking communication style of the decades from 1930 to 1960 was based on classical rhetoric, the scholars writing from the perspective of the style tended to establish evaluative criteria from classical rhetoric and to document their justification for using such criteria by references to the original sources. By the 1960s it was becoming clear that the attempt to move from style-specific criticism suitable for the classroom to scholarly work suitable to develop general knowledge about communication was formulary and barren. The analogy between the state of rhetorical criticism in the early 1960s and the practice of doing research within the quasi-paradigm of variable analytic studies of the 1970s is a striking one.

In 1965 Black published *Rhetorical Criticism: A Study in Method.* In the preface he noted:

> More recently Thonssen and Baird's admirable book, *Speech Criticism,* was published, and gave substance to the suspicion that the field of rhetoric had, in truth, not only a subject matter of its own, but a scholarly method as well. The practice of rhetorical criticism is by no means still where Thonssen and Baird found it in 1948, but the theoretical statements that have appeared in the intervening years have been too few, and many of those few too concise, with the result that there is an almost universal discontent in the profession—perhaps its surest sign of life.[41]

Black suggested that the purpose of his book was to "stimulate and expand the dialogue on rhetorical criticism." He was of the belief that the "options available to the critic need to be multiplied, and above all, that the prevailing mode of rhetorical criticism is profoundly mistaken."[42]

Black argued that the predominant mode of rhetorical criticism in the early 1960s was neo-Aristotelian and based upon a modification of classical rhetorical theory which was antique, parochial, and applicable only to a subclass of discourse. Black noted that criticism at what I called the third level of analysis in Chapter 3 was a contemporary development and that the classical rhetorical theorists were essentially developing style-specific theory.

> The critics of classical antiquity, whether composing rhetorics, poetics, or histories of art, seemed uninterested in reflecting on their own activities. To articulate the principles of Sophoclean tragedy or Roman forensic oratory was, for Aristotle and Cicero, the end and justification of their respective critical works. They assumed the mission of elevating intuitive acts of creation to the status of viable method. Their aim was to formulate technical principles that artists could use: to make creativity systematic. They wrote primarily, not for the critic himself, or for the auditor, but for the artist.[43]

Black went on to examine the tacit assumptions involved in the viewpoint of the neo-Aristotelian critic. He pointed out that one untenable assumption was that the classical rhetorical theory comprises an immutable and universal set of principles against which one can criticize all discourse in all cultures and all times. Black argued that "we can hardly expect the principles of rhetoric formulated two thousand years ago to be uniformly germane today."[44] Black emphasized the inadequacy of the Aristotelian rhetorical theory in terms of its focus upon the enthymeme and rational discourse and its inability to deal with exhortative forms of persuasion. Black evaluated the *Rhetoric* of Aristotle as containing "a system descriptive only of a subspecies of argumentative discourse."[45] He concluded:

> It should be clear by now that neo-Aristotelianism is founded upon a restricted view of human behavior, that there are discourses which function in ways not dreamed of in Aristotle's *Rhetoric*, and that there are discourses not designed for rational judges, but for men as they are. It is the task of criticism not to measure these discourses dogmatically against some parochial standard of rationality but, allowing for the immeasurably wide range of human experience, to see them as they really are.[46]

Although Black did not use the distinction that I drew in Chapter 3 between the style-specific theories about communication that aid practitioners at the second level and the explanatory theories aimed to create understanding at the third level, his argument implied a similar analysis. Black's incisive insight was to see that the neo-Aristotelian critics elevated a theory developed by Aristotle to "formulate technical principles that artists could use" to the level of general and universal theory. They took such concepts as the enthymeme and tried to "suggest some mysteriously deep importance and elusively rewarding utility" to them.[47] *Rhetorical Criticism* contained six chapters. The first four developed and amplified Black's argument in attacking the triviality and shortcoming of the practice of the history and criticism of public address.

Black's attack served to focus the discontent with the state of rhetorical criticism. By the early 1970s, Scott and Brock surveyed the state of scholarship devoted to rhetorical criticism and concluded that the field was in the process of shifting from the traditional viewpoint to new approaches. Arguing by analogy from Kuhn's analysis of paradigm shifts in science, they noted that a similar "paradigm shift" was taking place in rhetorical criticism. They concluded that "we are in the midst of a disintegrating tradition. Perhaps rhetorical criticism now is transitional; from it will grow a fresh tradition. Of the latter point, we cannot be certain; of the former we are convinced."[48] They organized their anthology on rhetorical criticism around "The Traditional Perspective" and two of the newer directions, "The Experiential Perspective" and "The Critical Perspective of the 'New Rhetorics.'"

Although there was a rearguard action and some scholars wrote in defense of the tradition, even they tended to use Black's term *neo-Aristotelianism* in their discussion, and the term itself tended during the 1970s to become pejorative.[49] The search for new directions culminated in part in a conference in 1976 on the topic "'Significant Form' in Rhetorical Criticism."[50] By 1976, humanistic scholarship in rhetorical history and criticism was beginning to reshape itself into new traditions. A flurry of articles, convention papers, and books discussed the current state of scholarship and suggested new methods and new directions for the future.[51] Although the field is still in considerable flux at the time of this writing, research and theory in the humanistic study of communication is beginning to take shape.

197

The Critique of the
History and Criticism of
Public Address

Among the important features of humanistic studies emerging in current discussions of rhetorical criticism and history is the clarification of the similarities and differences between criticism and historiography.

History and Criticism Compared and Contrasted

Some Preliminary Distinctions Baskerville argued in the late 1970s that history was as important in its own way as rhetorical criticism and that humanists were not giving historical studies their proper role in the discipline.[52] At approximately the same time, Gronbeck again raised the question *"Can one generally distinguish between the history and the criticism of rhetorical discourse* [emphasis Gonbeck's]?"[53]

What is the relationship between historiography and rhetorical criticism? Gronbeck drew a distinction based on whether or not the scholar found most of the confirming materials or the proof for the argument outside the discourse or within the rhetorical artifact. History, he continued, was subject to the tests of truthfulness, criticism to tests of consistency and insightfulness. History was descriptive causal, criticism was evaluative-advisory.[54]

Baskerville presented a thorough review of the question of the differences between rhetorical history and criticism. He concluded that there were differences in emphasis and used the writings of Ernest Wrage as an example of the usefulness of history. Wrage, according to Baskerville, advanced the thesis that "students of public address may contribute in substantial ways to the history of ideas." Speeches, according to Wrage, "because they are pitched to levels of information, to take account of prevalent beliefs, and to mirror tone and temper of audiences . . . serve as useful indices to the popular mind."[55] Since Wrage saw the history of communication as an important division of the practice of intellectual history, Baskerville argues that scholars who chide Wrage for being an incomplete rhetorical critic or for advocating a less than useful approach to rhetorical criticism simply do not understand that Wrage was advocating the writing of history, not of criticism. Baskerville's analysis implies that we should not judge historians according to the same criteria we use in evaluating rhetorical critics.

Historical Viewpoints Distinguished from Critical Viewpoints While both historian and critic have a scholarly viewpoint which plays an important role in their work, the details and components of the viewpoints differ. By *viewpoint* in this context I mean an assumptive system analogous to what some communication analysts called *perspectives* and what Cronkhite and Liska called *epistemological metaphors*. A historian's viewpoint might include a mixture of such notions as that great personalities bend the course of history, that money makes the world go around, and that words speak louder than actions. A critic's viewpoint might include a mixture of such notions as that rhetoric is a reflection of more basic historical forces (the situation is controlling), and that rhetoric and other features of experience act in a reciprocal relationship. The critic's viewpoint might include some assumptions about the artistic nature of communication, about the ethical canons to be used in evaluating discourse, and about the importance of discovering how discourse functions persuasively, how it functions to create a sense of community, or how it functions to deal with historical change. The critic's viewpoint will also include some general assumptions relating to techniques of criticism. How important is the rational side of the discourse, the argumentative structure, logical consistency, soundness of premises? How important is the dramatic dimension, the mythic foundations, the poetic strain?

Historical Explanation Distinguished from Critical Explanation　Critical explanatory structures tend to differ from historical structures. By *explanatory structures* in this context I mean something analogous to the general hypotheses and theories of social scientists, what Cronkhite and Liska called *explanatory metaphors*. The critics' explanatory structures will be different depending upon the level of analysis and the purpose of the criticism.

Just as much important theorizing in communication takes place at the second level of generating style-specific special theories, so also much important criticism takes place at the second level of Figure 3, p. 72. At the second level, specialists in a given communication style make expert evaluations of practice and continually relate the speaking they criticize to the theory which provides the rationale for the style. All teachers of communication, whether in an academic setting or not, practice criticism vital to a rhetorical community. Recall that a communication style consists of an interrelationship among practice (communicating in observable ways), criticism (public discussion of the strengths and weaknesses of the practice), and theory (developing systematic comments of a general nature about communication.) Criticism of day-to-day communication contributes to the style-specific theory in that, after a time, the critics come to agree on standards to use in judging the communication, and these standards become part of textbooks or handbooks to help practitioners.

The structures that serve as explanatory systems for criticism at the second level tend to take the stock form of beginning with criteria, moving to a description of the communication, and concluding with an evaluation. Critics with expert knowledge of style-specific theory pick a sample of discourse to evaluate in terms of the appropriate ideal or exemplar communication event. For example, the first step in criticizing discourse according to the public speaking style is to take a manageable number of criteria from current theory as represented by a contemporary textbook. The second step is to use the criteria to focus attention on the discourse to be criticized. The critic might describe the speech's main features in terms of an exemplar use of evidence. The critic might pick out items of evidence and sort them into some category system, such as evidence from authority, from real examples, and from statistical material. The third step in the critical process is to make an evaluation of the selected features of the discourse in terms of the ideals set forth in the theory. Thus, the critic might evaluate the evidence as sound because of the interpretation, source, and clarity of the statistical support.[56]

The same general critical process is used in all communication styles. The critic evaluating a communication event in the message communication style might select a criterion such as fidelity of information transmission and conduct a survey to describe the downward flow of communication in the hierarchy of an organization. The critic might conclude with the evaluation, for example, that the communication is poor because little information is transmitted without distortion from upper management to the workers. The critic of the relationship style makes similar kinds of evaluations. Evaluative criticism is necessary for the practice of any art. In addition, the joy of practicing an art well requires acts of appreciation in which a particularly fine specimen or event arouses warm feelings of esteem. Criticism as appreciation functions strongly at the level of style-specific criticism. Historical works seldom have structures of the kind which characterize most style-specific criticism of day-to-day communication.

Scholars, who in our specialized corporate society tend to be theorizers of communication, often write essays of criticism that are essentially the same as their day-to-day criticism of people who are learning communication styles. The scholarly essay is often more detailed, more precise, and more concerned with esoteric puzzles relating to the fine points of the style-specific theory than are the teacher's comments to a student. Yet the differences between such a scholarly essay and didactic comment in the classroom are only of degree and not of kind. To be sure, scholarly criticism of this sort often has a much larger element of appreciation in it than does the coaching of the classroom teacher. Scholars of any art form have become the connoisseurs, and they enjoy discussing examples of the art in terms of its finer points. To that extent an emphasis on criticism as appreciation is a valid way to explain its uses.

Scholars have not only used criticism to evaluate the art of communication, they have also used critical essays to enter into contemporary controversies and make a persuasive point in an ongoing public debate. Scholars have evaluated politicians, political parties, governmental communication, and pressure groups in terms of the quality of their communication. Often drawing upon the theory related to the public speaking communication style, they have pointed out the shoddy quality of reasoning, evidence, and honesty reflected in the communication of those whose programs or ideas they wish to counter.[57]

On occasion scholarly critics will attempt to improve the general quality of communication in a society. Their aim is to strive for a more objective stance and submit the communication on all sides of a contemporary controversy to careful criticism. They take a guardian role and keep a critical eye on communication. The structure of such work tends to involve description and evaluation, as does the style-specific criticism, but often the critic as guardian casts the explanation into the form of a problem-solution structure.[58] Thus, the rhetorical critic might document a sexist bias in language usage by describing the offending communication and then argue that the bias creates a significant problem. The critic might then go on to imply or specify a solution to eliminate the problem.

The final kind of scholarly rhetorical criticism aims at discovering knowledge about human communication that transcends communication styles and contexts and transitory issues currently under contention. Scholars criticizing public communication in this third way are analyzing communication practices from the perspective of the third level and seeking general understandings of human symbol-using analogous to social scientific investigators aiming to develop general theories of communication. In Campbell's words, "The academic critic explores and analyzes whatever acts will aid in explicating the essential processes of human symbolization."[59]

How does the rhetorical critic searching to illuminate human symbolizing in general proceed? In the first place, the critic does not ask questions such as "Is this a good example of communication in the public-speaking style?" Nor does the critic ask questions such as "In what ways are my opponents in this controversy guilty of unethical, inadequate, or shoddy communication?" Rather, the critic asks questions such as "How does communication function to divide individual from individual, group from group, and community from community? How does communication function to create a sense of community and integrate individuals and groups into larger cooperative units? How does it function to provide for social change and continuity?"

Usually the critic comes to an insight about human communication as a result of studying a body of discourse and practice, and the resulting structure is an amplification and variation upon the theme of that insight.

The structures which characterize the historical studies of rhetoric and public discourse are different from those critics use to explain their insights. Historical structures may take the form of biographical narratives that explain a given communication event in detail or some significant speaker's entire career. Historical studies may also have structures that examine persuasive movements and campaigns or explain artistic practices on the basis of communication episodes of similar artistic patterns. Thus historians might structure explanatory accounts in terms of the Southern Fire-Eating School of Oratory, or the Agrarian School of Barnyard Vituperation. Studies of communication styles along the lines of my analysis in Chapters 3 and 4 and Black's study of the sentimental style are illustrative of interpretations which concentrate on similar artistic patterns.[60] Structures that illuminate individual events or speakers or movements or stylistic groups are explanations from the perspective of the third level. However, they do not provide a general account of human symbol-using. Just as style-specific scholarly criticism can increase our appreciation of the artistic and aesthetic dimensions of a communication style, so can a historical study illuminate the nature of a specific rhetorical community and provide us with an understanding of why it came into being, grew and prospered, and finally declined.

Historical structures often provide a more general accounting of human communication by providing comparative studies of several historical style-specific practices and theories. One common structural type is the tracing of the lineage of rhetorical theory and practice. Thus a historian might trace the teaching practices in American departments in institutions of higher learning devoted to communication back through the content of mass media, journalism, public speaking, and written and oral communication courses to the teaching of rhetoric in nineteenth-century institutions, and back to the influence of such writers of antiquity as Aristotle. Another common structural type is the discovery of historical periods or epochs. A historian might portray the history of political persuasion in North America in terms of a period of nation building, a period of conflict management, a period of war mobilization, and a period of display.

In sum, I believe that an important dimension of the difference between history and criticism relates to the differing viewpoints and structures which the two kinds of humanistic scholarship exhibit.

The Use of History Distinguished from the Uses of Criticism   History and criticism differ in significant ways in terms of their function or use. Criticism often has a much clearer practical application and use than does history, and that helps account for the growing popularity of scholarly rhetorical criticism in the decade of the 1960s, when relevance was a key concept for many specialists in communication. Style-specific criticism is integral and necessary to the maintenance of the daily communication of any culture. Criticism that moves from the day-to-day evaluation essential to ordinary communication to the scholarly critique of communication either for partisan purposes or as the guardian of the quality of communication serves the practical and important purpose of correcting abuses and clarifying the often tacit influences of a culture's communication. Criticism from the perspective of the second level, important as it is, often loses its usefulness when the discourse which brought it into being fades from the scene. The communication criticism vital to the development of the intense small group sessions that helped bind the Oneida Community of perfectionism together in the nineteenth-century has faded into the past. It remains an interesting historical artifact.[61] The critical essay which delivers a polemic against the Nixon administration's communication in regard to the Vietnam War likewise proves ephemeral as that issue recedes into history. The metacriticism from the third level of analysis is more enduring and aims at discovering knowledge about communication styles and contexts.

Historiographers have suggested a number of uses for historical scholarship. First, the scholar satisfies a curiosity about the past. In the late 1970s a television series adapted from a book by Alex Haley entitled *Roots* gained the largest audience of any group of television shows up to that time. The series presented the family tree of one black American family from the time of the capture of the first male member in Africa in the eighteenth century.[62] As a result of the popularity of the series, a number of other families of different ethnic and racial backgrounds began to search for their pasts. The scholar tries to keep the record of the past straight. The uses of the record of the past for a person, a family, a community, a culture, or a nation are subtle but important.

Equally important is Becker's notion that any social collective, whether it is a pair of human beings joined together for a significant period of time, a small group, an organization, a movement, a community, or a nation, requires a collective memory; that without a collective memory there is no cohesion, no sense of groupness, no possibility for cooperation.[63] Without such a record, individuals and social collectives would suffer from a kind of amnesia. The group with a record of its past has an identity, a heritage, a culture. For members of a group without a record, the present has little meaning; the future has little purpose.

People recollect the past by means of legends, folklore, and rites and rituals as well as by means of scholarship. The other recollections perform much the same function as the records kept by scholars. Thus any social collective with a sense of its own identity has a group history composed partly of an authentic record and partly of fanciful reconstructions, which is essentially a synthesis of art, folklore, legend, scholarship, and religion. If a nation such as the United States does not have a history, it must manufacture one, and in this process the story of Pocahontas and John Smith, of George Washington and the cherry tree, and of Patrick Henry saying, "Give me liberty or give me death" may be as important as the scholar's more authentic record.

George Orwell's book *1984* explains in fictional terms the subtle importance of the historical record.[64] In his terrifying society one of the important ways of manipulating the future is to rewrite the record of the past. The controllers of society in *1984* continually rewrite the record. They cause names, dates, places, and events to appear or disappear in the record according to their needs as manipulators of the future. The practice of totalitarian societies provides evidence in support of Orwell's artistic insight that whoever controls the present controls the past and whoever controls the past controls the future. The Nazis rewrote the German past; in particular, they provided a new interpretation of the end of World War I, the Versailles Treaty, and the Weimar Republic. More striking is the way the leaders of the Soviet Union have erased and modified the record. Beria, Molotov, Stalin, even these recent names, have been erased from the record, stricken from avenue and street signs, removed from the maps as towns are renamed.

What distinguishes that portion of the record kept by the humanists from the rest is the ethical imperative that the scholar must, insofar as is humanly possible, develop and keep an authentic record. The scholar tries to keep the record straight. Those who wish to gain or keep power and control society often find the scholar a dangerous enemy. Since scholars try to keep an accurate historical record, they have a duty to enter all relevant material as evidence. Scholars thus will put in the record things that powerful groups would rather suppress. Scholars will not record the fictions that people would like to have in their common recollections. For these reasons the scholar clings tenaciously to the principle of academic freedom. Scholars know that without such freedom to write of the past the record will be tampered with.

Historians provide an important function when they display a complicated set of historical events in all their diversity—aiming only to illuminate the human behavior caught in the focus of their studies, with no explicit desire to generalize their findings to analogous events.

Finally, and most importantly in terms of the analysis of communicative behavior from the third level, historical studies that make comparisons of a range of communication styles within or across a culture within a specific time period or down through history provide general knowledge about communication. Here the analogy with studies of the history of science such as Kuhn's are illustrative. Kuhn's study illuminated scientific practices in general and provided an explanation for changes in scientific practice and thought. In similar fashion, historical studies of communication styles could serve to clarify the way human beings communicate in general.

History and criticism often are closely intertwined in humanistic scholarship in rhetoric and communication. Scott and Brock divide what they call the "traditional perspective" of rhetorical criticism into two strains, the "neo-Aristotelian and the historical." They suggest that "some critics weave the two approaches into a unified work, but often they stand quite separately." They go on to suggest that Nichol's essay "Abraham Lincoln's First Inaugural Address" is an "excellent job of . . . weaving history and rhetorical analysis together quite effectively."[65]

Baskerville is of the opinion that there are substantial differences related to the practice of historiography and criticism. He nonetheless concludes that:

> . . . given the practical nature of rhetorical discourse, its close relationship with audience and situation, it is inevitable that "history"—the weaving of facts regarding speaker, audience and occasion into some kind of meaningful narrative—will often constitute a part of, or a preliminary to an essay in rhetorical criticism. Thus, the familiar concept "history and criticism" or "historical-critical studies" is particularly appropriate to public address.[66]

Campbell and Jamieson also find a symbiotic relationship between history and generic rhetorical criticism. They note:

> A generic approach to rhetorical criticism would culminate in a developmental history of rhetoric that would permit the critic to generalize beyond the individual event which is constrained by time and place to affinities and traditions across time. It would move from the study of rhetors and acts in isolation to the study of recurrent rhetorical action. It would produce a critical history exploring the ways in which rhetorical acts influence each other. Such a "genealogy" would trace the imprint of form on form, style on style, genre on genre.[67]

Summary

Scholars interested in communication have often found philosophers, psychiatrists, literary critics, sociologists of the symbolic interactionist school, cognitive and humanistic psychologists, and critics of social theory stimulating and useful to their thinking about communication.

Humanists who draw a distinction between biophysical motion and human symbolic action have been particularly influential on communication theorists in recent decades. An important stream of thinkers who explain human symbolic action in dramatistic terms illustrates the way humanistic studies can relate to empirical investigations. The sociologists who have adapted Burke's dramatism to their work have often had an empirical bent. Goffman has applied a dramatistic framework for the interpretation of field studies of ordinary human interaction.

The symbolic convergence approach, which utilizes the rigor of social scientific methods to investigate the rhetorical visions constructed from the rhetorical critical analysis of messages, also illustrates the dramatistic melding of humanism and social science.

The history and criticism of public address stands out as one of the more longstanding and influential schools of humanistic study of communication. Beginning in the 1920s with the formation of new departments dedicated to the study and teaching of oral communication, the history and criticism of public address culminated in popularity and influence in the early 1960s. A number of scholars, led by Black, submitted the quasi-paradigm to a systematic critique, and its popularity began to wane. Although the field is still in considerable flux, new directions in research and theory in humanistic studies of rhetoric and communication are beginning to take shape.

Among the new developments is an increasing interest in the distinctions between history of communication and rhetorical criticism and an impulse to encourage more study and writing of history. History and criticism are related in that they both deal with the authentic records left by time and both follow essentially the same scholarly norms in testing evidence and presenting arguments. They differ in that they have differing scholarly viewpoints or perspectives and find different kinds of explanatory structures.

Criticism functions at both the second level of communication practice as an important practical adjunct to communication styles, and at the third level as a way to gain insights into human symbol-using which transcend styles. Histories may function at the second level as a way to create a sense of community for small groups or larger collectives of people but are also developed by scholars at the third level of analysis to transcend specific rhetorical communities and trace similarities and the rise and fall of movements and campaigns.

Despite their differences, history and criticism are closely related and work to supplement and enrich one another in the study of rhetoric and communication.

Notes

1. James E. Combs and Michael W. Mansfield, eds., *Drama in Life; The Uses of Communication in Society* (New York: Hastings House, 1976), p. xxix.
2. Herbert W. Simons, "In Praise of Muddleheaded Anecdotalism," *Western Journal of Speech Communication* 42 (1978): 22
3. See, for example, Thomas B. Farrell and James A. Aune, "Critical Theory and Communication: A Selective Literature Review," *Quarterly Journal of Speech* 65 (1979): 93–107.
4. Wayne M. Towers, "Lazarsfeld and Adorno in the United States: A Case Study in Theoretical Orientation," in Brent D. Ruben, ed., *Communication Yearbook I* (New Brunswick, N.J.: Transaction Books, 1977), pp. 133–145.
5. Simons, p. 21.
6. W. G. Runciman, *A Critique of Max Weber's Philosophy of Social Science* (Cambridge: Cambridge University Press, 1972), p. 43.
7. Romano Harré, "Some Remarks on 'Rule' as a Scientific Concept," in

Theodore Mischel, ed., *Understanding Other Persons* (Oxford: Basil Black-well, 1974), p. 148.

8. Kenneth Burke, "Dramatism," in Combs and Mansfield, eds., p. 10.

9. Quoted in Simons, p. 23.

10. See, for example, Hugh Dalziel Duncan, *Symbols in Society* (Oxford: Oxford University Press, 1968). For a bibliography relating to humanistic studies from a dramatistic viewpoint see Hugh Salziel Duncan, "Short Bibliography of Works on Symbolic Analysis that Relate form to Social Content," in Frank E.X. Dance, ed., *Human Communication Theory: Original Essays* (New York: Holt, Rinehart and Winston, 1967), pp. 310–332.

11. See, for example, Erving Goffman, *Asylums: Essays on the Social Situation of Mental Patients and Other Inmates* (Garden City, N.Y.: Anchor Books, 1961).

12. Erving Goffman, "On Face-Work: An Analysis of Ritual Elements in Social Interaction," in Combs and Mansfield, eds., p. 115.

13. Ibid., p. 118.

14. Ibid., p. 132.

15. Ibid., p. 132.

16. Ibid., p. 118.

17. The basic conceptualization is presented in Ernest G. Bormann, "Fantasy and Rhetorical Vision: The Rhetorical Criticism of Social Reality," *Quarterly Journal of Speech* 58 (1972): 396–407.

18. For some empirical reports of chaining fantasies, see Ernest G. Bormann, *Discussion and Group Methods: Theory and Practice*, 2nd ed. (New York: Harper & Row, 1975); Ernest G. Bormann, Linda Putnam, and Jerie Pratt, "Power, Authority, and Sex: Male Response to Female Dominance," *Communication Monographs* 45 (1978): 128–155; James W. Chesebro, John F. Cragan, and Patricia W. McCullough, "The Small Group Technique of the Radical Revolutionary: A Synthetic Study of Consciousness Raising," *Speech Monographs* 40 (1975): 136–146; Robert F. Bales, *Personality and Interpersonal Relations* (New York: Holt, Rinehart and Winston, 1970).

19. For a case study of the convergence process focusing on the sharing of one salient fantasy in the 1972 Presidential campaign, see Ernest G. Bormann, "The Eagleton Affair: A Fantasy Theme Analysis," *Quarterly Journal of Speech* 59 (1973): 143–159.

20. See, for example, Carl Wayne Hensley, "Rhetorical Vision and the Persuasion of a Historical Movement: The Disciples of Christ in Nineteenth Century American Culture," *Quarterly Journal of Speech* 61 (1975): 250–264; Richard J. Ilkka, "Rhetorical Dramatization in the Development of American Communism," *Quarterly Journal of Speech* 63 (1975); 31–39; Barbara Larson, *Prologue to Revolution: The War Sermons of the Reverend Samuel Davies* (Falls Church, Va.: Speech Communication Association, Bicentennial Monograph Series, 1978); Charles J. O'Fahey, "Reflections on the St. Patrick's Day Orations of John Ireland," *Ethnicity* 2 (1975): 244–257.

21. The Q-sort procedure involves selection of test items such as words, statements, cartoons related to the conceptions to be studied. These items are placed on cards and the subjects sort the cards into piles according to the extent of agreement with the item. Statistic analysis results in clustering those items subjects agree with in order to get a complex and coherent

depiction of the subjects' conceptual representation of the topic under study. See, for example, Ernest G. Bormann, Jolene Koester, and Janet Bennett, "Political Cartoons and Salient Rhetorical Fantasies: An Empirical Analysis of the '76 Presidential Campaign," *Communication Monographs* 45 (1978): 317–329; John F. Cragan and Donald C. Shields, "Foreign Policy Communication Dramas: How Mediated Rhetoric Played in Peoria in Campaign '76," *Quarterly Journal of Speech* 63 (1977): 274–289; David L. Rarick, Mary B. Duncan, David G. Lee, and Laurinda W. Porter, "The Carter Persona: An Empirical Analysis of the Rhetorical Visions of Campaign '76," *Quarterly Journal of Speech* 63 (1977): 258–273.

22. Cragan and Shields have moved in this direction in terms of marketing surveys. John F. Cragan, "Uses of Bormann's Rhetorical Theory in Applied Communication Research" (Paper delivered at the annual meeting of the Speech Communication Association, Minneapolis, November 1978).

23. For a foreign-policy speech prepared on this basis, see Cragan and Shields.

24. For one influential amalgam of philosophy, psychiatry, and literary analysis adapted to communication see Paul Watzlawick, Janet H. Beavin, and Don D. Jackson, *Pragmatics of Human Communication: A Study of Interactional Patterns, Pathologies, and Paradoxes* (New York: Norton, 1967); see also Carol Wilder, "The Palo Alto Group: Difficulties and Directions of the Interactional View for Human Communication Research," *Human Communication Research* 5 (1979): 171–186.

25. For a study of the way publicists have used the past for their current rhetorical purposes and the way historians have often used rhetorical devices for supporting contemporary political positions, see Ronald F. Reid, *The American Revolution and the Rhetoric of History* (Falls Church, Va.: Speech Communication Association, Bicentennial Monograph Series, 1978).

26. Herbert A. Wichelns, "The Literary Criticism of Oratory," in Donald C. Bryant ed., *The Rhetorical Idiom* (Ithaca: Cornell University Press, 1958), p. 35.

27. From an abstract of H. Clay Harshbarger, "Burke's Chief American Works" (Ph.D. Dissertation, Cornell University, 1929), in *Quarterly Journal of Speech* 16 (1930): 384.

28. Ibid., p. 386.

29. See Orville Hitchcock, "Albert Craig Baird," in Loren Reid, ed., *Public Address: Studies in Honor of A. Craig Baird* (Columbia, Mo.: University of Missouri Press, 1961) pp. xi–xix.

30. William Norwood Brigance, *A History and Criticism of American Public Address* (New York: McGraw-Hill, 1943), p. viii.

31. A. Craig Baird and Lester Thonssen, "Methodology in the Criticism of Public Address," *Quarterly Journal of Speech* 33(1947): 134.

32. Ibid., pp. 135–136.

33. Lester Thonssen and A. Craig Baird, *Speech Criticism: The Development of Standards for Rhetorical Appraisal* 1st ed. (New York: Ronald Press, 1948).

34. Thomas R. Nilsen, "Criticism and Social Consequences," *Quarterly Journal of Speech* 42 (1956): 173–178.

35. Leland M. Griffin, "The Rhetoric of Historical Movements," *Quarterly Journal of Speech* 38 (1952): 184.

36. Albert J. Croft, "The Function of Rhetorical Criticism," *Quarterly Journal*

of Speech 42 (1956): 283–291.

37. See also Earnest S. Brandenburg, "Quintilian and the Good Orator," *Quarterly Journal of Speech* 34 (1948): 23–29.

38. Wayland Maxfield Parrish, "The Study of Speeches," in Wayland Maxfield Parrish and Marie Hochmuth, eds., *American Speeches* (New York: Longmans, Green, 1954), p. 12.

39. James H. McBurney and Ernest J. Wrage, *The Art of Good Speech* (Englewood Cliffs, N.J.: Prentice-Hall, 1953), pp. 28–31.

40. Marie Hochmuth Nichols, ed., *A History and Criticism of American Public Address*, vol. 3 (New York: Longmans, Green, 1954).

41. Edwin Black, *Rhetorical Criticism: A Study of Method* (New York: Macmillan, 1965), pp. vii–viii.

42. Ibid., p. viii.

43. Ibid., p. 2.

44. Ibid., p. 124.

45. Ibid., p. 130.

46. Ibid., p. 131.

47. Ibid., p. 130.

48. Robert L. Scott and Bernard L. Brock, *Methods of Rhetorical Criticism: A Twentieth Century Perspective* (New York: Harper and Row, 1972), p. 13.

49. See, for example, J. A. Hendrix, "In Defense of Neo-Aristotelian Rhetorical Criticism," *Western Speech*, 32 (1968): 246–52.

50. *Spectra* 11 (August 1975): 6.

51. The discussions at the Kansas Conference were typical. See Karlyn Kohrs Campbell and Kathleen Hall Jamieson, *Form and Genre: Shaping Rhetorical Action* (Falls Church, Va.: Speech Communication Association, 1978).

52. Barnet Baskerville, "Must We All Be 'Rhetorical Critics'?" *Quarterly Journal of Speech* 63 (1977): 107–116.

53. Bruce E. Gronbeck, "Rhetorical History and Rhetorical Criticism: A Distinction," *Speech Teacher* 24 (1975): 310.

54. Ibid., pp. 309–320.

55. Baskerville, p. 109.

56. The process of style-specific criticism is explicated in detail in terms of the critical process of relating norms to observations in Lawrence W. Rosenfield, "The Anatomy of Critical Discourse," *Speech Monographs*, 35 (1968), 50–69. For a discussion of the criticism within the theory of communication styles in the classroom, see Walter R. Fisher, "Rhetorical Criticism as Criticism," *Western Speech*, 38 (1974), 75–80.

57. See, for example, Karlyn Kohrs Campbell, *Critiques of Contemporary Rhetoric* (Belmont, Calif., 1972); the issue is raised in extreme form in Robert P. Newman, "Under the Veneer: Nixon's Vietnam Speech of November 3, 1969," *Quarterly Journal of Speech* 56 (1970): 168–178 and discussed in the *Forum* of the *Quarterly Journal of Speech* for December 1970. Richard H. Kendall attacks the Newman article for being a polemic unsuitable for a scholarly journal in "A Reply to Newman," pp. 432–435, and Newman answers. The issue is raised in more subtle fashion by Forbes I. Hill, "Conventional Wisdom—Traditional Form: The President's Message of November 3, 1969," *Quarterly Journal of Speech* 58 (1972): 373–386 and discussed in the *Forum* of the same number by Karlyn Kohrs Campbell,

"'Conventional Wisdom—Traditional Form': A Rejoinder," pp. 451–454. Interestingly enough, the same speech was studied by Hermann Stelzner from the perspective of significant recurring form as an example of the mythic quest drama in "The Quest Story and Nixon's November 3, 1969 Address," *Quarterly Journal of Speech* 57 (1971): 163–172. For an essay outlining the rationale for criticism as polemic, see Philip Wander and Steven Jenkins, "Rhetoric, Society and the Critical Response," *Quarterly Journal of Speech* 58 (1972): 441–450. For an interesting commentary on Wander and Jenkins, see Lawrence W. Rosenfield, "The Experience of Criticism," *Quarterly Journal of Speech* 60 (1974): 489–496. The question of criticism as polemic came under heavy dispute and self-conscious evaluation in the early 1970s. Such dispute often signals a shifting perspective among scholars. Thus the impulse for a more enduring criticism raises questions about the use of criticism as polemic.

58. See, for example, Haig Bosmajian, "The Language of White Racism," in Haig Bosmajian, ed., *Readings in Speech*, 2nd ed. (New York: Harper and Row, 1971), pp. 205–215.

59. Karlyn Kohrs Campbell, "Criticism: Ephemeral and Enduring," *Speech Teacher* 23 (1974): pp. 13–14.

60. Edwin Black, "The Sentimental Style as Escapism, or The Devil with Dan'l Webster," in Campbell and Jamieson, eds., pp. 75–88.

61. For a handbook incorporating the style-specific theory of the Oneida group communication, see Murray Levine and Barbara Benedict Bunker, eds., *Mutual Criticism* (Syracuse, N.Y.: Syracuse University Press, 1975).

62. Alex Haley, *Roots* (Garden City, N.Y.: Doubleday, 1976).

63. See Carl Becker, *Everyman His Own Historian* (New York: Appleton-Century-Crofts, 1935).

64. George Orwell, *1984* (New York: Harcourt, Brace, 1949).

65. Scott and Brock, p. 21.

66. Baskerville, p. 116.

67. Campbell and Jamieson, p. 27.

9

Humanistic Studies and General Theories of Communication

In Chapter 8 I described the nature of historical and critical scholarship in rhetoric and communication and both drew some distinctions and pointed out some major similarities between the two. In this chapter I take up the question of what contributions history and criticism can make to the development of general theories of communication. To examine more closely a possible relationship between humanism and social science it is necessary to examine the ways in which humanists explain and account for their findings. To use the Cronkhite and Liska terminology, how do the *explanatory metaphors* of rhetorical critics and historians compare with those of the social scientists theorizing about communication?

Explanation in the Writing of Humanistic Studies

Interpreting the Authentic Record The humanist interprets the record of the past and gives it meaning and significance for the present. Henry Adams characterized the work of historians as undertaking "to arrange sequences,—

called stories, or histories—assuming in silence a relation of cause and effect."[1] When scholars create stories they also create interpretations. Historians, rhetorical critics, and media analysts create the scholarly equivalent of a rhetorical vision when they arrange sequences of events into narrative or dramatic form.

The community of scholars keeps an authentic record that at least in principle contains all the traces left by human activity. The scholar beginning a study must select from the record those materials that seem pertinent. By the very process of selection the individual begins to provide a unique interpretation. When the interpreter takes the selected material and abstracts from the welter of events certain personae to be the characters in a series of incidents and arranges those incidents into a sequence, the result is a further substantial slant to the account.

In the process of telling the story, the humanistic scholar inevitably characterizes the historical personages. If I am doing a study of the rhetoric of abolition and include in my narrative Thomas Jefferson's warnings against the continuation of slavery and omit other details of Jefferson's life relating to that institution, I provide one characterization of him. If I go on to dramatize his sexual relations with his slave Nancy and his subsequent treatment of their offspring, I create a different persona. The humanistic scholar will also characterize human action in terms of plans, intentions, motives. If I tell the story of network television news programming and attribute to the producers of such shows a motivation to serve the public interest, I provide one interpretation; if I attribute a motivation to achieve high ratings in order to make a profit, I provide another.

Scholars may concentrate on studying the authentic record for evidence relating to the avowed plans, intentions, and motives of the human actors. They might, for example, take Lincoln's stated reasons for coming out of retirement in 1854 as the compelling ones. In that case, Lincoln's motive was to save the Union. Scholars may also attribute reasons for human action to factors which are irrational, below the level of consciousness, and beyond the choice of the historical personages. Thus, I might examine Lincoln's behavior in terms of his loss of his natural mother as a child and his relationship to his stepmother.[2] Or I might examine the abolition movement in terms of its leaders being members of a social elite losing their status in society to a newly rising group of economic entrepeneurs and trying to reestablish their status.[3]

Finally, a humanistic scholar might attribute human action to broad inhuman forces which create compelling situations and thus coerce human beings into doing what they do. I might examine the communication that attempted to manage or resolve the conflict over slavery in the Senate of the United States in the years from 1820 to 1860 as so much ineffectual rhetoric divorced from the "realities" of the economic and social forces irresistibly pushing the North and South to an armed conflict. Furthermore, I might interpret the historical context in such a way that nothing that the speakers could have done in terms of their communication would have avoided the Civil War.

In Chapter 8 I pointed out the importance of the recollections of communities of people to their individual and group self-images and to their behavior. I argued that whoever controls the recollections will control the past and by controlling the past will control the future. Any group's recollections will include fictitious accounts of the past as well as nonfictitious accounts. The community will avow that some of the fictions are imaginative but they will mistakingly assume others to be factual. The scholars' role in contemporary North America is to keep watch on the community's nonfictitious accounts to assure that they are authentic and accurate.

The community of humanistic scholars consists of members who have many different viewpoints. They must of necessity select and arrange material from the past into what are often quite idiosyncratic interpretations of what has happened. How then can they agree upon and keep an authentic record?

The authentic record consists of the fragments of the past that are useful for the scholar. Among the fragments are coins, monuments, potsherds, arrowheads, temples, inscriptions, and all artifacts that can give insight into what human beings have done and thought. Some of the historical traces have been preserved because communities have from earliest times developed a collective memory. Some have been preserved by accident; some have been destroyed by accident.

Recent history is no exception. Valuable documents are lost or destroyed and others are altered or doctored. Some may be overlooked because the scholar lacked diligence or was unlucky. Thus, the past must always be reconstructed from the inferences a scholar can make and the insights drawn from traces left by the preceding generation.

The winnowing of time has already sampled the evidence that was once available to scholars. They can never be sure that what remains is representative, for time can be capricious. Often people with a vested interest systematically destroy historical evidence to wipe out information they think would be damaging to themselves, their family, or their friends. Nonetheless a record remains whether the artifacts, documents, electronic transcriptions, and other traces were saved by accident or by design. Some of the record is spurious and some is forged. The community of scholars has two important functions in regard to its guardian role. The first is the testing and evaluation of the historical traces to establish their authenticity. The Kensington Runestone of Minnesota is an example of an alleged historical trace with implications bearing on the discovery of America that has not been established as authentic and is generally discounted by the scholarly community. The second function is the testing and evaluation of the record of events contained in the authenticated traces to judge its accuracy. The first function is called *external criticism* and the second is called *internal criticism*, and the norms for conducting such evidential tests on historical sources are well established. The authentic record is the hard common core of scholarly agreement about the bare bones of human history.

The scholarly community studies the historical traces carefully, evaluating them and coming to agreement about their authenticity and meaning. To be sure, the events recorded in the traces are, for the most part, only indirectly verifiable, and some are more conclusively demonstrated than others for the community. Nonetheless, a community of agreement tends to emerge about the authentic record, and a scholarly work must be tied back to that record with footnotes in such a way that other scholars may check the accuracy of the citations and the interpretation of the traces.

When the scholar takes the historical traces and interprets them by fitting them into a plausible narrative, or setting up a typology or category system, or creating some other explanatory structure, he or she has room for creativity. Like the social scientist, the humanist is restricted in the range of creativity; the scientist is tied to laboratory or field observations and the humanist to the evidence of the past. As long as the humanists account for the authentic record in plausible fashion, they may construct structures to explain it in almost any way they wish. The best work of humanistic scholarship outreaches the merely competent because of its creative and apt explanatory structures. In Chapter 8 I compared and contrasted historical interpretative structures with the interpretations of rhetorical critics in general terms. Here I examine the nature of structure in more detail.

The Nature of Structure   Structure implies an organic form of interrelationships among the salient features of the material that provides so apt a fit of the observable record or the sources that the reader of the study is both persuaded and pleased by the scholar's new way of looking at the material. The structure provides an explanation that leads to an understanding of the subject under study.

Contrary to the assumptions of the scientific historians, the scholar does not find structure in the material as one might find a penny in the street because the penny happens to be there and any other passerby might find it was well. The scholar finds a structure that is a function of the authentic record, to be sure, but the structure is also an invention based upon the investigator's viewpoint and talent. Two scholars studying the same portion of the authentic record from different viewpoints will construct explanatory accounts that provide different structures and, thus, a different understanding of the events. Adam Smith and Karl Marx, studying economic events from different viewpoints, provided very different structures to explain them, and yet both wrote classical works of scholarship. The necessity of reinterpreting the authentic record stems from the possibility of finding different structure in the same events. Much of the excitement, interest, and educational value of humanistic study comes from participating in scholarly communication aimed at understanding, modifying, rejecting, or accepting the explanatory structures presented in scholarly papers, articles, and monographs.

The classical works of scholarship provide particularly apt, persuasive structures that seem universal enough to be applicable to other materials. The classical structures remain relevant and interesting to succeeding generations of scholars. Applying classical structures to new materials is a risky matter, however. When scholars apply the structure developed in the study of a particular part of the authentic record to the other events, the results may do violence to the material under study, because interpretive structures are closely tied to the specific materials they explain. Often the scholar will have to force new material into inappropriate molds in order to fit the derived structure without adaptation and modification. Marxist scholars who have used the structure of *Das Kapital* to explain diverse economic, historical, and cultural materials furnish an example of what can happen in this regard.

Few scholars have the genius to write classical studies; but unless the person has talent enough to find structure of some sort in the material, the result will not be a work of scholarship at all.

A powerful explanatory structure is what makes a work of scholarship live on through time. Such structures are imaginative works of the magnitude of Newton's theory in the natural sciences and can be considered the product of genius. The role of creativity in humanistic scholarship comes most strongly into play at the point of inventing an explanatory structure. But one need not look only to the grand landmarks to discover talented scholars producing apt and satisfying accounts of the subjects of their studies.

Wilbur Samuel Howell provides an excellent historical structure in his study "Ramus and English Rhetoric: 1574–1681." Howell selected this time period because he judged the "period between 1574 and 1681 witnessed the death of the medieval world and the birth of the modern world."[4] In this period, Howell found Ramus a transitional figure, not a rebel fighting medieval thought but rather a reformer who maintained the medieval outlook. Ramus insisted that the liberal disciplines should exist as separate and independent entities. He wished each subject to be rigidly defined. He found that rhetoric and dialectic overlapped in the invention and disposition of ideas. Ramus, whose primary interest was dialectic, tidied up this overlap by pruning from rhetoric the canons of invention and disposition. Rhetoric was then left with style and delivery as its province, since the fifth canon, memory, was also detached from rhetoric and made part of disposition in dialectic. When Ramus' dialectic was translated into English in 1574 by Roland MacIlmaine there was an English system of dialectic and rhetoric. Thomas Wilson was representative of this rhetoric. The collision between the native English dialectic and rhetoric and the Ramist theory resulted in a complete victory for the French invader. Howell found, however, that almost as soon as the Ramist reforms won the field, they became obsolete. The separation of the investigative responsibilities of speakers and writers from their presentational responsibilities took place at a moment in history when other forces were working to bring these responsibilities together. The rhetoric that develped under the influence of Ramus' reforms had little to say to "the brave young science" of the time. The scientists, the representatives of the newly born modern world, wanted a theory of communication adequate to needs of scientist talking to scientist and of scientist talking to the public.

The basic figures underlying this structure are those of death and birth, conflict and collision. The broad general framework or outer structure involves the death of medieval thought and the birth of modern thought. Within this main structure is the collision of the ideas of the reformer Ramus with the rhetoric of Thomas Wilson. The Ramist reforms won the fight in England, but the victory was hollow because developments within the broader structure were making the Ramist system obsolete.

Michael Halloran's study of the televised debate held in the House Judiciary Committee from July 24 through 31, 1974, on the proposed impeachment of Richard Nixon illustrated the way rhetorical critics also provide structure to explain and illuminate communication.[5] Halloran's viewpoint emphasized the whole series of televised reports as one "drama," as a way for society to both solve a problem and hold a mirror up to the community itself and by portraying main currents within the community dramatize the various forces at work to cause society to cohere or divide.

Halloran's structure divided the function of a public proceeding into (1) the discussion of important community problems leading to solutions which the public body has the official power to implement, and (2) the dramatic performance of a ritual of public communion. In the case of the House Judiciary Committee's proceedings these two functions came into conflict during the course of the televised debates on impeachment. The conflict encouraged the committee to allocate most of its time to the first of the five articles under consideration and resulted in the termination of the proceedings after the vote on Article I. In addition, the ritualistic features of the televised hearings encouraged the representatives to use a linguistic style of "rhythm and solemnity" and filled with the conventional forms of Congressional address. Finally, the emphasis on the ritualistic aspects of the hearings accounted for the effect of the communication of the opponents of the majority view. Halloran's explanatory structure, which portrayed the hearings as primarily a way for society to hold a mirror up to the community and dramatize its conflicts and values, was highlighted in his critical analysis of the speaking of minority members Sandman of New Jersey and Wiggins of California. Wiggins' role was central and crucial to the structure. Wiggins supported the basic legitimacy of the entire proceedings, and because he spoke as the loyal opposition he enabled the drama on television to enact the community's customs, laws, and established values for doing public business of the highest importance.

Halloran's structure is plausible and accounts for the authentic record. The committee did spend most of its time discussing the first article. The proceedings did seem anticlimactic after the first ballot. Many commentators in the community did applaud Wiggins for skillfully and honorably playing the role of loyal opposition. Sandman lost popularity and paid the price for stepping outside the drama and questioning the legitimacy of the proceedings. Another critic whose viewpoint saw the hearings as essentially a matter of conducting Congressional business might well invent a structure which judged them to be ineffectual or poor in terms of decision-making because of the distribution of time and the quality of the argument. However, Halloran's structure emphasizing the overriding purpose of the television sessions (tacit as it may have been) as performing a ritual of community cohesion provided a different evaluation of the quality of the communication. Halloran implied that judged according to the needs of the community, the communication event of the impeachment proceedings on television was excellent.

Halloran's structure to explain the television proceedings exhibited another characteristic of good humanistic scholarship in that others will see new applications for his structure. Another scholar wishing to examine another televised committee hearing or public meeting of some governmental body with the power to make decisions might decide they were analogous to the televised debates on impeachment and take Halloran's structure as a starting place to examine the discourse. Halloran restricted the scope of his generalizations to public proceedings that were "official business session[s] of a representative body."[6] But he otherwise implied that his conclusions would apply to any such proceedings across time and cultures.

Humanistic scholarship can be thought of as "objective" and "scientific" insofar as scholars have developed a method for gathering evidence and testing documents so that they can reach general agreement about the truth or falsity of specific statements of fact that relate to the authentic record.

Humanistic scholarship can be thought of as "subjective" and "artistic" insofar as scholars approach their task with different viewpoints and varying talent for discovering structure in their materials. As the historian Frederick Marcham once told members of the Eastern Public Speaking Conference, "And while we seek as much as we can of an authentic record, our claim to respect as scholars, shall we say as artists, lies in our ability to illuminate the fragments left to us with the light of our imagination."[7]

Derived Structure Versus Unique Structure. The question of method in rhetorical criticism is related to the explanatory structure critics use in their work. The neo-Aristotelian critics tended to derive their structures from previous scholarship. Thus, they came to adopt methodological norms that allowed them to ask a similar set of questions relating to speaker, speech, audience, and occasion about almost any oration. Other critics have taken a structure derived from the work of Kenneth Burke, or linguists, or literary critics, or social scientists, and applied them to the objects of their study. Derivative structures pose problems for the humanistic scholar. Gronbeck argued that his taxonomy of documentary films had avoided *the tendency to impose externalized frames from other studies* [emphasis Gronbeck's]."[8] Black would accept a derivative structure if it had been assimilated by the critic.

> A critic who is influenced by, for example, the Burkean pentad and who, in consequence of that influence, comes to see some things in a characteristically dramatistic way—that critic is still able to function in his own person as the critical instrument, and so the possibility of significant disclosure remains open to him. But the would-be critic who has not internalized the pentad, who undertakes to "use" it as a mathematician would use a formula—such a critic is certain (yes *certain!*) to produce work that is sterile [emphasis Black's].[9]

Rosenfield argued even more strongly against the scholar who approached the critical object with a "set of values" or "any other system categories." Such a person, according to Rosenfield, "does not engage in a critical encounter so much as he processes perceptual data." His "'mentality' is that of the mail room clerk sorting parcels into pre-established, discrete, empty bins. But he would be wrong to equate such hollow data processing with thinking, let alone experiencing anything."[10]

The lure of comparative work is nonetheless strong for a number of rhetorical critics, as exemplified in the growing interest in genre criticism. If comparative work is useful, then programmatic studies from some common viewpoint employing a common set of technical critical terms make a good deal of sense. A number of years ago Mouat argued for a unified approach to rhetorical criticism. He wrote not to "make a brief for a particular set of principles that will bind rhetorical concepts but rather to urge that there be a single set of principles." Such unification of rhetorical principles would enable rhetorical critics to "participate in a symposium or in a series of studies, so that unnecessary divergencies, confusions, and cross purposes can be minimized."[11] Wasby noted that the critical emphasis on the idiosyncratic in communication resulted in studies that are "difficult for anyone to integrate in order to develop general explanations or theories."[12] After quoting Wasby, Simons went on to call for criticism that would develop a social science of rhetorical choice and suggested a rigorous common method of definitions and theoretical explanations. Certainly any critic who hopes to use rhetorical criticism as an avenue to the development of a general theory must encourage programs of studies based upon a common viewpoint and some commonality of method.[13]

The issues of method and generalization are closely interrelated in that some critics would argue that the function of criticism is to illuminate the specific and unique and others would search for mythic overarching and recurring patterns.

Generalization in the Writing of Humanistic Studies

Social scientists have long been concerned with the nature of generalizations about human behavior. Are lawful generalizations possible? If possible, can generalizations about human action be universal? Are theories of a middle range more likely than broad all-encompassing Newtonian-type theories? Are probability generalizations possible and useful? Much of the material in Parts II and III of this book has related to issues concerning the nature and extent of generalizations about human communication.

Humanists have also been concerned with the possibility of generalization in their studies. For the most part, social scientists have assumed that some form of generalization, no matter how limited, is a prerequisite for a scientific theory. Humanists, on the other hand, sometimes raised the issue of whether or not generalizations of any sort are either possible or desirable. The role of generalization in humanistic scholarship is basic to a consideration of the ways in which humanism can contribute to the development of general theories of communication.

Generalization in the Writing of History Philosophers of history have thoroughly explored the issue of generalization in the writing of history. Recently, rhetorical critics have become more self-conscious about the advantages and disadvantages of seeking to generalize their findings and to develop theoretical structures of considerable scope based upon their work. Many of the arguments relating to generalizations in the writing of history have a bearing on generalizations in the writing of rhetorical criticism.

Writers on historiography tend to agree that it is very difficult for a humanistic scholar to avoid a minimum level of generalization.[14] The use of language implies some generalization. Without some general syntactical and semantical rules, communication is difficult if not impossible. The method for critical external and internal examination of historical artifacts also contains a set of rules,—i.e., generalizations. If a scholar wishes to emphasize and illuminate the unique nature of the communication under study, he or she must explain the special and unique by at least an implied comparison with the norm, the average, or the general run-of-the-mill.[15]

The major issues, however, relate to the possibility of much broader generalizations than the minimum required for writing and interpreting historical events. Gottschalk has provided an interesting and useful taxonomy of historians in terms of their willingness to generalize. He called the first category "the school of the unique" and characterized them as "those who make generalizations only if they are unaware that they are doing so and try to eliminate the ones of which they are aware." Next is the category of "the school of the strictly limited generalization." Members of the school are aware that they are making generalizations but limit them "strictly to the exposition of the historical subject matter under investigation and of that subject matter only in its own setting." Gottschalk called the next category "the school of generalization on the basis of trends." Members of the school deliberately try to go beyond the subject matter under investigation in order to make comparisons and point out relationships with antecedent, concurrent, and subsequent events and make broad interpretative syntheses, although they limit their generalizations to interrelated trends. Gottschalk's fourth category is "the school of generalization on the basis of comparison." Members of the school not only develop interpretations based upon interrelated trends but go beyond the events under study to draw analogies with events at other places or other times in the past whether they were closely interrelated or not. The fifth category consists of "the school of generalizations that have validity for prediction or control." These are the humanistic scholars searching for generalizations analogous to those of Newton. They venture "propositions about past trends or analogies in such general or abstract terms as to leave the implications, if they do not indeed state explicitly, that their propositions may be extrapolated to events in the future." The final group at the extreme end of the continuum Gottschalk characterized as "the school of the cosmic philosophies of history." The members of the sixth school "propound philosophies that are intended to provide a cosmic understanding of the course of human events past and to come."[16]

Aydelotte has provided a useful summary of four major argumentative positions in regard to historical interpretation and generalization that are equally applicable to humanistic scholarship in communication. The first argument is that a generalization can only take the form of a covering law and because of the complexity of historical forces such generalization is impossible for humanists. The second is that no final proof can be provided for any general statement and historians ought therefore to confine themselves to telling a story based upon the authentic record. The third argument is that historians should confine themselves to insight and speculation. The best of historical insight stems from talent, wisdom, and maturity and not from labored documentation or from method. Historical generalization should be "personal, subjective, intuitive, speculative, and impressionistic." The last argument is that historians gain little from formal procedures and that the recital of statistical evidence cannot take us deeper into "the heart of reality" and that the attempts to formulate generalizations based upon formal statistical methods have been "trivial and inconsequential." Aydelotte develops the four arguments essentially to counter them and to develop his own position, which suggests that theories of a "middle range" are possible and useful and can be forwarded by statistical methods in historical analysis.[17]

Historians who specialize in the study of rhetoric and communication have not devoted a great deal of attention to the problem of generalization. They seem, at the moment, to be more concerned with reasserting the usefulness of the historical study in scholarship relating to communication. Probably when they come to raise the issues regarding their special problems they will have to take a stand on some of the same questions that have concerned historians in general. Rhetorical critics, on the other hand, have begun a serious dialogue on the nature of generalization within criticism. A strong impulse to study enduring features of rhetorical discourse and to search for recurring significant forms developed after the attack on neo-Aristotelian criticism. Scholars published a growing number of studies of rhetorical myth, metaphor, genre, and fantasy themes and types. The impulse expressed itself in the Kansas Conference on Significant Form in Rhetorical Criticism, which was called to consider "recurring patterns in discourse or action including among others, the repeated use of images, metaphors, arguments, structural arrangements, configurations of language."[18]

Generalization in the Writing of Rhetorical Criticism   Simons, in a paper for the Kansas Conference, called for a scientific approach to rhetorical criticism to discover generalized findings that could be integrated into a theory of communication. Simons suggested, "Rather than haggling over the level at which some thing becomes a genre as opposed to a family or species, we might better recognize that genres 'exist' at various levels of abstraction, from the very broad to the very specific."[19] When Simons went on to suggest a taxonomy of genres arranged in a "hierarchical" scheme he reflected the tradition in the natural sciences of searching for theoretical structures based upon concept laws, a tradition which I discussed in Chapter 5. A number of scholars have argued that the discovery of generalizations about rhetorical events in terms of the discovery of recurring patterns that can be placed into genres and related to one another is a useful and important form of rhetorical criticism. Campbell and Jamieson, for example, state:

> Recurrence of a combination of forms into a generically identifiable form over time suggests that certain constants in human action are manifest rhetorically.

One may argue that recurrence arises out of comparable rhetorical situations, out of the influence of conventions on the responses of rhetors, out of universal and cultural archetypes ingrained in human consciousness, out of fundamental human needs, or out of a finite number of rhetorical options or commonplaces. Whatever the explanation, the existence of the recurrent provides insight into the human condition.[20]

Simons was of the opinion that the new generic scholarship "bids fair to producing a social science of rhetorical choice, one that delimits strategic and stylistic options in the face of situational and purposive restraints."[21] Campbell and Jamieson were tentative but did note, "Ideally, theory develops out of and is tested by criticism. Whether or not that is true of generic concepts, these and other criticisms have raised the questions which have become so exigent in contemporary rhetorical criticism."[22]

The process of inductively arriving at generalizations in the form of genres raises the possibility of a taxonomy of genres with explanatory and, perhaps, predictive power. If we have developed a taxonomy of rhetorical genres based upon concept laws and one of the categories is the mass-media apologia and we know that the president is going on television in a situation which creates exigencies that are part of the defining criteria for a mass-media apologia, we could then anticipate if not predict important features of the president's message.

Scholars who would argue for a taxonomy based upon generic concept laws would be analogous to historians of the school which Gottschalk noted wished to develop "generalizations that have validity for prediction or control."

Humanistic scholars in rhetoric and communication have not developed concept laws like *oxygen* and *iron* or *snails* and *crabs*. For the most part they have worked out stipulated definitions that describe pigeonholes into which units of discourse may or may not fit or into which they may fit only partially. Gronbeck's taxonomy of "Celluloid Rhetoric" illustrated the method of clarification by classification as it relates to humanistic scholarship. Gronbeck divided documentary film into two genera, poetic and real, and further divided each genus into three species. The poetic genus consisted of romance, melodrama, and morality play. Each species exhibited sufficient special criteria relating to content and treatment to distinguish it from the others. Gronbeck's taxonomy was not scientific. He categorized some films as romances with confidence, for they exhibited the defining criteria, but with others he was more tentative. Some films exhibited some but not all of the defining criteria and could therefore be considered only partial members of the genre.[23]

If the classifications of messages into genres do not result in lawful generalizations, what might be the purpose of the search for recurring patterns and genres? Scholars who argue that comparisons of samples of discourse with one another can serve to illuminate each are analogous to the historians Gottschalk characterizes as "the school of generalization on the basis of comparisons" whose members develop interpretive structures based upon interrelated trends and who go beyond the events under study to draw analogies with events at other places or other times in the past whether they are closely interrelated or not.

Generalization Related to Situational Constraints   One of the important issues relating to generalization in humanistic scholarship in communication was expressed by Simons as follows: *"Rhetorical genres will emerge most clearly when rhetorical practices are most constrained by purpose and situation* [emphasis Simons']." Simons attributed the position to Black, Rosenfield, Bitzer, Hart, and Jamieson among others. In Simons' view, "rhetorical practices do not cluster together into identifiable genres by accident; rhetoric as a pragmatic, adaptive art, is highly constrained by purpose and situation—and these constraints are often quite similar for different rhetors facing different audiences at different times."[24]

The critic whose viewpoint includes the notion that, as Simons put it, "in statistical terms purpose and situation account for the greatest common variance among rhetorical practices" will proceed as Measell did in his study of Lincoln and Pitt to search out first the historical context to discover the constraints of situation. Having documented the historical analogue, Measell next searched for the commonalities that both Lincoln and Pitt shared and assumed that when similar situational constraints exist, then a similar body of discourse of a repressive nature will be associated with them.[25] Such a critic will, of necessity, write a good bit of historical background for any study, and as Measell illustrated, the historical situation will generally come first in the structure which comes to account for the rhetoric.

Another position on the issue of the relationship between situation and rhetoric is that expressed by Simons, who suggested that a cyclical or dialectical relationship between historical events and rhetorical discourse is a better viewpoint and more likely to be fruitful for critical investigation.[26] The notion that situation effects rhetoric which then affects the subsequent course of events is a venerable one in rhetorical criticism. Essentially the effects criterion of the first edition of *Speech Criticism* emphasized such a pattern.[27] Thonssen and Baird argued that the critic could not understand a piece of rhetorical discourse until the audience, historical background, specific occasion, speaker's previous biography, and specific purpose were documented. Once the speech was accounted for in terms of the context from which it arose, then the critic's task was to complete the analysis by discovering the speech's effect, immediate and long-range, on the unfolding of history.

My own position on the question of whether or not historical analogues drawn from diverse cultures that flourished in remote as well as in more recent times are likely to exhibit similar rhetorical forms is that they are not. Since I would stress the importance of the social reality created by rhetoric, my perspective on this question illustrates yet a third viewpoint.

My position is that the critical viewpoint that divorces rhetoric from what "really counts" too often sends the critic searching for the "real" moving forces of history. Such critics search for social, economic, or other forces to account for what is "really happening" and tend to see rhetoric thrown up by these forces as rationalization or a way to keep the public misled in order to cut down unrest. The Marxist position and indeed all economic-determinism viewpoints have been very influential in supporting the notion that "ideology," which is in their terms usually synonymous with rhetoric, is a smokescreen or an aura surrounding the material forces which determine the march of history.

Critical viewpoints that divorce rhetoric from what really counts are, in some respects, sophisticated versions of the folk wisdom that "if you want to know what a politician is up to, watch his feet, not his mouth." Marvin Meyers, a trained historian but an inspired amateur in rhetorical criticism, remarks of the position that "politics is reduced to a hoof-or-mouth question; and only school children and the gulls of Buncombe County attend to political talk. Journalists, historians, all astute men of affairs will watch the shifting feet." Interestingly enough, some rhetorical critics, perhaps because they aspire to be astute men of affairs, also prefer to watch the shifting feet, even though one would think they would be the first to emphasize the importance of what is said. Meyers, in the preface to his book *The Jacksonian Persuasion*, argues against the emphasis on the shifting feet. He notes that political behavior is "vastly more complicated than the 'realists,' folk or academic, imagine." He maintains:

> Persuasion is not one thing—mere talk—and conduct another—"reality." The paradox of Jacksonian Democracy is not to be resolved by simple separation and elimination. This book is an attempt to define the relationship, placing persuasion in the foreground and conduct in the background. Another writer might reverse the view. In the end the two accounts must meet.[28]

The critic with the viewpoint that the feet are more important than the mouth uses the important stuff, whether sociological analysis or historical interpretation or economic principles or political theory, to account for rhetoric. The critic validates the rhetorical analysis with criteria from investigations that reveal such "real" historical forces as class structure and conflict and economic interests. Measell established the analogy between Pitt and Lincoln first on historical grounds and then searched for rhetorical similarities, as though rhetoric were the dependent effect and historical forces the cause of discourse. The notion that "the situation is the source and ground of rhetorical activity" is a popular one. The concept of *situation* needs careful explication, however. Simons was right in charging that too often the critical terms central to a critic's work have been "woefully inadequate." Particularly I would agree with his charge that "when pressed to indicate what one means by rhetorical situation" the response too often has been "to use such equally ambiguous terms as 'climate,' 'atmosphere,' 'occasion,' or 'set of exigences.'"[29]

Rhetoric can be viewed as situational in two distinct ways. In one sense of the term *situation*, a speaker always faces some idiosyncratic aspects of audience, occasion, topic, and so forth. The speaker giving a funeral eulogy in North America in the 1980s discusses a unique individual and is somewhat constrained by that person's biography. Audiences will differ. The setting for the eulogy will have unique aspects. The speaker may have a somewhat unusual purpose for delivering the eulogy. The immediate occasion will contain novel features. To say that rhetoric is situational in the sense that each specific occasion is to some extent unique is commonplace and does little for the critic searching for significant recurring rhetorical forms. Indeed, the idiosyncratic nature of the situation makes the discovery of analogues more difficult and mitigates against the discovery of genres.

In another sense of the term *situation*, a speaker at any time and in any culture faces a context analogous to other situations in other cultures at other times. That is, all funeral orations in all times and all cultures share a common set of distinguishing characteristics, so they can be called a genre.

There is a tension if not a contradiction between the situational emphasis of the method and the search for a significant form as a recurring pattern. Just as situational ethics tends to restrict the application of ethical insights such as "Thou shalt not kill," so too emphasis on the exigencies of the rhetorical situation mitigates against the discovery of general recurring patterns related to situations. Yet it is the second sense of situation as archetypal historical contexts that results, often if not invariably, in analogous rhetorical forms that are the bases for genre criticism as a way to lawful knowledge.

On occasion, critics following the general assumption that rhetoric springs from situation will accept a historical or sociological definition of a movement or campaign and then turn to the discourse associated with that group and try to find common rhetorical characteristics. Thus we get the rhetoric of black power, of isolationism, of the New Left, of feminism, an so forth. Movements defined on historical, sociological, or political grounds are seldom rhetorically homogeneous. My study of the reform speakers of the three decades prior to the American Civil War revealed two distinct rhetorical movements working for abolition, the rhetoric of agitation and the rhetoric of conversion. On other grounds, historians have often lumped the people involved in the two rhetorical movements together as "the abolition movement."[30]

A critical approach that puts the emphasis on the symbolic side of the equation has much to recommend it. Some critics should begin with the assumption that the rhetoric is a crucial factor in the way a community generates and sustains its social reality and that the community's social action follows or mirrors its symbolic action.[31] The historical situation, the here-and-now problems facing a group of rhetors, does have an influence on discourse in that the rhetoric must often account for it or have a plausible mechanism for ignoring it. Nonetheless, most of the time, the symbolic interpretations of similar events vary a great deal. Indeed, some rhetorical visions are so bizarre that outsiders evaluate them as "crazy" or out of touch with reality. In the 1950s, for example, the rhetorical vision of a group on the far right characterized Dwight Eisenhower as a communist and discounted evidence to the contrary as the result of communists' changing appearances through their control of the media.

Creative Insight and the Writing of Humanistic Studies

To this point I have been stressing the viewpoint of scholars who interpret events in terms of explanatory structures incorporating generalizations.

Another group of rhetorical critics are more analogous to historians who make the argument which Aydelotte summarized that historical generalizations ought to be personal, subjective, intuitive, and speculative. Rosenfield, for instance, urged as a proper stance one in which the critic would "release himself, letting the phenomena 'speak to him' through their luminosity."[32] Black, in a foreword to a reprinting of *Rhetorical Criticism* in 1978, expressed a similar position. Behind the writing of the book, he wrote, "was an idea that was too dimly understood by its author to possess the book as firmly as it would if the book were to be written now. That idea is that critical method is too personally expressive to be systematized." In terms of methodology, Black placed criticism "near the indeterminate, contingent, personal end of the methodological scale." Black saw the critic as the "sole instrument of observation" and the result is, "We value criticism that gives us *singular* access to its subject." Black's emphasis on personal engagement with the object of criticism and with providing singular access to it was coupled with the notion that the "function of criticism in shaping the ways in which an object will be apprehended brings the style of critical writing to transcend mere embellishment, and to acquire probative force."[33] Scott and Brock noted one of the emerging schools of rhetorical criticism following the demise of neo-Aristotelianism to be the experiential.[34]

Critics of the experiential school emphasize the literary nature of criticism as a humanistic art. The critic throws an idiosyncratic light on the discourse because of personal engagement with the material. The critical insight must be more than what others would routinely see to be justified. The criterion of intersubjective agreement is not simply ignored; it is self-consciously rejected as ensuring trivial criticism. However, the emphasis on the personal singular access to the rhetoric does not free the critic from the demands of humanistic scholarship in some important regards.

> The critic's public should, in principle, be able to verify for itself that the critical object can be apprehended as the critic proposes without offering reason, and that the critic's way of apprehending the object yields moral understanding of it.[35]

Scholarship that examines rhetorical and communicative episodes from the viewpoint of bringing creativity and talent to bear on the unique aspects of the experience in the hope of providing the reader with a singular perception of the critical object is unlikely to make a direct contribution to general communication theories.

The explanatory force of creative insight tends to be based upon empathy. The writing of criticism or history that concentrates on a singular engagement with the unique elements in a situation or object functions much as imaginative literature does in enlarging the understanding. Much as a play or novel might enable one to empathically and vicariously participate in a human experience, so too can creative humanistic scholarship provide us with a greater than routine engagement with a historical event or a rhetorical object.

In addition to empathic understanding, the creative humanist may provide the reader with a way of apprehending communication that creates moral or aesthetic understanding. Moral and ethical judgments play an important role in research, theory, and applications in the natural and social sciences. Communication theorists might well benefit from the reading of scholarship based upon creative insight which opens a new window on communication. Society in general will probably be better served if our communication theorists are well read in the humanities as well as the natural and social sciences. Yet those who do not wish to generalize any more than necessary are unlikely to make a direct contribution to general communication theories.

Humanistic Generalization and General Communication Theories

225

Humanistic
Generalization and
General
Communication
Theories

The most direct contributions to general communication theory will come from humanistic scholars willing to generalize their findings to a greater or lesser degree. Some rhetorical critics have been willing to advance only modest forms of generalizations involving similarities in two communicative episodes. Rosenfield, for example, made a comparative study that drew an analogue between Nixon and Truman.[36] Others have suggested generalizations that cover a somewhat broader class of communicative episodes, as Ware and Linkugle did in describing a genre of apologia.[37] Rosenfield's analogue study is drawn from the practice of two speakers using the same communicative style. Similarities among mass-media apologists in twentieth-century North America may well be due to their being types drawn from a common style.

Some humanistic scholars have made generalizations that clearly transcend styles. They have argued that basic recurring communicative patterns are universal to the human condition and have put forward archetypes, recurring mythic structures, and genres as ways to generalize across styles, cultures, and historical epochs. Freud's account of sexual dynamics and complexes in terms of Greek mythology is a pattern of generalization often followed by psychiatrists and psychoanalysts. Stelzner has applied the mythic pattern of a hero going on a quest to a presidential speech of Richard Nixon's.[38] King's study of the rhetorical responses of elites in danger of losing power, my study of the rhetorical uses of evil, and Gronbeck's analysis of the rhetoric of political corruption are other examples of generalizations that span communication styles.[39]

One reason many social scientists have found Burke's writings intriguing may well be that he did suggest universal patterns of symbol-using. Duncan, for example, took Burke's notion of hierarchy and elaborated it into a coherent set of axioms which he assumed to express invariable relations. Duncan noted that "if we refuse to believe that symbols, like Jung's engrams or Freud's memory-traces, are 'derived' from some kind of archaic heritage or archetypes which are passed on through the 'collective unconscious,' then we must show how symbols do affect social relationships." The explanation "must *begin* with questions of *how* symbolic laws operate in social communication [emphasis Duncan's]."[40]

Duncan argued:

Social order is always expressed in some kind of hierarchy. This differentiates men and women in ranks determined by age, sex, family lineage, skill, ownership, or authority, which are scaled in some kind of social ladder. Such differentiation is always resolved through appeals to some universal "higher" principle superior to local principles in which ultimate principles are "latent," or struggling to perfection.[41]

Duncan elaborated on the symbolic laws relating to hierarchy with axioms such as the following:

Hierarchy is expressed through the symbolization of superiority, inferiority, and equality, and of passage from one to another.

Hierarchy functions through persuasion, which takes the form of courtship in social relations.

The expression of hierarchy is best conceived through forms of drama which are both comic and tragic.[42]

The scope of Duncan's generalizations included all groups of human beings who have, are now, or will in the future coalesce into a social order. He asserted that "social order is always expressed in some kind of hierarchy."[43] Duncan's axioms are generalizations in the proper linguistic form to serve as laws in a general theory of communication. The generalization that social order's always expressed as hierarchy resembles the generalization that water when heated will always boil.

If we compare Duncan's axioms with the touchstone of the Newtonian type of hypothetico-deductive theory, however, we discover that the generalizations do not function like laws of nature such as that water when heated always boils. The same analysis that I applied to the variable analytic studies and the consistency hypotheses in Chapter 7 to indicate why they were not covering laws applies with even greater force to the generalizations of humanistic scholars.

Humanistic generalizations, even such broad ones as Duncan's axioms, cannot function as do the generalizations that are laws of nature. The historians searching for what Gottschalk characterized as generalizations that have "validity for prediction and control" cannot serve to engineer the future. Publicists and propagandists engrossed in political and economic battles have often taken such generalizations and used them for the purposes of policy argument. For example, some took the generalization "The appeasement of aggressive totalitarian nations always leads to war" and predicted that since the appeasement of Hitler at Munich led to war, the appeasement of Stalin at Berlin would lead to war.[44] But without suitable quantification, the deductive features of Newton's theory are impossible for historical generalizations. The generalization that appeasement of aggressors always leads to war and the axioms of Duncan's dramatistic account of hierarchy are like the generalizations of cognitive dissonance in that they cannot yield prediction and control or new hypotheses for investigations by means of mathematical computations as Newton's theory can.

Some critics have used quantitative content analysis procedures and counted message elements, and a growing number of historians have recently been using statistical interpretations of quantitative historical data.[45] Nonetheless, humanists are less likely than social scientists to quantify concepts by means of reliable and valid operational procedures which can be replicated from study to study. Without data which fulfill the assumptions of the mathematics employed in computations, the derived theorems and conclusions will not apply to future observations. Rhetorical criticism is often hermeneutic and exegetical in its method. Humanists are more likely than social scientists to draw conclusions from premises by the exegetical form of argument indicated by the social scientific and theological "reasoning" outlined in Figure 6, p. 174.

An equally important difference between covering laws and humanistic generalization stems from the humanistic method of interpreting the authentic record which puts a premium on providing unique and singular account. My discussion of the use of structures derived from previous scholarship indicates the extent to which humanists often denigrate a work which "slavishly" borrows its explanatory structure from a previous study and applies it without modification to new material. The hypothetico-deductive theory is analogous to an interpretative structure in humanistic scholarship. In the practice of normal science the structure of the theory becomes the basic interpretative frame. The community of scientists apply their theory over and over again to new materials. A scientist in the Newtonian tradition who replicated a study and found the same results as earlier studies might add useful information to the puzzle-solving. A social scientist who replicated a study and applied and tested the same interpretative structure could likewise make a contribution to research. By contrast, a historian or rhetorical critic who replicated a study by examining exactly the same material, using the same interpretative structure and arriving at the same conclusions would make little contribution. Other scholars would be likely to characterize such a study as derivative and redundant. The justification for a humanist's dealing with material previously studied is the possiblility of providing a new interpretative structure.

Humanistic Generalizations as Hypotheses for Scientific Investigations How then can humanists and social scientists be brought together in fruitful cooperation in terms of communication theories and hypotheses? Bowers suggested that humanists can derive generalizations from their studies which then serve as hypotheses for rigorous social scientific investigations.[46] The assertion of an invariable relationship by Burke or Duncan may invite an empirical testing such as that provided by Tompkins and his associates when they took Burke's generalizations about hierarchy and used them as a basis for a study of "the inherent characteristics of formal organizations."[47]

Simons called for a "scientific approach to the study of genres" by rhetorical critics. He urged the use of scientific methods to develop a "theoretical coherence to the speculative generalizations of individual critics, help verify (or disprove) their claims by subjecting them to controlled tests, and ultimately guide the interpretation and evaluation of particular rhetorical artifacts."[48] Simons recommended that critics develop theories that are logically rigorous, that allow predictions, that are "confirmed when tested in the real world," and that permit "control over phenomena." In addition, the theories ought to be "'elegant' in the sense that verifiable predictions can be derived from a few general principles" and they ought to be comprehensive for a "broad range of phenomena."[49]

Miller noted that the historical debates within the community of scholars interested in rhetoric and communication were "chiefly characterized by acrimonious rivalry, exaggerated claims and counterclaims, mutual lack of understanding, and absence of much real, substantive stocktaking." He argued that by the mid-1970s the arguments seemed "at best, a quaint historical episode or, at worst, a professional anachronism."[50] He warned against overreacting in the opposite direction and failing to make useful distinctions between humanism and social science.

> Any such tendency to view scholarly distinctions as redundant and unnecessary seems as misguided as most prior dabbling in superficial rivalry and controversy. *Distinctions among various approaches to inquiry are useful and important, not because they demonstrate that one approach is inherently better than others, but because they illustrate the complexity of the phenomena that speech communication scholars seek to understand and illuminate the various kinds of questions that can be asked about these phenomena* [emphasis Miller's].[51]

Miller distinguished humanism from social science not on the basis of method but on the basis of purpose. If the scholar was observing communication episodes primarily to develop "empirical statements that possess generalized predictive and/or explanatory validity" the result would be a scientific study of communication. If the scholar was observing the communication episodes primarily to illuminate the communication involved in order to understand it or to make ethical or aesthetic judgments about it, then the result would be humanistic study of communication. He argued that both the humanist and the social scientist might study the same events and might even use the same methodology such as content analysis but still be distinguished profitably on the basis of goals. Miller would classify the historian searching for laws which allow for prediction and control as a social scientist. Given his stipulated definitions, Miller concluded that:

> . . . each of these motives for question-asking can enrich our understanding of various aspects of the total speech communication process. But in addition, the fruits of each can merge with the other in a symbiotic fashion As a result of intensive humanistic investigation of a specific communicative event, the scientist may gain information that enables him to posit a new hypothesis about the relationship between two or more communicative variables. An attempt to assess the ethics of some communicative transaction may be aided by the findings of a scientific study.[52]

Miller was well advised to emphasize the usefulness of distinguishing between humanism and social science, but his distinction based on the investigator's purposes seems awkward. Shields and Cragan pointed out some difficulty in Miller's formulation in terms of discovering the covert motives of investigators.[53] Miller suggested that in the give-and-take of scholarly controversy the motivations of individuals would come clear. But a set of stipulated definitions that result in classifying scholars seeking to find genres or historical generalizations as scientists would confuse the issues almost as much as it would clarify them.

If we adopted Miller's stipulated definitions to distinguish scientists from humanists we would blur other important distinctions, such as those relating to the humanist's use of the traces of the past as evidence compared to the social scientist's systematic observations and those relating to the differing viewpoints and explanatory structures which also serve to explain the differences between social scientists and humanists.

The idea that humanistic studies might serve to turn up hypotheses that could, in turn, serve as the basis for social scientific investigations is plausible and has been the case on occasions in the past. Too often, social scientists have selected hypotheses drawn from special style-specific theories, but that need not be. Social scientific methodologies have been and might well be used profitably in the future to study areas that humanistic scholarship has revealed to be generalizable across styles.

The Symbiotic Relationship of Social Science and Humanism

My own position is that some of the more exciting and fruitful work in communication theorizing in the last decade has been in terms utilizing the contributions of humanists and social scientists in a symbiotic relationship of greater complexity than the one of having humanists do the preliminary spade-work to discover hypotheses for social scientists to test subsequently.

Simons noted one important way that rhetorical criticism could contribute to communication theory: "While other students of persuasion are busy determining the differential effects of varied rhetorical choices, critics can be breaking new ground by developing theory and conducting research about the factors influencing those choices."[54] Humanistic studies can make a strong contribution to those communication theorists whose work stresses the importance of studying the meaning of the symbolic actions to the people who are involved in their enactment. A complete account of a communication episode requires the work of humanists and social scientists studying the details of the communication that are style-specific to a given community.

The social scientist making an ethnographic study of the practices of a linguistic community such as Philipsen's study of speaking "like a man" in Teamsterville and the humanist making a critical analysis such as Black's study of the sentimental oratory of the nineteenth century can both make an important contribution to the understanding of human communication.[55] They both contribute to *verstehen* in the Weberian tradition by giving insight into the rules, customs, norms, and general usage of a specific community.

If we know that there is a general tendency in human interaction for people to do "face-work" in Goffman's terms, we understand something about communication. A given community, however, is likely to have a "unique character" because "its standard set of human-nature elements is pitched and combined in a particular way."[56] Humanists who study style-specific communication practices help explain the unique way which a given rhetorical community pitches and combines its standard set of human-nature elements.

Ethnographic studies of the communication practices of communities by means of fieldwork or by studies of ordinary language and conversations also provide an understanding of the unique character of the communication community. The methods of some of the investigators making ethnographic and ordinary language studies resemble those of rhetorical criticism. Hermeneutics in its traditional sense as well as in its more contemporary social scientific meaning is essentially the critique of language and communication.[57]

The work of those who study style-specific communication from either a humanistic or social scientific perspective can be enriched by humanistic studies that discover recurring patterns or generalize across communication styles. Blending the research results from humanistic and social scientific studies at both the second and the third level can provide a full understanding of human behavior and human symbolic action.

The interplay of humanistic and social scientific studies and theorizing can be illustrated by contemporary work in small group communication. Recall the Burke and Duncan formulation of the generalized tendency of all social order to be expressed in some kind of hierarchy. Assuming that generalization to be useful, we could study small groups in laboratory and field settings to discover whether or not they structured their roles into a hierarchical form. Shaw summarized a number of small group studies as follows:

> When several individuals come together for the first time and begin to interact, these consistent individual differences begin to appear. Some persons talk more than others; some exert more influence upon the group's decisions; some are generally more active than others; some appear to elicit greater respect from other group members; and so on. . . . Each position is evaluated by the members of the group, including the occupant, in terms of its prestige, importance, or value to the group. Although several positions may enjoy equal status, there almost always exists status differences such that the group structure is hierarchical.[58]

For small group communication settings in contemporary North America, at any rate, empirical social scientific studies support the generalization that the social order is characterized by hierarchy. Such a generalization provides a partial explanation, but for full understanding we need to have a richer theory. Since I have previously argued that Shaw's attempts to use the variable analytic quasi-paradigm and develop Newton-like hypotheses proved relatively barren, we need to look for alternative theoretical structures.

Nofsinger suggested that a better model for communication theories might be Darwin's explanation of the patterns of evolution. He wrote, "We must study, interpret, and compare specific instances. We must have the details! Darwin and [Wallace] probably would not have devised the theory of evolution merely from a general impression that life abounds in variety."[59]

Darwin provided an explanatory structure to account for the facts of evolution. Just as a later historian might study the same portion of the record and provide a much different explanatory structure than an earlier one, so might another scientist study the fossil record and provide a different explanatory structure than the one suggested by Darwin.

Darwin's explanatory structure consisted of the generalization that nature produced more life than the environment could sustain, which always resulted in a battle for survival. Those life forms which were best adapted to their environment survived. The survival of the fittest provided a selective process that assured that only the best individuals in terms of adaptation would have progeny. Since survival of the fittest did not account for all the facts, Darwin added the generalization that sexual preference served to select out certain characteristics for survival. Bright plumage evolved for male birds in some species because it was sexually attractive even though it was not well adapted for camouflage purposes.

An account of the emergence of hierarchy in small groups could take a form somewhat like Darwin's explanation of the facts of evolution. The theory could consist of a generalization that there is a tendency in small groups of people working together to specialize. The process underlying the specialization is that the total communicative influence in a group is in the direction of encouraging individuals to specilize in such a way that they will maximize the effective use of their talents to best achieve the group's purposes. Assume that some speech act is important to the effectiveness of the group and that all the members can perform the act but some are better than others. The group would encourage the member who was best at it to specialize in that particular communicative function. Since the tendency to make maximum use of member resources does not explain all the facts, a corollary generalization might be needed. For example, a corollary generalization might be that the communication in groups creates a shared cultured that includes common values and that these shared values influence the way members assign prestige and status to one another.[60]

With the addition of an explanatory structure in the Darwinian form we have a richer explanation of the role of hierarchy in small group communication. We not only have the evidence of social scientific investigations which document the generalization for a specific domain (small group communication) but we have also a process account which explains why the hierarchy came into being. Much detail is still missing from the explanation, however. Assume that to the general findings I now add detailed case studies of specific groups. My extensive case studies provide information analogous to that gathered by ethnographic studies of larger communities. On the basis of case studies I search for recurring patterns that cut across groups and find in contemporary North America a cluster of such groups that fall into a communication style similar to the relationship style outlined in Chapter 4. The patterns also reveal another style similar to the message communication style.[61]

We can now add to the general theory of small group communication the details of the style-specific special theories. Using the two theories, we get a yet fuller account of the communication of any given group. We might note that a particular group is a business meeting in a corporate setting and in the pragmatic style. The hierarchical structure of the group is explained in terms of the general theory of specialization and status emergence. The details of the specialization are explained in terms of the exemplar communication model and the specific tasks the group performs. We might examine how good—that is, how close to the ideal type—this particular group is and explain it further in terms of its relative artistic excellence. We could next make a rhetorical criticism of the communication in a series of meetings as Sharf did by applying a Burkean analysis to some small group communication or as others have done by applying fantasy theme analysis. [62]

When we blend all of the elements from humanistic and social scientific theories and studies together, we understand not only what Goffman called the "traffic rules of social interaction" and "the code the person adheres to in his movement across the paths and designs of others," but we also get insight into where the group members are going and why they want to get there. We also can explain why they are ready to follow the code or why they choose to break the rules. [63]

In my example of small group communication theory the humanistic insight that hierarchy is central to social order was documented by rigorous social scientific investigations. A general explanatory account not in the form of Newton but along the lines of Darwin provided understanding as to why the hierarchy came into being in the small group setting. Case-study observations that noted details of individual groups revealed the presence of special theories of small group communication relating to communities practicing styles of communication. These stylistic features were supplemented by rhetorical criticism of the communication in the group.

The same pattern of theorizing could develop for larger communities. Instead of case studies the social scientific investigations could be ethnographic studies or naturalistic studies of communication. The humanistic study of the rhetorical communities could discover patterns that generalize across styles and provide the basis for social scientific investigations that could culminate in general theories. The application of general theories and the special theories to given episodes could be supplemented by field-study descriptions of the communicative behavior and rhetorical criticisms of the messages.

When investigators apply the general and special communication theories which relate to a communication episode and add detailed ethnographic or historical and critical studies to actual communication episodes within a given community, they provide an understanding of the symbolic behavior in a way that a covering law theory by itself could not. On the other hand, the kind of understanding provided by such a complex accounting for communication would not allow the investigators to predict and control events.

I might follow the procedure outlined above in studying a given task-oriented small group and come to a rich understanding of their communication. My understanding might have practical applications in that I could help them approximate the exemplar model of good communication in the style they are practicing by intervening in the sessions, giving advice, evaluating the communication, and coaching the group on ways to improve. My efforts to improve the artistry and effectiveness of the task-oriented small group would be facilitated by my understanding of what was going on. But the application of special and general theories would not enable me to predict and control the communication and the way their group would evolve in the same way that I could control the trajectory of a bullet by the application of the laws of Newton to the problem. Freely falling objects on the surface of the earth do not pause and say, as a student once said to me when I was coaching her in an attempt to improve her group, "I understand. I know what I ought to do but I'll be damned if I'll do it."

Summary

The humanist interprets the record of the past and gives it meaning and significance for the present. The community of humanists keeps an authentic record by performing two important guardian functions: (1) testing and evaluating the historical traces to establish their authenticity, and (2) testing and evaluating the evidence contained within the authenticated traces to judge their accuracy and usefulness as evidence about the nature of historic events.

When a scholar takes the historical traces and interprets them, he or she has room for creativity. The humanist is restricted to the evidence of the past as authenticated by the scholarly community's tests of external and internal criticism of sources. As long as humanists make plausible accounts of the authentic record they may construct explanations in creative fashion.

Structure implies an organic form of interrelationships among the salient features of the historical record that provides so apt and plausible a fit that the reader of the study is provided with a new understanding of the events. The scholar finds a structure that is a function of the authentic record, but the structure is also an invention based upon the investigator's viewpoint and talent. A powerful explanatory structure is what makes a work of humanistic scholarship live on through time.

Derivative structures pose a problem for humanistic scholars. A historian or critic who applies the structure developed in a prior study may have difficulty because the interpretative structure is closely tied to the specific materials of the original study. The scholar may do violence to the new material by forcing it into inappropriate molds in order to make it fit the derived structure. One group of rhetorical critics avoids the use of derived structure. Comparative work does imply some commonalities of viewpoint and structure, and another group of rhetorical critics encourage the creative application of systems of analysis in order to further programs of research and the development of genres and taxonomies.

The community of historians and critics is divided on the question of the possibility and advisability of generalizations in their work. The scholars tend to fall along a continuum from those at one extreme who stress the unique and singular nature of humanistic scholarship to those on the other who seek generalizations that allow for prediction and control of human events. In rhetorical criticism the problem of generalization is related to the assumptions that scholars make about the importance of situational restraints. Some scholars have as part of their viewpoint the assumption that situational constraints control rhetorical choice and method and that since communicative situations tend to recur, each situation results in a rhetorical type or genre. Others have a viewpoint that sees a reciprocal relationship in that situations constrain rhetoric but rhetoric shapes future situations. A third position reflects the viewpoint that communication creates social reality and the resulting social situations.

The rhetorical critics who stress creative insight and strive for a personal and unique engagement with the critical object provide the reader with an opportunity for empathic understanding and the apprehension of moral or aesthetic judgments.

Rhetorical critics who seek generalizations which transcend communication styles provide the most direct contributions to the development of general theories of communication. Some humanists have made broad generalizations about communicative events, but such generalizations are not the same as the covering laws of a Newtonian theory and they cannot provide the same kind of understanding, prediction, and control of events.

Some philosophers of communication have suggested that humanistic and social scientific studies can be brought into fruitful cooperation by using the generalizations of humanists to furnish the hypotheses for social scientists. Social scientists have, in the past, developed their hypotheses from humanistic studies, but they have often selected topics drawn from style-specific theories that restrict their domain to a particular rhetorical community.

The interplay between humanistic scholarship and social scientific studies and theorizing can be much more complex than the linear one in which humanists discover topics and social scientists investigate them. The work of those who study style-specific communication from either a humanistic or social scientific perspective can be enriched by humanistic studies that discover recurring patterns that generalize across styles. Blending the research results from humanistic and social scientific studies at both the second and the third level can provide a full understanding of human behavior in the tradition of Weber's concept of *verstehen*.

Verstehen provides insights into events that include the communicators' rhetorical choices and why they made them as well as their actual communicative behavior. The kind of complex accounting for communication that would result from a blending of humanism and social science would not, however, allow for the prediction and control of events. The model of the Newtonian hypothetico-deductive theory is too simple to deal adequately with the complexity of human symbolic action. The actors who play out their communication episodes at the second level reflect upon their behavior and their communication in order to establish rules, customs, stylistic theories, and critical procedures. From time to time they change their styles and rules and sometimes choose not to conform to the rules or follow the dictates of style.

A total account of communicative behavior that explains not only general features of human symbol-using but also provides understanding of the details of specific episodes will require both special and general theories, as detailed in the previous chapters. The total account of communication might well include humanistic studies which supplement social scientific investigations to explain how human beings acquire competence in language, in styling communication, in developing rules, and in making choices about strategy and tactics, and, indeed, about whether or not to conform to communication-related conventions.

Notes

1. Henry Adams, *The Education of Henry Adams: An Autobiography* (Boston: Houghton-Mifflin, 1918), p. 382.
2. A group of scholars developing accounts of events from a psychohistorical viewpoint have sometimes analyzed the relationships among family members as part of their interpretative structure. Vol. 5, no. 2 of *The Journal of Psychohistory* (1977) is devoted to studies of President Carter, and several essays in that number examine his childhood. See particularly David R. Beisel, "Toward a Psychohistory of Jimmy Carter," pp. 201–238.
3. For a brief presentation of the "status revolution" thesis, see David Donald, "Abolition Leadership: A Displaced Social Elite," in Richard O. Curry, ed., *The Abolitionists; Reformers or Fanatics?* (New York: Holt, Rinehart and Winston, 1965), pp. 42–48.
4. Wilbur Samuel Howell, "Ramus and English Rhetoric: 1574–1681," *Quarterly Journal of Speech* 37(1951): 299–310.
5. Michael Halloran, "*Doing Public Business in Public,*" in Karlyn Kohrs Campbell and Kathleen Hall Jamieson, eds., *Form and Genre: Shaping Rhetorical Action* (Falls Church, Va.: Speech Communication Association, 1978), pp. 118–138.
6. Ibid., p. 119.
7. Frederick George Marcham, "History and Speech: Collaborative Studies, Present and Future," *Quarterly Journal of Speech* 35 (1949): 288.
8. Bruce Gronbeck, "Celluloid Rhetoric: On Genres of Documentary," in Campbell and Jamieson, eds., p. 156.
9. Edwin Black, "Author's Foreword," *Rhetorical Criticism: A Study in Method* (Madison: University of Wisconsin Press, 1978), p. xii.
10. Lawrence W. Rosenfield, "The Experience of Criticism," *Quarterly Journal of Speech* 60 (1974): 491.
11. Lawrence H. Mouat, "An Approach to Rhetorical Criticism," in Donald C. Bryant, ed., *The Rhetorical Idiom* (Ithaca, N.Y.: Cornell University Press, 1958), p. 165.
12. Stephen L. Wasby, "Rhetoricians and Political Scientists: Some Lines of Converging Interest," *Southern Speech Journal* 36 (1971): 237.
13. Herbert Simons, "'Genre-alizing' About Rhetoric: A Scientific Approach," in Campbell and Jamieson, eds., pp. 33–50.
14. For a discussion of the issue from a historian's point of view, see Louis Gottschalk, "Categories of Historiographical Generalization," in Louis Gottschalk, ed., *Generalization in the Writing of History* (Chicago: University of Chicago Press, 1967), pp. 113–129.
15. Ibid., p. 114.
16. Ibid., pp. 113–114.
17. William O. Aydelotte, "Notes on the Problem of Historical Generalization," in Gottschalk, ed., p. 146.
18. *Spectra* 11 (August 1975): 6.

19. p. 37.

20. Karlyn Kohrs Campbell and Kathleen Hall Jamieson, "Form and Genre in Rhetorical Criticism: An Introduction," in Campbell and Jamieson, eds., pp. 26–27.

21. Simons, p. 33.

22. Campbell and Jamieson, p. 18.

23. Gronbeck, pp. 139–161.

24. Simons, p. 41; see particularly Lloyd F. Bitzer, "The Rhetorical Situation," *Philosophy and Rhetoric* 1 (1968): 1–14; and Kathleen Jamieson, "Generic Constraints and the Rhetorical Situation." *Philosophy and Rhetoric* 6 (1973): 162–170.

25. James Measell, "A Comparative Study of Prime Minister William Pitt and President Abraham Lincoln on Suspension of Habeas Corpus," in Campbell and Jamieson, eds., pp. 87–102.

26. Simons, p. 48, footnote 36.

27. Lester Thonssen and A. Craig Baird, *Speech Criticism: The Development of Standards for Rhetorical Appraisal* (New York: Ronald Press, 1948).

28. Marvin Meyers, *The Jacksonian Persuasion: Politics and Belief* (Stanford: Stanford University Press, 1960), pp. v, vi, viii.

29. Simons, p. 42.

30. Ernest G. Bormann, "The Rhetoric of Abolition," in Ernest G. Bormann, ed., *Forerunners of Black Power: The Rhetoric of Abolition* (Englewood Cliffs, N.J.: Prentice-Hall, 1971), pp. 1–38.

31. Cathcart makes a strong case for the rhetorical definition of movements rather than for the critic relying on definitions based on historical, sociological, or political grounds. See Robert S. Cathcart, "New Approaches to the Study of Movements: Defining Movements Rhetorically," *Western Speech* 36 (1972): 82–88; see also Charles A. Wilkinson, "A Rhetorical Definition of Movements," *Central States Speech Journal* 27 (1976): 88–94.

32. Rosenfield, p. 494.

33. Black, pp. x–xiii.

34. Robert L. Scott and Bernard L. Brock, *Methods of Rhetorical Criticism: A Twentieth Century Perspective* (New York: Harper & Row, 1972), p. 15.

35. Black, pp. xii–xiii.

36. Lawrence W. Rosenfield, "A Case Study in Speech Criticism: The Nixon-Truman Analog," *Speech Monographs* 35 (1968): 435–450.

37. B.L. Ware and Wil A. Linkugel, "They Spoke in Defense of Themselves: On the Generic Criticism of Apologia," *Quarterly Journal of Speech* 59 (1973): 273–283.

38. Hermann G. Stelzner, "The Quest Story and Nixon's November 3, 1969 Address," *Quarterly Journal of Speech* 57 (1971): 163–172.

39. Andrew A. King, "The Rhetoric of Power Maintenance: Elites at the Precipice," *Quarterly Journal of Speech* 62, (1976): 127–134; Ernest G. Bormann, "Fetching Good Out of Evil: A Rhetorical Use of Calamity," *Quarterly Journal of Speech* 63 (1977): 130–139; Bruce E. Gronbeck, "The Rhetoric of Political Corruption: Sociolinguistic, Dialectical, and Ceremonial Processes," *Quarterly Journal of Speech* 64 (1978): 155–172.

40. Hugh Duncan, "Axiomatic Propositions," in James E. Combs and Michael W. Mansfield, eds., *Drama in Life: The Uses of Communication in Society* (New York: Hastings House, 1976), p. 30.

41. Ibid., p. 33.
42. Ibid., pp. 34, 35, 36.
43. Ibid., p. 33.
44. For a discussion of such generalizations and the general problem of historical generalizations as related to laws of nature, see Morton A. Kaplan, *On Historical and Political Knowing: An Inquiry Into Some Problems of Universal Law and Human Freedom* (Chicago: University of Chicago Press, 1971).
45. See, for example, Roderick Floud, *An Introduction to Quantitative Methods for Historians* (Princeton: Princeton University Press, 1973); William O. Aydelotte, Allan G. Bogue, and Robert William Fogel, eds., *The Dimensions of Quantitative Research in History* (Princeton: Princeton University Press, 1972).
46. John Waite Bowers, "The Pre-Scientific Function of Rhetorical Criticism," in Thomas R. Nilsen, ed., *Essays on Rhetorical Criticism* (New York: Random House, 1968), pp. 126–145; See also Bruce Gronbeck, "Rhetorical History and Rhetorical Criticism: A Distinction," *Speech Teacher* 24 (1975): 309–320.
47. Phillip K. Tompkins, Jeanne Y. Fisher, Dominic A. Infante, and Elaine L. Tompkins, "Kenneth Burke and the Inherent Characteristics of Formal Organizations," *Speech Monographs* 42 (1975): 135–142.
48. Simons, p. 34.
49. Ibid., pp. 35–36.
50. Gerald R. Miller, "Humanistic and Scientific Approaches to Speech Communication Inquiry: Rivalry, Redundancy, or Rapproachement," *Western Speech Communication* 39 (1975): 230.
51. Ibid., p. 231.
52. Ibid., p. 238.
53. Donald C. Shields and John F. Cragan, "Miller's Humanistic/Scientific Dichotomy of Speech Communication Inquiry: A Help or Hindrance?" *Western Speech Communication* 40 (1976): 278–281; "Miller Replies," pp. 281–283.
54. Simons, p. 44.
55. Gerry Philipsen, "Speaking 'Like a Man' in Teamsterville: Culture Patterns of Role Enactment in an Urban Neighborhood," *Quarterly Journal of Speech* 61 (1975): 13–22; Edwin Black, "The Sentimental Style as Escapism, or The Devil with Dan'l Webster," in Campbell and Jamieson, eds., pp. 75–86.
56. Erving Goffman, "On Face-Work: An Analysis of Ritual Elements in Social Interaction," in Combs and Mansfield, eds., p. 132.
57. For a discussion of some contemporary approaches to hermeneutics, see Leonard C. Hawes, "Toward a Hermeneutic Phenomenology of Communication," *Communication Quarterly* 25 (1977): 30–41.
58. Marvin E. Shaw, *Group Dynamics: The Psychology of Small Group Behavior* (New York: McGraw-Hill, 1971), pp. 234–235.
59. Robert E. Nofsinger, Jr., "A Peek at Conversational Analysis," *Communication Quarterly* 25 (1977): 20.
60. For an amplification of this emergence theory of small group communication, see Ernest G. Bormann, *Discussion and Group Methods: Theory and Practice*, 2nd ed. (New York: Harper & Row, 1975), Part II, "Theory."
61. For a description of the consummatory and pragmatic styles of small group

communication, see Bormann, pp. 29–47.

62. Barbara F. Sharf, "A Rhetorical Analysis of Leadership Emergence in Small Groups," *Communication Monographs* 45 (1978): 156–172. For a rhetorical criticism using fantasy theme analysis, see Ernest G. Bormann, Jerie Pratt, and Linda Putnam, "Power, Authority, and Sex: Male Response to Female Leadership," *Communication Monographs* 45 (1978): 119–155.

63. Goffman, p. 118.

238

Humanistic Studies and
General Theories of
Communication

10

Afterword: Summary and Future Directions for Communication Theory

The scholars whose main intellectual focus is the study of human communication have achieved a level of sophistication in research methodology and theorizing that bodes well for the future. Twenty years ago, social scientific investigations in communication were sometimes methodologically naive when compared to those of social science in general. Since that time the level of training in social scientific methods for communication researchers has risen dramatically. The communication researchers who have received their training in the last decade have usually been well prepared in applied statistics, often knowledgeable in the foundations of statistics, and conversant with research design, data collection, and the problems of quantification.

In preparing this manuscript I surveyed the literature in communication and such cognate disciplines as philosophy, psychology, sociology, and psychiatry. My conclusion is that the research design and general methodological sophistication in communication compares favorably with the best work in social science in general. Sophistication and talent in research design and method are not guarantees of success, but they are prerequisites.

Even as late as the 1960s many communication scholars were relying almost entirely on conceptualizations and explanatory structures borrowed from other disciplines. They were citing social psychologists and sociologists in their articles without being cited in return, which they often took to be indicative of second-class academic status. From time to time they published in the journals of other disciplines and often interpreted such publication as more prestigious than similar publications in communication journals.

In the 1970s communication theorists found less need to document their ideas with allusions to works from other fields. The footnotes in this book could have been more liberally sprinkled with the names of philosophers, sociologists, and psychologists with only a tangential interest in communication. The student of communication who wishes to specialize in a given area of theorizing ought to read the pertinent materials from other fields in depth. However, a survey of communication theory such as this one no longer has to rely heavily on such material, because the literature on communication deals with the same ideas cogently and in direct application to human communication.

By the 1980s the general intellectual climate for scholars in communication had changed markedly for the better. Throughout the pages of this book I have documented the fact that a number of creative theorists and philosophers of communication emerged from within their own ranks in the 1970s. These seminal thinkers began to write about communication in ways which broke new ground, and fewer and fewer of them continued the derivative path of trying to apply assumptive systems, explanatory structures, and technical terminology from other disciplines to communication research and theory.

Publications in such journals as *The Quarterly Journal of Speech, Communication Monographs*, and *Human Communication Research* are now of high quality and compare favorably with those in the best of the social scientific journals.

Further evidence of research maturity is furnished by the fact that more and more communication scholars are receiving grants in support of their research. They are doing so in competition with other social scientists; governmental funding agencies and national foundations are increasingly supporting communication research, further testifying to the general excellence of such work.

The field of applied communication has grown even more rapidly than basic research. Courses in communication have grown in number and importance. More and more students have been drawn to the study at both the undergraduate and graduate levels. The demand for continuing education and for consulting in communication from all the corporate structures in society has grown rapidly in the last two decades.

Meantime the controversies within the community of scholars interested in rhetorical and communication theory and research have largely burned themselves out. Much of the conflict was unproductive quibbling over such "issues" as whether "data-crunching mechanics" could ever be expected to make a contribution to the intellectual development of literate and humane people, or whether the anachronistic "word games" of the rhetoricians could ever be expected to make a contribution to significant knowledge about communication or to the real needs of the late twentieth century. Although some brushfires of irritation break out from time to time, remindful of the old flaming antagonism, the newer generations of both humanists and social scientists seem eager to cooperate and to explore possible integration of effort.

Ironically, while so much progress in terms of quality of training, and of acceptance by the intellectual community and the general public characterized the 1970s, the decade, as we have seen, was also characterized by a widespread feeling that something was amiss with the state of communication theorizing. The publications discussing the state of the art reflected an increasing feeling of unease and a lessening of excitement about the research results. There was an ebbing of the heady feeling that theorists were in the vanguard of important developments and on the verge of theoretical breakthroughs that would soon bring about ways to predict and control human behavior. What was an impulse in the 1960s had become by the late 1970s a concerted effort to submit the entire research and theorizing enterprise to a thorough critique.

The impulse began in the 1960s with the awareness that, despite decades of effort, the theoretical payoff of social scientific investigations in communication was not up to the promise. According to the scenario of the development of hypothetico-deductive theories, after extensive investigations, low-level laws of nature would emerge that would, in turn, guide future investigations, and before too long, theoreticians would formulate covering laws that encompassed the low-level generalizations. When the realities of communication research failed to match the script, a number of theoreticians began to search for the source of the problem. They decided that what was needed was the work of synthesizers and integrators of research results. The mid-1960s saw a spate of theoretical essays summarizing research results.

When the efforts at synthesis failed to produce theories, some troubled scholars turned to critical examination of the details of social scientific methodology utilized in the research efforts. They asked whether laboratory studies were inherently unable to duplicate real-life communicative situations, whether the details of quantification in terms of reliability and validity were adequate, whether the statistical models were appropriate and of sufficient power, and whether the selection of subjects, the control of biases, and the demand characteristics of the experiments were sufficient. To some extent the current high quality of training in statistical procedures and foundations, the use of computer technology, and the design of social scientific experiments among communication researchers stem from the careful critique of research method of the period.

Finally, in the 1970s, the impulse turned to the examination of the research perspectives and to a philosophical analysis of the assumptive systems underlying research and theorizing in communication. The impulse became a movement directed against the specific target of behaviorism but also against the more general social scientific climate of logical positivism. Although many of those examining the foundations of research and theory were against behaviorism and logical positivism, they were divided as to more useful perspectives, viewpoints, and philosophical assumptions for communication. Some argued for a phenomenological viewpoint, some for pragmatism, some for constructivism, and some for idealism. Others argued that the particular viewpoint a scholar adopted was less important than that scholars search their practices and viewpoints and bring the tacit assumptions into view for analysis and critique and develop a coherent and consistent personal viewpoint. Some argued for a more specific set of assumptions within a scholarly viewpoint based upon a systems perspective or a rules perspective.

The decade of turmoil in the 1970s added excitement and purpose to the enterprise of communication theory and research. The conflicts of this time seemed productive in cutting away conceptualizations and research practices that had demonstrated their triviality. The battle was no longer between humanist and social scientist over turf or for status; now the fight was over ideas— over the portion of its work that the intellectual community holds most dear. To some, the controversies seemed analogous to religious warfare in passion and in quibbling over minor theological points. Miller and Berger developed the analogy of religious conversion in an essay in which they surveyed the scene and portrayed it in terms of "the lost souls responsible for promulgating heathen research practices of old are urged to repent and to accept the word of the philosophical and scientific messiahs who have come to save them."[1]

My survey of these intellectual developments has not been even-handed. I have taken my stand in the controversy and expressed my position, particularly in Chapter 7. The community of scholars must always keep a vigilant watch on the research practices of its members to ensure that technique is sound and careful, yet the problems with communication research have not been confined to inept or inadequate research methods. The scholarly community needs to examine, periodically, its philosophical roots, yet the problems with communication research have not been mainly the result of misguided philosophical perspectives. The difficulties, to my mind, stemmed from a middle-range problem between global perspectives and the specific nuts-and-bolts details of method. The major difficulty in research and theorizing in the middle decades of the twentieth century was the widespread popularity and influence of the quasi-paradigm of the variable analytic approach to the study of communication and its associated quasi-hypothetico-deductive theorizing.

A number of those critiquing communication research and theory are coming to recognize that the quasi-paradigm is an identifiable tradition. They are also discerning its shortcomings and are ceasing their own research programs in the tradition as well as speaking out against its influence. For example, Delia gathered together previous critiques and organized them with additional material of his own to demolish the usefulness of the concept of *source credibility*, one of the central concepts of attitude change research. Many communication scholars find it difficult to separate the practice of the quasi-paradigm from the scientific method in general. Once it is clear that the attitude change studies, for example, represent one very limited way to do research, then ways to study communication that do not rely on such concepts as *relevant*, *independent* and *dependent variables*, and *controls* become more feasible.

Communication theorists and researchers moved into the 1980s with a growing vacuum created by the sagging importance of the variable analytic studies. Fewer and fewer young scholars were applying the quasi-paradigm; less and less research within the tradition was being reported at conventions and published in journals. The result was a considerable amount of experimentation with new perspectives, new viewpoints, new conceptualizations, and new ways to gather and interpret data.

Humanists in rhetorical studies had gone through a similar period of malaise in regard to the widespread study of the history and criticism of public address at midcentury and had come to reject the neo-Aristotelian approach to rhetorical criticism. The 1980s found the scholars in rhetorical theory and criticism moving in new directions and dealing with communication in ways that brought them into cooperation with some of the new trends in social scientific studies of communication.

My faith in futurists has been thoroughly shaken in the last thirty years as predictions about the greening of America are followed by the new conservatism, as predictions about the desperate need for new Ph.D.s are followed by a severe shortage of jobs for people holding the doctorate, as predictions about rapidly expanding enrollments in higher education are followed by a loss of students, and the subsequent gloomy predictions of a rapid loss of students are followed by a slight rise in enrollments. My consideration of future directions in communication theory, therefore, will be in terms not of predictions of the future but of current developments that seem on their face to hold promise for the future. Undoubtedly some developments that I will overlook or that are now beyond my ken will become the wave of the future. My analysis will not predict what pathways scholars will follow, but rather will discuss what turnings seem worth taking given the current intellectual landscape.

New Directions in Special Communication Theories

One of the major difficulties with the current state of communication theorizing is the widespread confusion of special and general theories. Scholars who yearn for general theories and who try to supply the lack with special theories continually demand that style-specific artistic formulations, so useful in teaching and consulting and improving communication, act like general theories in explaining, describing, predicting, and controlling. They may criticize the exemplar model of the message communication style because it is linear or lacks the complexity to account for all the dynamic interrelationships that universally characterize communication events. They may try to derive hypotheses for research from it, and when it fails to perform as a hypothetico-deductive general theory would, they become disgruntled with it.

If we keep the distinction between special and general theories clearly in mind, then we can make a more sensible evaluation of the overall quality of the special communication theories.

The academically popular special communication theories are functioning effectively. Indeed, much of the success of those working in the field of communication stems from the practical usefulness of the special theories. Scholars rely on the special theories in their classes, in their work as consultants in business and industry, and in working with educational and health organizations. The growth in student enrollments and the increasing number of thriving communication consultants testifies to the usefulness and importance of their work helping people more closely approximate the exemplars of the various communication styles which are widespread in our culture.

Theater is sometimes called the "fabulous invalid" because observers often view the institution with alarm and predict its demise. The public speaking communication style qualifies as the fabulous invalid among contemporary special communication theories. When the public speaking style was identified with the rhetorical faction in the controversies of the 1960s, many opponents argued that it was passé, that people no longer gave public speeches, and that it was not academically respectable to coach students in the style since such courses had no content. The rise of the relationship communication style also posed a challenge to courses in public speaking.

The public speaking situation remains an important communication context in North American society. Americans continue to go to lectures, political rallies, and ceremonial occasions that call for an extended address in the public speaking style. New variants of the style grew up around the electronic media, and a particularly widespread variation called the "presentation" came to be a central communication episode in the organizational context. There were some tendencies in contemporary society that encouraged specialists to take over the major duties associated with important public speaking occasions such as committees of ghostwriters to prepare the messages. On the other hand, the increasing use of presentations to make sales overtures to clients, to brief people, to make proposals for new services and product development, and to urge organizational change forced more and more people to give their own speeches. People in the appropriate organizational positions often had to give the presentation in order for it to have maximum impact.

The message communication style, with its emphasis on task-oriented communication, was well adapted to business meetings, task force deliberations, and all the problem-solving and decision-making small group and two-person episodes that characterize corporate society. In general, much of the formal business of organizations is carried on by deliberations in the message communication style. Information transmission is important to cooperative effort, and coordination depends upon it. The generality of the message communication model is both a strength and a weakness. Its strength is that theorists can adapt it to two-person episodes, small group meetings, public audiences, and mass-media communication. Its weakness is that such generality means that detailed advice and coaching to improve high-fidelity transmission of information must come from the experience of the instructor and from careful analysis of specific contexts. The attempt on the part of some scholars in organizational communication to develop a standardized method to evaluate the quality of communication in organizations is evidence of the need to gather specific information in order to apply the message communication model in that setting.

The message communication style was well adapted to the felt needs of many people working in corporate contexts. They often defined their communication problems in terms of lack of understanding, communication breakdowns, and barriers that stopped the flow of information. The style focused attention on features of communication context and process which mitigated against effective transmission of information, and this met the felt needs of people directly. The associated weakness was that the style tended to neglect the social dimension of communication. Practitioners working with the information problems could not ignore human relations and often developed additional material to deal with interpersonal problems. The style's main focus, however, remained on the transmission of information.

Communication scholars demonstrated considerable skill and flexibility in accommodating the new developments in society to formulate the third major academic style, that of relationship communication. Perhaps the fact that neither the public speaking style nor the message style provided a full-blown model of both content and relationship created a sense of need which the sensitivity, growth, and encounter group movement began to fill. The theoretical literature in both journals and textbooks through the 1960s and early 1970s reveals the way theoreticians grappled with questions about what was the nature of "interpersonal communication" and how it might be used in classes and workshops. One can trace how various innovations and exercises were incorporated into courses and handbooks and how various issues came under dispute and were resolved until the style matured and the details fell into place. By the late 1970s such writers as Stewart could provide a consistent and complete description of the exemplar communication model in terms of four basic characteristics, with each of the characteristics firmly grounded in philosophical foundations.[2]

My survey of special communication theories is not complete, although the three I have emphasized are among the most important. Academic theoreticians have dealt with the communication styles associated with bargaining, negotiating, threatening, and coercing to some extent; they have probably not given them the attention that their importance in contemporary society might justify. Theoreticians dealing with special communication theories have had some concern with communication relating to negotiations and conflict in general. The message communication style must almost be stood on its head to accommodate "hard-line" negotiating in such conflict areas as labor relations, legal litigation, and international disputes. Conflict situations often put a premium on bluff, falsehood and half-truth, simulated tantrums, threats, and other techniques to inhibit high-fidelity transmission of information.

Academicians have also been concerned to some extent with the mass-media communication styles associated with persuasion in behalf of products, candidates, and political, social, and religious positions. They have studied and made some preliminary analyses of the marketing research preparation, the development of scenarios or campaign themes, the intricacies of what is called "name identification" or "image-building," and the planning and implementation of campaign details such as media buys, saturation techniques, and peaking strategies.

Communication theorists have largely refrained from the formulation of propaganda, negotiation, and coercion styles into special theories that they can present in classes and workshops. Often they found the ethical dimension of such practices troublesome, and the academic climate tended to discourage courses in how to intimidate your opponent, how to win the best settlement for your side, or how to lie and bluff at the negotiating table. The widespread need for communication styles appropriate to conflict settings, of course, results in considerable nonacademic attention to such matters. People do specialize in negotiating techniques and do become experts in running promotional, advertising, and political campaigns. They develop exemplar models for their efforts, coach newcomers in apprentice roles, and write how-to-do-it articles and memos.

Another group of communication practices deal with various uses of group communication settings to convert individuals to new visions and new lifestyles. Currently such communication tends to be called *consciousness raising*. The practice is age-old and academicians have periodically expressed some interest in it, but communication theorists have not developed a special theory related to the conversion style.

When informal communication practices evolve into discernible styles of communication, they become candidates for academic study. On occasion, as was the case with the relationship style, scholars took a hand in the development of a special style-specific theory, with courses and other teaching and coaching sessions, and with standards for criticism. They were in the forefront of the puzzle-solving controversy among those concerned with the style. In my judgment the most promising of the informal communication styles for future directions in constructing special communication theories relates to the mass-media campaigns in persuasion, promotion, and propaganda. Courses in advertising, public relations, and political persuasion are already providing the framework for such theorizing. A special theory related to bargaining and negotiating communication contexts is also a possible future direction.

Since special communication theories have large artistic elements, they are amenable to changes by conventional definitions and stylistic innovation in the exemplar communication models. Like all style-related matters, special communication theories are susceptible to rapid shifts and fads. Some of the shifts may be essentially changes in terminology, such as when some writers relabeled the public speaking style *public communication*. Other changes may be more substantial, as when scholars under the influence of the growing popularity of the relationship style began to expand the message communication style to incorporate more consideration of relationship elements in task-oriented communication. When I wrote a book with three colleagues in the early 1960s, my coauthors and I thought that the term *interpersonal* in the title referred to oral communication directed to another person who was physically present.[3] Our alternative to the term *interpersonal communication* was *face-to-face communication*. By the 1970s, many were using the term *interpersonal* to mean the relationship communication style. By the 1980s a number of writers were using the term *interpersonal* for the relationship style, the message communication style, and for general theories dealing with a few people participating in face-to-face communication episodes.[4]

Academic theoreticians of communication have both the leisure and the motivation to modify, change, or radically alter formulations relating to the artistic special theories. They write many textbooks and often seek some attractive alternative formulation to catch attention. They puzzle over the usefulness of the special theories in practical settings and try to improve them in their own teaching and coaching and consulting. When they hit upon a better formulation, they exchange news and notes in convention programs, in informal conversations, and in newsletters and journals. The special theories are always in dynamic process.

Problems with the special theories often stem from confusing the special theories with general theories, as when in the 1960s some partisans of the message style argued that the public speaking style was based upon prescriptive advice rather than descriptions of communication; they failed to realize that their style was equally prescriptive. Confusing special theories with general theories encourages scholars to try to integrate elements from several different styles into a whole that takes the best from each. Such integration may be useful, but if the theoreticians are not careful they may try to force together elements from different special theories which do not fit comfortably together. The relationship style's emphasis on nonmanipulative, open, trusting communication is difficult to reconcile with the public speaking style's emphasis on persuasive speaking. The relationship style emphasizes the notion that you "cannot not communicate," whereas the message communication style emphasizes intentional transmission of information.

In general, the special theories, despite some problems, have been a major strength in the academic study of the field. Communication scholars make a strong contribution by thinking through the assumptions of the special theories, developing innovations to make them more useful or aesthetic, establishing their boundaries, and assuring that they are internally consistent. If the scholars continue their generally good work in the development of special communication theories, they should be able to continue their efficient teaching and consulting for the benefit of the ongoing communication in society.

New Directions in General Communication Theories

In earlier chapters of this book I highlighted some of the arguments for alternative approaches to theory and research in communication that evolved from the general critique of the 1970s. Most of the newer developments are still in an embryo stage in terms of research. My necessarily brief evaluation of their promise at this stage of their development will be conjectural and suggestive rather than definitive. Some central issues are emerging. The rationales for some of the intriguing new lines of inquiry are unclear, and in some instances the investigators themselves do not seem sure of their assumptive bases. Still, some of the new approaches seem to be aiming for general theories which function like laws of nature in expressing causal connections expressed either in probability generalizations or in invariable relations. They would design such general theories to allow anticipation of events in the case of probability accounts or prediction in the case of invariable relations. Such theories could also be used to control with more or less precision the unfolding of communication events.

Other scholars seem embarked upon research and theorizing based on a rationale that would search for general theories capable of providing understanding and thus an explanation, but would ground such explanations on the conventional nature of much communication-related activity. Human choice and decision-making would be central to these explanations, and the theorists would not expect their general theories to allow predictions or control of events.

Although the controversies over proper theorizing make this feature of the future less clear-cut, some scholars seem to be aiming for general theories based upon an image of human nature. Others seem to be aiming for theories that are based upon unfolding patterns in social collectives.

In the following analysis I will examine some of the more intriguing developments and raise some of the questions growing out of the analysis in earlier chapters of theorizing in communication.

New Directions in the Study of Styles and Strategies   One of the most useful insights of Kuhn's interpretative structure to explain the modern developments in science is his idea that to shift from one scientific paradigm to another is to experience a drastic shift in world view—a shift as spectacular as the shift of perception in an optical illusion. The shift from the quasi-paradigm of the variable analytic tradition to some other research perspective may not be quite as drastic, but the analogy to the optical-illusion shift is still a striking one.

In order to shift out of the quasi-paradigm, investigators and theorists must cease thinking in terms of *variables*. The master concept of *variable*, along with its subsidiary concepts such as *controlled variables*, *manipulated variables*, and *independent* and *dependent variables*, are all central to the variable analytic program. Equally important is the concept of a *hypothesis* that focuses the design of the investigation and asserts a tentative relationship among the variables under study. The testing of hypotheses leads to the first qualifying term in the characterization of a hypothetico-deductive theory. The last term of such a characterization implies mathematical computations among the hypotheses to integrate them into a consistent system, and from them, to apply the theory to practical problems and to reveal new hypotheses for critical experimental testing.

Those investigators who continue to think and write in terms of variables, controls, and hypotheses will have great difficulty breaking out of the world view of the quasi-paradigm.

The irony is that twentieth-century physics and chemistry no longer set up their investigations in terms of testing hypotheses and manipulating variables. An intriguing recent experiment in quantum mechanics will serve to illustrate my point. One of the perplexing issues that have surrounded the theory of quantum mechanics in physics is the possibility that the observer can have an effect on the state of the particle under observation. Some have taken that possibility and, by analogy, argued that it is evidence of the weakness of causal argument even in the most fundamental of the natural sciences. Recently a number of studies have thrown some light upon that question, and the investigations indicate how the experiments of modern physics differ from the variable analytic design.

The experiment is designed so two protons are brought together to form what is called a *singlet state*. Protons carry an intrinsic angular spin momentum. In the singlet state the two protons must exhibit angular spin momentums that point in opposite directions. One proton may have a spin pointing up, and if it does then the other's spin must point down in order for the protons to be in the singlet state. The theory provides only that the spins be complementary; it gives no prediction as to the actual spin of either proton. The experimenters use three pieces of equipment lined up along the flight of each proton. The first is a telescope, which emits a signal if a suitable pair of protons is detected on the two paths. Next in line is a spin filter, which, for instance, might allow only protons with an up spin to pass. Finally, each path ends with a detector, which provides a signal whenever a proton passes through the filter and reaches it. The investigators set up the alignment of equipment so that one filter-detector array is much closer to the origin of the singlet state than the other. When the investigators get a signal that two protons in the singlet state are in flight toward the filter-detectors, they have no way of computing from quantum mechanics which is spinning up and which is spinning down. Each has a 50-50 chance of spinning up. As soon as the first proton hits the nearer filter-detector, however, the investigators may get a reading. Assume the filter allows spin-up protons through and the investigators get a signal. As long as the second proton remains in flight, its spin is formally undetermined, but the experimenters can make up their minds about the second proton when they get a reading on the first. They know the second is spin-down even before its spin is measured. Einstein originally proposed the experiment as a thought experiment, but seven such experiments have recently been performed, and five have supported the predictions of quantum mechanics. My point is not to present some esoteric findings from quantum mechanics but to indicate how far the physicists have departed from testing hypotheses by manipulating and controlling variables. What the investigators did in the experiment described above was to set up an environment such that it was likely that some protons would come along in a singlet state, and when they got a signal that such a phenomenon was in view, they observed it.

The physicists still work from an assumption that "nowhere in quantum mechanics can the observer's knowledge alter the outcome of a real measurement. The second spin may be indeterminate until it is decided by a distant measurement, but it could not be definitely up at first and later definitely down. There is no hint of 'mind over matter.'"[5]

The rejection of the quasi-paradigm of the variable analytic studies does not require the rejection of empiricism nor the rejection of hope for theories which contain causal arguments.

What are some of the directions theorists are taking to move from variables to other conceptualizations for rigorous investigations? Miller and Burgoon, in a review and commentary on persuasion research, after noting that the variable analytic paradigm was on the wane, went on to examine several examples of more promising lines of investigation. They suggested in particular the two important and promising concepts of *communicator style* and *persuasive message strategies*. Miller and Burgoon summarized recent studies related to both concepts and suggested that style and strategy may be a more fruitful way to view persuasion in the future.[6] If investigators do not fall into the trap of recasting these concepts into the form of *variables* to be manipulated in order to discover their effect on paper-and-pencil attitude scores, these two lines of investigation look most promising.

Style may well be the key to studies of communication in the next decade. My analysis of special communication theories earlier in the book is based on style as the central controlling rationale. Making style a central construct shifts our world view from the mechanical analogy of objects setting one another in motion by acting at a distance or by colliding, and focuses our attention on the artistic elements in human communication. Miller and Burgoon place the construct of *communicator style* in the general framework of interpersonal attraction and the initial perceptions of attractiveness. Geier and Pratt have done some work on the influence of communicator style on the emergence of leaders in zero-history leaderless group discussion.[7] Norton and his associates have explored the construct in considerable detail, particularly in relation to varied styles of speakers.[8]

Communication style either of individuals or of communities opens up the investigator's vision to encompass a number of new developments in other areas of communication study. Solomon's study from a sociolinguistic perspective of the style of Carter's *Playboy* interview illustrates how rhetorical criticism and sociolinguistics can be brought into concert to explain a complicated mass-media communication episode. She summarized the modern sociolinguistic study of the social implications of variations and shifts in style. Integrating the concept of style with the Hymes tradition of communicative competence, Solomon suggested, "Each individual possesses a linguistic repertoire from which to choose the level of style best suited to a particular situation."[9] She made a rhetorical criticism of Carter's *Playboy* interview during the 1976 presidential campaign on the basis of an analysis of two kinds of code-switching.

Persuasive strategy is another construct that can open up investigation and theorizing in persuasion and shift it away from the attitude-change exemplar. Miller and Burgoon refer to a Marwell and Schmitt study that developed a typology of sixteen compliance-gaining message strategies such as arguing that if the others comply, people will value them, or will think better of them, or they will feel better about themselves, or they will be punished or rewarded, and so forth.[10] Miller and his associates subsequently did further work in terms of examining the relationship between strategy and situations.[11]

Many rhetorical critics have used strategy as a controlling construct, and the potential for integrated and symbiotic work with social scientists in regard to theorizing about persuasive strategies is strong. King, in a study of elites in danger of losing power, developed a general typology of persuasive strategies that have been used historically by endangered power holders.[12] He noted such strategies as *"Crying Anarchy"* and *"The Official Betrayal Alibia"*. Gronbeck's study of the rhetoric of political corruption illustrates the possibilities of integrating humanistic with social scientific analysis of strategy. Although his essay is more of a first step establishing a framework to begin to study strategies, it relates directly to the construct *strategy*. Gronbeck draws from Hymes and the social linguists, from cognitive psychologists, from ethnomethodologists such as Garfinkel, from sociological analysis of social rule, from symbolic interactionists, from political scientists, and from Kenneth Burke and Duncan. Like King, Gronbeck has "baldly asserted some explanatory generalizations regarding the need for destroying evil periodically so as to reinforce cultural identity."[13]

Delia and his associates at Illinois are developing a comprehensive and detailed research program in which communicative strategy is a central concept.

Starting with a critique of the philosophical assumptions they saw guiding social scientific research in communications, the Illinois group formulated their own assumptive system, which they characterized as *constructivism*. From that viewpoint, they undertook a series of investigations in the communicative development of children. Their preliminary studies of children led them to a consideration of the development of children's ability to adopt rhetorical strategies as they matured. The program then expanded to consider strategies in ordinary conversations and in other communication.

The Illinois research group brought three sets of conceptualizations to bear on the problem of explaining the way children develop communicative competence. One component related to the communicative development of children and incorporated Kelly's view of cognitive processes. The implied image of human beings in the conceptualization is that each individual develops a system of cognitive structures which channel behavior. The construct systems are dynamic and undergo changes with maturation. The Illinois group does not accept the stages of development account, which considers maturation of communication competence to move through a universal pattern for all individuals. Clark and Delia noted that much of the research at Illinois "has been directed toward the study of the relationship of developmentally defined differences in psychological structure (e.g., cognitive complexity, construct abstraction) and the use of communicative strategies varying in sensitivity to individuality of perspectives and listener adaption."[14]

A second component in the conceptualization of the development of communicative competence in children was the account of how individuals come to an "acquisition of constructs guiding communicative conduct employed in common within a given speech community."[15]

A third component was a conceptualization of the interactive episodes that characterize ongoing communication. Here the Illinois group "follows such sociologically oriented symbolic interactionists as Blumer in giving attention to contextually emergent constraints."[16]

The constructivist account of communication involved explaining the way children develop communicative competence as their personal cognitive processes evolve to greater complexity and as they learn the rules, norms, and customs of the communication games of their rhetorical communities. Within the context of commonly shared conventions, individuals with idiosyncratic cognitive processes (which do exhibit some common patterns) engage in episodes during which they continually generate shared conceptions about the norms and rules governing the specific communication event and during which they construct and reconstruct a common social reality.

Strategy becomes central in the course of explaining the unfolding of specific communication episodes.

Clark and Delia noted:

> . . . . as a general perspective on communication development, it [constructivism] aims at incorporating interpretative, behavioral, cultural, and situational processes and structures within an integrated framework. Thus, we see the development of purposive, strategic message formulation—rhetorical competence—as only one aspect of communicative development. However, giving this aspect of communicative development systematic attention is important . . .because it provides a focus in which all the processes and structures involved in communication can be clearly seen.[17]

The Illinois group has used ethnographic studies, conversational analysis, and laboratory studies in examining rhetorical strategies. Clark and Delia outlined the possible integration of rhetorical theory relating to lines of argument and issue analysis to the constructivist study of strategies. They also suggested that genre rhetorical criticism might well make a contribution along the lines of ethnographic studies.

Their moves toward theory-building have tended in the direction of developing typologies or taxonomies of rhetorical strategies. Arguing by analogy to the *topoi* of classical rhetoric, Clark and Delia recommended the development of a more sophisticated typology of strategies firmly grounded in humanistic and social scientific research.[18]

Ethnolinguistic and Naturalistic Studies of Communication The interest in field studies and in naturalistic studies of ordinary talk has been increasing rapidly. Studies of rhetorical communities are central to the scientific study of special communication theories. In addition, such studies can discover rules, norms, and customs associated with various communication contexts and episodes within a specified community.

Scholars embarking on such studies need to be quite clear in their own minds whether they are charting a group's communication in order to discover its symbolic reality, much as an anthropologist might study a cultural community in a South Seas island to understand and explain it, or whether they hope to build a general theory covering many communities. In Chapter 9 I reported Nofsinger's notion that the collection of ethnographic studies of a variety of rhetorical communities would provide the necessary details so that, like Darwin, subsequent theoreticians could develop general theories to account for the observed similarity and variety.

If they are seeking general theories, they might well ask if they hope to account for the diversity and unity among rhetorical communities on the basis of some individual characteristics of *Homo sapiens* passed on genetically, or whether they are seeking for some general characteristics of social communities passed on through the collective unconscious or genetically through social traits which relate to bonding, hierarchical social order, and other social processes that permitted human collectives to adapt to their environment and thus contribute to the survival of the species.

Theories based upon an image of human beings might include such constructs as an expanded version of the language-acquisition device that some linguists used to account for the way people learn languages. A device enabling human beings to acquire communicative competence might be hypothesized that included the ability to take a sample of a given communication episode and draw generalized rules and norms from it. The individual might then try to conform to the rule in another episode that seems similar, modify the inference if the rule seemed inappropriate, and so forth.

Communication scholars recommending a rules perspective for the development of theory should ask analogous questions about their formulations. If they conduct their studies of the conventional rules of a community to provide insight into specifics about the people who are part of that community, they provide one kind of explanation. If they conduct their studies in order to explain the way people develop and conform or fail to conform to rules in general, they provide another kind of explanation. Again they might provide either an image of human beings to account for their general theory, or a model of social processes to do so. Cushman and his associates, as I indicated in Chapter 2, have put forward a model of human beings that assumes a rational decision-making process based upon thinking in the form of the practical syllogism.

The same questions arise for those investigators involved in conversational analysis and the study of such concepts as *turn-taking* and *utterances* and *utterance pair sequences*. If they are studying these features of conversations to discover something about the rhetorical community in which the subjects participate, then, like the anthropologist studying a culture, they can explain the turn-taking norms and rules of a limited number of people in a particular historical period. However, if they hope to develop general theories relating to turn-taking and the nature of utterance pair sequences, then they must demonstrate that such patterns are part of a universal human condition or at least of a number of rhetorical communities.

For those investigators like Nofsinger who hope to collect enough ethnographic data to begin to make comparative studies across communication styles, the present body of research is too small to provide the basis for general theories. Certainly such an approach will provide a much more comprehensive explanation of human communication than could be provided under the best of circumstances by the variable analytic approach. Whether it will produce such theories remains to be seen. For those who would provide an accounting for a universal human nature on the basis of the sampling of conversation or other communication events, the development of theoretical tests should come much sooner.

In general, the investigations based upon a human-action perspective and studying communication practices in all their diversity and complexity are moving in promising directions.

The Systems Studies of Communication The investigators aiming to develop a general systems theory of communication are not far enough along in their studies for a judgment of their potential. As an epistemological metaphor, the systems perspective has considerable attraction for communication theorists who see interrelated communication as a process.

The systems accounts do emphasize explanations based on the patterns which characterize collectives rather than those based on images of human beings. The systems perspective has led researchers in the direction of studying groups and organizations over time. The investigators have often searched for patterns in terms of networks through which messages flow or of systematic content changes over time. Some of the studies have involved massive data collection procedures. Even in the restricted scope of the small group discussion as a system, Fisher and his associates have collected communication interacts and double-interacts in searches for patterns which involved coding large numbers of units. [19]

Theoreticians using the systems perspective need to decide whether their generalizations will be style-specific, related to individual rhetorical communities, or applicable to larger domains cutting across communities and cultures.

Dramatism and General Communication Theory In Chapter 9 I used dramatism as an example of how humanistic and social scientific scholarship could come into productive relationship in terms of general communication theories. My viewpoint, which is sympathetic to dramatism, has been reflected throughout the book in my accounts of rhetorical criticism, history, and special and general communication theories.

There is no need here to recapitulate my previous discussions about dramatism. The assumptive system of symbolic convergence does emphasize the importance of considering the meanings of the symbolic action to the actors involved in the communication episodes. Other features are also important, however. Subconscious or unconscious forces may account for the symbolic convergence process. The assumptive system also concentrates on communication features of collectives. The basic explanatory generalization relates to the dynamic process of sharing group fantasies. That hypothesis is assumed to include all human collectives in the past, now, and in the future, regardless of cultural differences and rhetorical style. Ethnographic studies, Q-sort studies, and survey investigations can serve to chart the nature of shared fantasies and common rhetorical visions. The collection of such data provides the necessary detail for discovering patterns which cut across rhetorical communities. Rhetorical criticisms can serve the same purpose.

Rational and logical argument follows the sharing of rhetorical visions with their associated value systems and social realities. Argument depends upon some final common ground upon which the disputants can agree. Different logical forms are created and validated by the symbolic convergent process.

Dramatism has considerable potential to provide understanding along the lines I sketched in Chapter 8 in regard to explaining small group communication by a blending of general and specific communication theories. The general theories of symbolic convergence may well take the form of Darwin's account of the facts of evolution. Elsewhere I have conjectured that in terms of mass-media communication, symbolic convergence might develop a theoretical structure analogous to meteorological theories.[20]

The State of the Art

There seems to be a tendency to have more "state of the art" papers than "state of the science" papers, and that may be well advised in the case of communication theory. Communication theory in the latter part of the twentieth century remains both an art and a social science. Under the generic term *communication theory*, scholars have included a hodgepodge of concepts, definitions, hypotheses, typologies, taxonomies, and terminologies. Some of the material consisted of special theories with an artistic component. Other material was designed to function as a general theoretical account of communication.

General theorizing about communication is in a state of transition as older formulations fade in popularity and new perspectives guide social scientific investigation. Because of the current turmoil and the transitory state of communication theorizing, this book could not provide an integrated description of the agreed-upon theories. What I have done is sketch the history which brought the field to this point of transition, summarize the material often included in communication theory, analyze its component parts, and provide the reader with a method for critical analysis and evaluation.

As research approaches and theoretical formulations evolve and change, the ability to make a critical analysis of the unfolding scene and to discern a good communication theory when one comes across it will remain an important goal of a sound education in communication theory and practice.

Notes

1. Gerald R. Miller and Charles R. Berger, "On Keeping the Faith in Matters Scientific," *Western Journal of Speech Communication* 42 (1978): 44.
2. See particularly John Stewart, "Foundations of Dialogic Communication," *Quarterly Journal of Speech* 64 (1978): 183–201.
3. Ernest G. Bormann, William S. Howell, Ralph G. Nichols, and George L.

Shapiro, *Interpersonal Communication in the Modern Organization* (Englewood Cliffs, N.J.: Prentice-Hall, 1969).

4. See, for example, the section on interpersonal communication in the annual communication yearbooks published by the International Communication Association. A typical overview is that by Charles R. Berger, "Interpersonal Communication Theory and Research: An Overview," in Brent D. Ruben, ed., *Communication Yearbook I* (New Brunswick, N.J.: Transaction Books, 1977), pp. 217–228.

5. Reported in the "Science and the Citizen" section of *Scientific American* 239 (July 1978): 78. The report is entitled "Esse Est Percipi" and is on pp. 72–78. I have taken the example from this report.

6. Gerald R. Miller and Michael Burgoon, "Persuasion Research: Review and Commentary," in Brent D. Ruben, ed., *Communication Yearbook 2* (New Brunswick, N.J.: Transaction Books, 1978), pp. 29–47.

7. John Geier, "A Descriptive Analysis of an Interaction Pattern Resulting in Leadership Emergence in Leaderless Group Discussion" (Ph.D. dissertation, University of Minnesota, 1968); Jerie Pratt, "A Case Study Analysis of Male and Female Leadership Emergence in Small Groups" (Ph.D. dissertation, University of Minnesota, 1979).

8. Robert W. Norton, "Foundations of a Communicator Style Construct," *Human Communication Research* 4 (1978): 99–112; Robert W. Norton and Loyd S. Pettigrew, "Attentiveness as a Style of Communication: A Structural Analysis," *Communication Monographs* 46 (1979): 13–26; Robert W. Norton, "Communicator Style and Teacher Effectiveness," in Ruben, ed., *Communication Yearbook I*, pp. 525–542.

9. Martha Solomon, "Jimmy Carter and *Playboy*: A Sociolinguistic Perspective on Style," *Quarterly Journal of Speech* 64 (1978): pp. 173–174.

10. Miller and Burgoon, pp. 41–44.

11. Gerald R. Miller, Frank Boster, Michael Roloff, and David Seibold, "Compliance-Gaining Message Strategies: A Typology and Some Findings Concerning Effects of Situational Differences," *Communication Monographs* 44 (1977): 37–50.

12. Andrew A. King, "The Rhetoric of Power Maintenance: Elites at the Precipice," *Quarterly Journal of Speech* 62 (1976): 127–134.

13. Bruce E. Gronbeck, "The Rhetoric of Political Corruption: Sociolinguistic, Dialectical, and Ceremonial Processes," *Quarterly Journal of Speech* 64 (1978): 171.

14. Ruth Anne Clark and Jesse G. Delia, "*Topoi* and Rhetorical Competence," *Quarterly Journal of Speech* 65 (1979): 190.

15. Ibid., p. 191.

16. Ibid., p. 192.

17. Ibid., p. 193.

18. Ibid., pp. 199–206.

19. See, for example, Donald G. Ellis and B. Aubrey Fisher, "Phases of Conflict in Small Group Development: A Markov Analysis," *Human Communication Research* 1 (1975): 195–212.

20. Ernest G. Bormann, "Generalizing About Significant Form: Science and Humanism Compared and Contrasted," in Karlyn Kohrs Campbell and Kathleen Hall Jamieson, eds., *Form and Genre: Shaping Rhetorical Action* (Falls Church, Va.: Speech Communication Association, 1978), pp. 66–67.

Name Index

Subject Index